AGELESS
BODY,
TIMELESS
MIND

AGELESS BODY, TIMELESS MIND

The Quantum Alternative to Growing Old

DEEPAK CHOPRA, M.D.

Harmony Books / New York

Published by Harmony Books, a division of Crown Publishers, Inc.,
201 East 50th Street, New York, New York 10022. Member of the Crown
Publishing Group. Random House, Inc. New York, Toronto, London, Sydney,
Auckland.

HARMONY and colophon are trademarks of Crown Publishers, Inc.
Manufactured in the United States of America

Library of Congress Cataloging-in-Publication Data
Chopra, Deepak.
Ageless body, timeless mind : the quantum alternative to growing old / by
Deepak Chopra.
p.   cm.
Includes index.
ISBN 0-517-59257-6 (hc) : $22.00
1. Longevity.   2. Mind and body.   3. Vitality.   4. Aging.   5. Holistic
medicine.   I. Title.
RA776.75.C48   1993
612.6'8—dc20   93-16766   CIP

ISBN 0-517-59257-6
10 9 8 7 6

CONTENTS

ACKNOWLEDGMENTS

This book was made possible by the loving support and encouragement of the following people:

The friends who form my staff at Quantum Publications—Roger, Gita, Carol, Mara, Steve, Bob, Joe, and Jimmy. Your genuine caring inspires my work every day.

My wife and children, whose love is manifested in so many ways but particularly in their unstinting patience and understanding.

My agent, Muriel Nellis, whose sage guidance has shaped every step in my career as a writer.

My editor, Peter Guzzardi—this book was his vision to begin with, and only he knows what ingenuity and patience it took before these pages lived up to his high ideal.

Wayne Dyer, who offered me his devoted friendship and challenged me to new heights.

And my loving parents, the best examples of graceful aging I have ever known.

Thank you all. I hope this book reflects your best hopes for me and the future of mankind.

People don't grow old.
When they stop growing, they
become old.
ANONYMOUS

If you were to destroy in mankind the
belief in immortality, not only love
but every living force maintaining
the life of the world would at once
be dried up.
DOSTOEVSKY

I move with the infinite in Nature's power
I hold the fire of the soul
I hold life and healing
RIG VEDA

Look at these worlds spinning
out of nothingness
That is within your power.
RUMI

PART ONE

---

*The Land
Where No One
Is Old*

I WOULD LIKE YOU to join me on a journey of discovery. We will explore a place where the rules of everyday existence do not apply. These rules explicitly state that to grow old, become frail, and die is the ultimate destiny of all. And so it has been for century after century. However, I want you to suspend your assumptions about what we call reality so that we can become pioneers in a land where youthful vigor, renewal, creativity, joy, fulfillment, and time-lessness are the common experience of everyday life, where old age, senility, infirmity, and death do not exist and are not even enter-tained as a possibility.

If there is such a place, what is preventing us from going there? It is not some dark continental landmass or dangerous uncharted sea. It is our conditioning, our current collective worldview that we were taught by our parents, teachers, and society. This way of seeing things—the old paradigm—has aptly been called "the hypno-sis of social conditioning," an induced fiction in which we have collectively agreed to participate.

Your body is aging beyond your control because it has been programmed to live out the rules of that collective conditioning. If there is anything natural and inevitable about the aging process, it cannot be known until the chains of our old beliefs are broken. In order to create the experience of ageless body and timeless mind, which is the promise of this book, you must discard ten assumptions about who you are and what the true nature of the mind and body is. These assumptions form the bedrock of our shared worldview. They are:

1. There is an objective world independent of the observer, and our bodies are an aspect of this objective world.
2. The body is composed of clumps of matter separated from one another in time and space.
3. Mind and body are separate and independent from each other.
4. Materialism is primary, consciousness is secondary. In other words, we are physical machines that have learned to think.
5. Human awareness can be completely explained as the product of biochemistry.
6. As individuals, we are disconnected, self-contained entities.
7. Our perception of the world is automatic and gives us an accurate picture of how things really are.
8. Our true nature is totally defined by the body, ego, and personality. We are wisps of memories and desires enclosed in packages of flesh and bones.
9. Time exists as an absolute, and we are captives of that absolute. No one escapes the ravages of time.
10. Suffering is necessary—it is part of reality. We are inevitable victims of sickness, aging, and death.

These assumptions reach far beyond aging to define a world of separation, decay, and death. Time is seen as a prison that no one escapes; our bodies are biochemical machines that, like all machines, must run down. "At a certain age," Lewis Thomas once affirmed, "it is in our nature to wear out, to come unhinged, and to die, and that is that." This position, the hard line of materialistic science, overlooks much about human nature. We are the only creatures on earth who can change our biology by what we think and feel. We possess the only nervous system that is aware of the phenomenon of aging. Old lions and tigers do not realize what is happening to them—but we do. And because we are aware, our mental state influences what we are aware of.

It would be impossible to isolate a single thought or feeling, a single belief or assumption, that doesn't have some effect on aging, either directly or indirectly. Our cells are constantly eavesdropping on our thoughts and being changed by them. A bout of depression can wreak havoc with the immune system; falling in love can boost it. Despair and hopelessness raise the risk of heart attacks and cancer, thereby shortening life. Joy and fulfillment keep us healthy and extend life. This means that the line between biology and psychology can't really be drawn with any certainty. A remembered stress, which is only a wisp of thought, releases the same flood of destructive hormones as the stress itself.

Because the mind influences every cell in the body, human aging is fluid and changeable; it can speed up, slow down, stop for a time, and even reverse itself. Hundreds of research findings from the last three decades have verified that aging is much more dependent on the individual than was ever dreamed of in the past.

However, the most significant breakthrough is not contained in isolated findings but in a completely new worldview. The ten assumptions of the old paradigm do not accurately describe our reality. They are inventions of the human mind that we have turned into rules. To challenge aging at its core, this entire worldview must be challenged first, for nothing holds more power over the body than beliefs of the mind.

Each assumption of the old paradigm can be replaced with a more complete and expanded version of the truth. These new assumptions are also just ideas created by the human mind, but they allow us much more freedom and power. They give us the ability to rewrite the program of aging that now directs our cells.

The ten new assumptions are:

1. The physical world, including our bodies, is a response of the observer. We create our bodies as we create the experience of our world.
2. In their essential state, our bodies are composed of energy and information, not solid matter. This energy and

information is an outcropping of infinite fields of energy and information spanning the universe.

3. The mind and body are inseparably one. The unity that is "me" separates into two streams of experience. I experience the subjective stream as thoughts, feelings, and desires. I experience the objective stream as my body. At a deeper level, however, the two streams meet at a single creative source. It is from this source that we are meant to live.

4. The biochemistry of the body is a product of awareness. Beliefs, thoughts, and emotions create the chemical reactions that uphold life in every cell. An aging cell is the end product of awareness that has forgotten how to remain new.

5. Perception appears to be automatic, but in fact it is a learned phenomenon. The world you live in, including the experience of your body, is completely dictated by how you learned to perceive it. If you change your perception, you change the experience of your body and your world.

6. Impulses of intelligence create your body in new forms every second. What you are is the sum total of these impulses, and by changing their patterns, you will change.

7. Although each person seems separate and independent, all of us are connected to patterns of intelligence that govern the whole cosmos. Our bodies are part of a universal body, our minds an aspect of a universal mind.

8. Time does not exist as an absolute, but only eternity. Time is quantified eternity, timelessness chopped up into bits and pieces (seconds, hours, days, years) by us. What we call linear time is a reflection of how we perceive change. If we could perceive the changeless, time would cease to exist as we know it. We can learn to start metabolizing non-change, eternity, the absolute. By doing that, we will be ready to create the physiology of immortality.

9. Each of us inhabits a reality lying beyond all change. Deep inside us, unknown to the five senses, is an innermost core of being, a field of non-change that creates personality, ego, and body. This being is our essential state—it is who we really are.

10. We are not victims of aging, sickness, and death. These are part of the scenery, not the seer, who is immune to any form of change. This seer is the spirit, the expression of eternal being.

These are vast assumptions, the makings of a new reality, yet all are grounded in the discoveries of quantum physics made almost a hundred years ago. The seeds of this new paradigm were planted by Einstein, Bohr, Heisenberg, and the other pioneers of quantum physics, who realized that the accepted way of viewing the physical world was false. Although things "out there" appear to be real, there is no proof of reality apart from the observer. No two people share exactly the same universe. Every worldview creates its own world.

I want to convince you that you are much more than your limited body, ego, and personality. The rules of cause and effect as you accept them have squeezed you into the volume of a body and the span of a lifetime. In reality, the field of human life is open and unbounded. At its deepest level, your body is ageless, your mind timeless. Once you identify with that reality, which is consistent with the quantum worldview, aging will fundamentally change.

Ending the Tyranny of the Senses

Why do we accept anything as real? Because we can see and touch it. Everyone has a prejudice in favor of things that are reassuringly three-dimensional, as reported to us by our five senses. Sight, hearing, touch, taste, and smell serve to reinforce the same message: things are what they seem. According to this reality, the Earth is flat, the ground beneath your feet is stationary, the sun rises in the east and sets in the west, all because it seems that way to the senses. As long as the five senses were accepted without question, such facts were immutable.

Einstein realized that time and space are also products of our five senses; we see and touch things that occupy three dimensions, and we experience events as happening in sequential order. Yet Einstein and his colleagues were able to remove this mask of appearances. They reassembled time and space into a new geometry that had no beginning or end, no edges, no solidity. Every solid particle in the universe turned out to be a ghostly bundle of energy vibrating in an immense void.

The old space-time model was smashed, replaced by a timeless, flowing field of constant transformation. This quantum field isn't separate from us—it *is* us. Where Nature goes to create stars, galaxies, quarks, and leptons, you and I go to create ourselves. The great advantage of this new worldview is that it is so immensely creative—the human body, like everything else in the cosmos, is constantly being made anew every second. Although your senses report that you inhabit a solid body in time and space, this is only the most superficial layer of reality. Your body is something far more miraculous—a flowing organism empowered by millions of years of intelligence. This intelligence is dedicated to overseeing the constant change that takes place inside you. Every cell is a miniature terminal connected to the cosmic computer.

From this perspective, it hardly seems possible that human beings could age at all. Weak and helpless as a newborn baby appears, it is superbly defended against time's ravages. If a baby could preserve its nearly invulnerable immune status, we would all live at least two hundred years, according to physiologists' estimates. If a baby could preserve its glistening smooth arteries, as supple as silk, cholesterol would not find anywhere to lodge, and heart disease would be unknown. Each of a newborn's 50 trillion cells is limpid as a raindrop, without a trace of toxic debris; such cells have no reason to age, because nothing inside them has begun to disrupt their perfect functioning. A baby's cells are not really new, however—the atoms in them have been circulating through the cosmos for billions of years. But the baby is made new by an invisible intelligence that has come together to shape a unique life-form. The timeless field has invented a new dance step, the pulsating rhythms of a newborn's body.

Aging is a mask for the loss of this intelligence. Quantum physics tells us that there is no end to the cosmic dance—the universal field of energy and information never stops transforming itself, becoming new at every second. Our bodies obey this same creative impulse. An estimated 6 trillion reactions are taking place in each cell every second. If this stream of transformation ever stopped, your cells would fall into disorder, which is synonymous with aging.

Day-old bread goes stale because it just sits there, prey to humidity, fungus, oxidation, and various destructive chemical processes. A chalk cliff crumbles over time because wind and rain beat it down, and it has no power to rebuild itself. Our bodies also undergo the process of oxidation and are attacked by fungi and various germs; they are exposed to the same wind and rain. But unlike a loaf of bread or a chalk cliff, we can renew ourselves. Our bones don't just store calcium the way chalk does—they circulate it. Fresh atoms of calcium constantly enter our bones and leave them again to become part of blood, skin, or other cells as the body's needs demand it.

In order to stay alive, your body must live on the wings of change. At this moment you are exhaling atoms of hydrogen, oxygen, carbon, and nitrogen that just an instant before were locked up in solid matter; your stomach, liver, heart, lungs, and brain are vanishing into thin air, being replaced as quickly and endlessly as they are being broken down. The skin replaces itself once a month, the stomach lining every five days, the liver every six weeks, and the skeleton every three months. To the naked eye, these organs look the same from moment to moment, but they are always in flux. By the end of this year, 98 percent of the atoms in your body will have been exchanged for new ones.

A huge proportion of this endless change works to your benefit. Only one enzyme out of millions reacts with an amino acid less than perfectly; the rarest neuron among billions misfires; on a strand of DNA coded with billions of pieces of genetic information, just one might fail to repair itself correctly when damage occurs. These rare mistakes are imperceptible, and you would think that they could not count for much. The human body is like a great Shakespearean actor who can play Hamlet a thousand times and stumble over just one syllable. But the invisible cracks in the body's perfection do count. The precision of our cells falters by slow degrees. The ever-new becomes slightly less new. And we age.

Beginning at age 30 and moving at the snail's pace of 1 percent per year, the average human body starts to come unhinged: wrinkles appear, the skin loses its tone and freshness, muscles start to sag. Instead of indicating three times more muscle than fat, the ratio starts to become equal, eyesight and hearing taper off, bones thin and become brittle. Stamina and endurance steadily decline, making it harder to perform as much work as before. Blood pressure rises, and many biochemicals shift away from their optimal levels; the most worrisome to doctors is cholesterol, which gradually rises over the years, marking the insidious progress of heart disease, which kills more people than any other affliction. On other fronts, cellular mutations begin to run out of control, creating malignant tumors that strike one person in three, mostly after age 65.

Over time, these various "age changes," as gerontologists call them, exert massive influence. They are the thousand tiny waves that bring in the tide of old age. But at any given moment, aging accounts for only 1 percent per year of the total change taking place inside your body. In other words, 99 percent of the energy and intelligence that you are composed of is untouched by the aging process. In terms of the body as process, eliminating this 1 percent of dysfunction would wipe out aging. But how do we get at this 1 percent? To answer that, we must find the control switch that manipulates the body's inner intelligence.

The new reality ushered in by quantum physics made it possible for the first time to manipulate the invisible intelligence that underlies the visible world. Einstein taught us that the physical body, like all material objects, is an illusion, and trying to manipulate it can be like grasping the shadow and missing the substance. The unseen world is the real world, and when we are willing to explore the unseen levels of our bodies, we can tap in to the immense creative power that lies at our source. Let me expand on the ten principles of the new paradigm in light of this hidden potential waiting beneath the surface of life.

1. There is no objective world independent of the observer.

The world you accept as real seems to have definite qualities. Some things are large, others small; some things are hard, others soft. Yet none of these qualities means anything outside of your perception. Take any object, such as a folding chair. To you the chair isn't very large, but to an ant it is immense. To you the chair feels hard, but a neutrino would whiz through it without slowing down, because to a subatomic particle the chair's atoms are miles apart. The chair seems stationary to you, but if you observed it from outer space, you would see it revolving past you, along with everything else on Earth, at a thousand miles per hour. Likewise, anything else you can describe about the chair can be completely altered simply by changing your perception. If the chair is red, you can make it appear black by looking at it through green glasses. If the chair weighs five pounds, you can make it weigh two pounds by putting it on the moon or a hundred thousand pounds by putting it in the gravitational field of a dense star.

Because there are no absolute qualities in the material world, it is false to say that there even is an independent world "out there." The world is a reflection of the sensory apparatus that registers it. The human nervous system takes in only the most minute fraction, less than one part per billion, of the total energy vibrating in the environment. Other nervous systems, such as that of a bat or a snake, reflect a different world, coexisting with ours. The bat senses a world of ultrasound, the snake a world of infrared light, both of which are hidden from us.

All that is really "out there" is raw, unformed data waiting to be interpreted by you, the perceiver. You take "a radically ambiguous, flowing quantum soup," as physicists call it, and use your senses to congeal the soup into the solid three-dimensional world.

The eminent British neurologist Sir John Eccles pierces the sensory illusion with one startling but irrefutable assertion: "I want you to realize that there is no color in the natural world and no sound—nothing of this kind; no textures, no patterns, no beauty, no scent. . . ." In short, none of the objective facts upon which we usually base our reality is fundamentally valid.

As disturbing as this may sound, there is incredible liberation in realizing that you can change your world—including your body—*simply by changing your perception.* How you perceive yourself is causing immense changes in your body right now. To give an example: In America and England, mandatory retirement at age 65 sets an arbitrary cutoff date for social usefulness. The day before a worker turns 65, he contributes labor and value to society; the day after, he becomes one of society's dependents. Medically, the results of this perceptual shift can be disastrous. In the first few years after retirement, heart attack and cancer rates soar, and early death overtakes men who were otherwise healthy before they retired. "Early retirement death," as the syndrome is called, depends on the perception that one's useful days are over; this is only a perception, but for someone who holds it firmly, it is enough to create disease and death. By comparison, in societies where old age is accepted as part of the social fabric, elders remain extremely vigorous—lifting, climbing, and bending in ways that we do not accept as normal in our elderly.

If you examine old cells, such as ones that form liver spots on the skin, through a high-powered microscope, the scene is as devastated as a war zone. Fibrous streaks run here and there; deposits of fat and undiscarded metabolic wastes form unsightly clumps; dark, yellowish pigments called lipofuscin have accumulated to the point where they litter 10 to 30 percent of the cell's interior.

This scene of devastation was created by subcellular processes that went wrong, but if you look through less materialistic lenses, you will see that old cells are like maps of a person's experience. Things that made you suffer are imprinted there, along with things that brought you joy. Stresses you long ago forgot on the conscious level are still sending out signals, like buried microchips, making you anxious, tense, fatigued, apprehensive, resentful, doubtful, disappointed—these reactions cross the mind-body barrier to become part of you. The clogged, toxic deposits in old cells don't appear uniformly; some people acquire much more than others, even when there is little genetic difference between them. By the time you reach age 70, your cells will look unique, mirroring the unique experiences you processed and metabolized into your tissues and organs.

Being able to process the raw, chaotic vibrations of the "quantum soup" and turn them into meaningful, orderly bits of reality opens up enormous creative possibilities. However, these possibilities exist only when you are aware of them. While you are reading this book, a huge portion of your consciousness is engaged in creating your body without your participation. The so-called involuntary or autonomic nervous system was designed to control functions that have slipped out of your awareness. If you began walking down the street in a daze, the involuntary centers in your brain would still be coping with the world, keeping on the lookout for danger, poised to activate the stress response at a moment's notice.

A hundred things you pay no attention to—breathing, digesting, growing new cells, repairing damaged old ones, purifying toxins, preserving hormonal balance, converting stored energy from fat to blood sugar, dilating the pupils of the eyes, raising and lowering blood pressure, maintaining steady body temperature, balancing as you walk, shunting blood to and from the muscle groups that are doing the most work, and sensing movements and sounds in the surrounding environment—continue ceaselessly.

These automatic processes play a huge part in aging, for as we age, our ability to coordinate these functions declines. A lifetime of unconscious living leads to numerous deteriorations, while a lifetime of conscious participation prevents them. The very act of paying conscious attention to bodily functions instead of leaving them on automatic pilot will change how you age. Every so-called involuntary function, from heartbeat and breathing to digestion and hormone regulation, can be consciously controlled. The era of biofeedback and meditation has taught us that—heart patients have been trained in mind-body laboratories to lower their blood pressure at will or to reduce the acid secretions that create ulcers, among dozens of other things. Why not put this ability to use in the aging process? Why not exchange old patterns of perception for new ones? There are abundant techniques, as we will see, for influencing the involuntary nervous system to our advantage.

2. *Our bodies are composed of energy and information.*

To transform the patterns of the past you must know what they are made of. Your body appears to be composed of solid matter that can be broken down into molecules and atoms, but quantum physics tells us that every atom is more than 99.9999 percent empty space, and the subatomic particles moving at lightning speed through this space are actually bundles of vibrating energy. These vibrations aren't random and meaningless, however; they carry information. Thus, one bundle of vibrations is coded as a hydrogen atom, another as oxygen; each element is in fact its own unique code.

Codes are abstract, and so ultimately is our cosmos and everything in it. Chasing the physical structure of the body down to its ultimate source dead-ends as molecules give way to atoms, atoms to subatomic particles, and these particles to ghosts of energy dissolving into an empty void. This void is mysteriously imprinted with information even before any information is expressed. Just as thousands of words exist silently in your memory without being spoken, the quantum field holds the entire universe in unexpressed form; it has been that way since the Big Bang, when billions of galaxies were compressed into a space millions of times smaller than the period at the end of this sentence. Yet even before that infinitesimal dot, the structure of the universe existed in unmanifest form.

The essential stuff of the universe, including your body, is non-stuff, but it isn't ordinary non-stuff. It is thinking non-stuff. The void inside every atom is pulsating with unseen intelligence. Geneticists locate this intelligence primarily inside DNA, but that is only for the sake of convenience. Life unfolds as DNA imparts its coded intelligence to its active twin, RNA, which in turn goes out into the cell and imparts bits of intelligence to thousands of enzymes, which then use their specific bit of intelligence to make proteins. At every point in this sequence, energy and information have to be exchanged or there could be no building life from lifeless matter.

The human body derives its primary energy by burning sugar, which is transported to the cells in the form of glucose, or blood sugar. The chemical structure of glucose is closely related to common table sugar, sucrose. But if you burn table sugar, you don't get the exquisite, complex structures of a living cell; you just get a charred lump of ash and traces of water and carbon dioxide in the air.

Metabolism is more than a burning process; it is an intelligent act. The same sugar that remains inert in a sugar cube supports life with its energy because the body's cells infuse it with new information. The sugar may contribute its energy to a kidney, heart, or brain cell, for example. All of these cells contain completely unique forms of intelligence—the rhythmic twitching of a heart cell is completely different from the electrical discharges of a brain cell or the sodium exchanges of a kidney cell.

As marvelous as this wealth of diverse intelligence is, at bottom there is one single intelligence shared by the whole body. The flow of this intelligence keeps you alive, and when it ceases to flow, at the moment of death, all the knowledge stored in your DNA is rendered useless. As we age, this flow of intelligence becomes compromised in various ways. The specific intelligence of the immune system, the nervous system, and the endocrine system all start falling off; these three systems are now known by physiologists to function as the master controls of the body. Your immune cells and endocrine glands are outfitted with the same receptors for brain signals as your neurons are; therefore, they are like an extended brain. Senility cannot be looked upon, then, simply as a disease confined to our gray matter; when intelligence is lost in the immune or the endocrine system, senility of the whole body is creeping in.

Since all this happens at an unseen, unmanifest level, the losses go unnoticed until they have progressed to a very late stage and are expressed as a physical symptom. The five senses cannot go deep enough to experience the billions of quantum exchanges that create aging. The rate of change is at once too fast and too slow: too fast because individual chemical reactions take less than 1/10,000th of a

16

second, too slow because their cumulative effect will not show up for years. These reactions involve information and energy on a scale millions of times smaller than a single atom.

Age deterioration would be unavoidable if the body was simply material, because all material things are prey to entropy, the tendency of orderly systems to become disorderly. The classic example of entropy is a car rusting in a junkyard; entropy breaks down the orderly machinery into crumbling rust. There is no chance that the process will work the other way—that a rusty scrap heap will reassemble itself into a new car. But entropy doesn't apply to intelligence—an invisible part of us is immune to the ravages of time. Modern science is just discovering the implications of all this, but it has been imparted for centuries through spiritual traditions in which masters have preserved the youthfulness of their bodies far into old age.

India, China, Japan, and to a lesser extent the Christian West have given birth to sages who realized their essential nature as a flow of intelligence. By preserving that flow and nurturing it year after year, they overcame entropy from a deeper level of Nature. In India, the flow of intelligence is called *Prana* (usually translated as "life force"), which can be increased and decreased at will, moved here and there, and manipulated to keep the physical body orderly and young. As we will see, the ability to contact and use Prana is within all of us. A yogi moves Prana using nothing more than attention, for at a deep level, attention and Prana are the same—life is awareness, awareness is life.

3. Mind and body are inseparably one.

Intelligence is much more flexible than the mask of matter that hides it. Intelligence can express itself either as thoughts or as molecules. A basic emotion such as fear can be described as an abstract feeling or as a tangible molecule of the hormone adrenaline. Without the feeling there is no hormone; without the hormone there is no feeling. In the same way, there is no pain without nerve signals that transmit pain; there is no relief from pain without endorphins that fit into the pain receptors to block those signals. The revolution we call mind-body medicine was based on this simple discovery: Wherever thought goes, a chemical goes with it. This insight has turned into a powerful tool that allows us to understand, for example, why recent widows are twice as likely to develop breast cancer, and why the chronically depressed are four times more likely to get sick. In both cases, distressed mental states get converted into the biochemicals that create disease.

In my medical practice, I can see two heart patients afflicted with angina pectoris, the typical squeezing, breathless pain that is typical of heart disease. One patient will be able to run, swim, and perhaps even mountain-climb, totally ignoring his pain or not even having any, while the other nearly faints with pain when he gets up out of his armchair.

My first instinct will be to look for a physical difference between them, but I might or might not find anything. Cardiologists expect anginal pain to appear when at least one of the three coronary arteries is 50 percent blocked. This blockage is almost always in the form of an atheroma, a lesion on the inside of the arterial wall built up by dead cells, blood clots, and fatty plaque. The 50 percent blockage is only a rule of thumb, however. Some angina patients are disabled by pain when they have only a single small lesion barely obstructing blood flow in one artery, while other patients suffering from massive, multiple blockages of up to 85 percent have been known to run marathons. (Angina is not always caused by physical blockage, I should add. Arteries are lined with a layer of muscle cells that can go into spasm and squeeze the vessel closed, but this is a highly individual reaction.)

In mind-body terms, my two patients are expressing their different interpretations of pain. Every patient stamps his condition with a unique perspective, and pain (or any other symptom) emerges into awareness only after it interacts with all the past influences at work in the mind-body system. There is no single response for all people or even for the same person at two different times. Pain signals are raw data that can be turned to many purposes. High-exertion athletics, such as long-distance running, subject an athlete to pain that he interprets as a sign of accomplishment ("no pain, no gain"); but the same pain, inflicted under other circumstances, would be completely unwelcome. Track runners admire a coach who pushes them to their limits; they might hate the same treatment in boot camp.

Medicine is just beginning to use the mind-body connection for healing—defeating pain is a good example. By giving a placebo, or dummy, drug, 30 percent of patients will experience the same pain relief as if a real painkiller had been administered. But the mind-body effect is much more holistic. The same dummy pill can be used to kill pain, to stop excessive gastric secretions in ulcer patients, to lower blood pressure, or to fight tumors. (All the side effects of chemotherapy, including hair loss and nausea, can be induced by giving cancer patients a sugar pill while assuring them that it is a powerful anticancer drug, and there have been instances where injections of sterile saline solution have actually led to remissions of advanced malignancy.)

Since the same inert pill can lead to such totally different responses, we must conclude that the body is capable of producing *any* biochemical response once the mind has been given the appropriate suggestion. The pill itself is meaningless; the power that activates the placebo effect is the power of suggestion alone. This suggestion is then converted into the body's intention to cure itself. Therefore, why not bypass the deception of the sugar pill and go directly to the intention? If we could effectively trigger the intention not to age, the body would carry it out automatically.

We have extremely exciting evidence to prove that such a possibility exists. One of the most dreaded diseases of old age is Parkinson's, a neurological disorder that produces uncontrollable muscle movements and a drastic slowing down of bodily motions such as walking, eventually resulting in a body so stiff that the patient cannot move at all. Parkinson's has been traced to an unexplained depletion of a critical brain chemical called dopamine, but there is also a simulated Parkinson's caused when the dopamine-producing cells of the brain have been destroyed chemically by certain drugs. Imagine a patient afflicted with this type of Parkinson's in an advanced stage of frozen motion. Trying to walk, he can only take a step or two before halting in place, as stiff as a statue.

However, if you draw a line on the floor and say, "Step over that," the person will miraculously be able to walk right over it. Despite the fact that the production of dopamine is completely involuntary and its stores are seemingly exhausted (as shown by the fact that his brain cannot signal his leg muscles to take another step), merely by having the intention to walk, the brain is awakened. The person may freeze again after only a few seconds, but again you can ask him to step over an imaginary line, and his brain will respond. By extension, the infirmity and inactivity exhibited by many old people is often just dormancy. By renewing their intention to live active, purposeful lives, many elderly people can dramatically improve their motor abilities, strength, agility, and mental responses.

Intention is the active partner of attention; it is the way we convert automatic processes into conscious ones. Using simple mind-body exercises, almost any patient can learn in a few sessions to convert a racing heartbeat, asthmatic wheezing, or free-floating anxiety into a more normal response. What seems out of control can be brought back into control with the proper technique. The implications for aging are enormous. By inserting an intention into your thought processes, such as, "I want to improve in energy and vigor every day," you can begin to assert control over those brain centers that determine how much energy will be expressed in activity. The decline of vigor in old age is largely the result of people *expecting* to decline; they have unwittingly implanted a self-defeating intention in the form of a strong belief, and the mind-body connection automatically carries out this intention.

Our past intentions create obsolete programming that seems to have control over us. In truth, the power of intention can be reawakened at any time. Long before you get old, you can prevent such losses by consciously programming your mind to remain youthful, using the power of your intention.

4. *The biochemistry of the body is a product of awareness.*

One of the greatest limitations of the old paradigm was the assumption that a person's awareness doesn't play a role in explaining what is happening in his body. Yet healing cannot be understood unless the person's beliefs, assumptions, expectations, and self-image are also understood. Although the image of the body as a mindless machine continues to dominate mainstream Western medicine, there is unquestionable evidence to the contrary. Death rates from cancer and heart disease are provably higher among people in psychological distress, and lower among people who have a strong sense of purpose and well-being.

One of the most publicized medical studies in recent years was conducted by Stanford psychiatrist David Spiegel, who set out to prove that the mental state of patients did not influence whether they survived cancer. He felt, as many clinicians do, that assigning importance to a patient's beliefs and attitudes would do more harm than good, because the thought "I caused my cancer" would cause feelings of guilt and self-recrimination. Spiegel took eighty-six women with advanced breast cancer (their disease was basically beyond help with conventional treatment) and gave half of them weekly psychotherapy combined with lessons in self-hypnosis. By any measure this represents minimal intervention—what could a woman do in an hour's therapy per week, time she must share with several other patients, to combat a disease that is inevitably fatal in advanced stages? The answer seemed obvious.

However, after following his subjects for ten years, Spiegel was stunned to find that the group receiving therapy survived on average twice as long as the group that received none. It was doubly telling that only three women were alive by this late date, all of them from the therapy group. This study is startling because the researcher expected no effect at all. But a decade of similar findings came in from other researchers. A meticulous 1987 study from Yale, reported by M. R. Jensen, found that breast cancer spread fastest among women who had repressed personalities, felt hopeless, and were unable to express anger, fear, and other negative emotions. Similar findings have emerged for rheumatoid arthritis, asthma, intractable pain, and other disorders.

Dominated by the old paradigm, doctors hold a prejudice against such results. As Larry Dossey points out in his insightful book *Medicine and Meaning,* "The dominant message, incessantly preached from the editorial pages of medical journals and the podiums of medical schools, is that the 'inherent biology of the disease' is overwhelmingly important and that feelings, emotions, and attitudes are simply along for the ride." What the new paradigm teaches us is that emotions are not fleeting events isolated in mental space; they are expressions of awareness, the fundamental stuff of life. In all religious traditions the breath of life *is* spirit. To raise or lower someone's spirits means something fundamental that the body must reflect.

Awareness makes a huge difference in aging, for although every species of higher life-form ages, only humans know what is happening to them, and we translate this knowledge into aging itself. To despair of growing old makes you grow old faster, while to accept it with grace keeps many miseries, both physical and mental, from your door. The commonsense notion "You're only as old as you think you are" has deep implications. What is a thought? It is an impulse of energy and information, like everything else in Nature. The packages of information and energy that we label trees, stars, mountains, and oceans could be called Nature's thoughts, too, but in one important respect our thoughts are different. Nature is stuck with her thoughts once their pattern has been fixed in place; things such as stars and trees follow a growth cycle that runs automatically through the stages of birth, development, decay, and dissolution.

We, however, are not stuck in our life cycle; being aware, we participate in every reaction that takes place inside us. The problems arise when we don't take responsibility for what we're doing. In his book *The Holographic Universe,* Michael Talbot draws a brilliant comparison with King Midas: Because everything he touched turned to gold, Midas could never know the actual texture of anything.

Water, wheat, flesh, or feathers all turned into the same hard metal the instant he touched them. In the same fashion, because our awareness turns the quantum field into ordinary material reality, we cannot know the true texture of quantum reality itself, either through our five senses or by thinking about it, for a thought also transforms the field—it takes the infinite possibilities of the void and shapes a specific space-time event.

What you call your body is a specific space-time event too, and by experiencing its materiality, you miss the Midas touch that converts pure abstract potential into a solid thing. Unless you become *aware of awareness,* you won't be able to catch yourself in the act of transformation.

5. Perception is a learned phenomenon.

The power of awareness would make no difference in our lives if Nature had outfitted us all with the same responses to experience. Clearly, this didn't happen; no two people share the same perception of anything. The face of your beloved may be the face of my worst enemy, the food you crave may cause nausea in me. These personal responses have to be learned, which is where differences originate. Learning is a very active use of the mind, leading to very active changes in the body. Perceptions of love, hate, delight, and nausea stimulate the body in extremely different directions. In short, our bodies are the physical results of all the interpretations we have been learning to make since we were born.

Some transplant patients report an uncanny experience after receiving a donated kidney, liver, or heart. Without knowing who the organ donor was, they begin to participate in his memories. Associations that belonged to another person start being released when that person's tissues are placed inside a stranger. In one instance, a woman woke up after a heart transplant craving beer and Chicken McNuggets; she was very surprised, because she had never before wanted either. After she began to have mysterious dreams in which a young man named Timmy came to her, she tracked down the donor of her new heart, which had come from the victim of a fatal traffic accident; when she contacted his family, it turned out that the victim was a young man named Timmy. The woman was stunned to discover that he'd had a particular fondness for drinking beer and had been killed on his way home from McDonald's.

Rather than seeking a supernatural explanation for such incidents, one could see them as confirmation that our bodies are made of experiences transformed into physical expression. Because experience is something we incorporate (literally, "make into a body"), our cells have been instilled with our memories; thus, to receive someone else's cells is to receive their memories at the same time.

Your cells are constantly processing experience and metabolizing it according to your personal views. You don't just funnel raw data through your eyes and ears and stamp it with a judgment. You physically *turn into* the interpretation as you internalize it. Someone who is depressed over losing his job projects sadness everywhere in his body—the brain's output of neurotransmitters becomes depleted, hormone levels drop, the sleep cycle is interrupted, neuropeptide receptors on the outer surface of skin cells become distorted, platelet cells in the blood become stickier and more prone to clump, and even his tears contain different chemical traces than tears of joy.

This whole biochemical profile will alter dramatically when the person finds a new job, and if it is a more satisfying one, his body's output of neurotransmitters, hormones, receptors, and all other vital biochemicals, down to DNA itself, will start to reflect this sudden turn for the better. Although we assume that DNA is a locked storehouse of genetic information, its active twin, RNA, responds to day-to-day existence. Medical students at exam time show a decreased output of interleukin 2, a critical chemical in the immune response that fights cancer. The production of interleukin 2 is controlled by messenger RNA, which means that the student's anxiety over passing his exams is speaking directly to his genes.

This point reinforces the great need to use our awareness to create the bodies we actually want. Anxiety over a medical exam eventually passes, as does depression over a lost job, but the aging process has to be countered every day. Your interpretation of how you are aging is critical to what happens over the next four, five, or six decades. In neurological terms, a brain signal is just a set of energy fluctuations. If you are in a coma, these signals are meaningless; when you are alert and aware, the same signals are open to infinite creative interpretations. Shakespeare was not being metaphorical when he wrote Prospero's line "We are such stuff as dreams are made on." The body is like a manifest dream, a 3-D projection of brain signals as they transform themselves into the state we call "real."

Aging is nothing but a set of misguided transformations, processes that should remain stable, balanced, and self-renewing but deviate from their proper course. This appears as a physical change, yet what has really happened is that your awareness—whether in your mind or your cells doesn't matter—deviated first. By becoming aware of how that slippage occurred, you can bring your body's biochemistry back into line. There is no biochemistry outside awareness; every cell in your body is totally aware of how you think and feel about yourself. Once you accept that fact, the whole illusion of being victimized by a mindless, randomly degenerating body falls away.

6. Impulses of intelligence constantly create the body in new forms every second.

Creating the body in new forms is necessary in order to meet the changing demands of life. A child's view of reality, for example, contains much that is unfamiliar, and until he learns more about the world, his body expresses itself in untrained and uncoordinated behaviors. At 3 months old, a baby cannot tell the difference between a staircase and a painting of a staircase. His brain hasn't grasped what an optical illusion is. By 6 months, his reality has changed; babies can recognize optical illusions by that age, and using that knowledge, their bodies are better able to negotiate three-dimensional space (mirrors don't look like holes in the wall, real stairs are to be climbed but not paintings of stairs, roundness is different from flatness, etc.). Making this perceptual shift isn't just mental; a whole new way of using eyes and hands has been achieved, and the physical dimensions of various brain centers for shape recognition and motor coordination are affected.

As long as new perceptions continue to enter your brain, your body can respond in new ways. There is no secret of youth more powerful. As one 80-year-old patient of mine succinctly put it, "People don't grow old. When they stop growing, they become old." New knowledge, new skills, new ways of looking at the world keep mind and body growing, and as long as that happens, the natural tendency to be new at every second is expressed.

In the quantum world, change is inevitable, aging isn't. The chronological age of our physical bodies is beside the point. The youngest-looking 50-year-old has molecules that are the same age as those of the oldest-looking 50-year-old. In both cases the chronological age of the body could be stated as 5 billion years (the age of the various atoms), or 1 year (the time it takes for these atoms to replace themselves in our tissues), or 3 seconds (the time taken for a cell to turn over its enzymes for processing food, air, and water).

In truth, you are only as old as the information that swirls through you, and this is very fortunate. You can control the informational content of the quantum field. Although there is a certain amount of fixed information in the atoms of food, air, and water that make up each cell, the power to transform that information is subject to free will. One thing you can own free and clear in this world is your interpretation of it. There are remarkable medical cases of young children, for example, who feel so unloved that they stop growing. This syndrome, called psychosocial dwarfism, occurs among severely abused children who convert their lack of love and affection into depleted growth hormone, in defiance of the fact that growth hormone is supposedly released on a preprogrammed schedule imprinted into every child's DNA. In these cases the power of interpretation overrides the genetic imprint, causing a change in the body's informational fields.

Interpretations arise from a person's self-interaction. You experience this as internal dialogue. Thoughts, judgments, and feelings are ceaselessly swirling through one's mind: "I like this, I don't like that, I'm afraid of A, I'm not sure of B," etc. Internal dialogue is not random mental noise; it is generated from a deep level by your beliefs and assumptions. A core belief is defined as something you assume is true about reality, and as long as you hold on to it, your belief will hold your body's informational fields to certain parameters—you will perceive something as likable or unlikable, distressing or enjoyable, according to how it fits your expectations.

When someone's interpretation changes, a change in his reality also takes place. In the case of children suffering from psychosocial dwarfism, putting them into a loving environment proves more effective than administering growth hormone (their belief in being unwanted and unworthy can be so strong that their bodies will not grow even when hormones are injected into them). However, if loving foster parents can transform the children's core belief about being unlovable, they can respond with bursts of naturally produced growth hormone, which sometimes brings them back to normal height, weight, and development. When they see themselves differently, their personal reality is altered at a physiological level. This is a powerful metaphor for how our fear of aging and our deep belief that we are meant to grow old may get transformed into aging itself, as a self-fulfilling prophecy generated by a withering self-image.

To escape this prison, we need to overturn the beliefs supported by fear. In place of the belief that your body decays with time, nurture the belief that your body is new at every moment. In place of the belief that your body is a mindless machine, nurture the belief that your body is infused with the deep intelligence of life, whose sole purpose is to sustain you. These new beliefs are not just nicer to live with; they are true—we experience the joy of life through our bodies, so it is only natural to believe that our bodies are not set against us but want what we want.

7. Despite the appearance of being separate individuals, we are all connected to patterns of intelligence governing the cosmos.

You and your environment are one. Looking at yourself, you perceive that your body stops at a certain point; it is separated from the wall of your room or a tree outdoors by empty space. In quantum terms, however, the distinction between "solid" and "empty" is insignificant. Every cubic centimeter of quantum space is filled with a nearly infinite amount of energy, and the tiniest vibration is part of vast fields of vibration spanning whole galaxies. In a very real sense, your environment is your extended body: With every breath, you inhale hundreds of millions of atoms of air exhaled yesterday by someone in China. All the oxygen, water, and sunlight around you are only faintly distinguishable from that which is inside you.

If you choose, you can experience yourself in a state of unity with everything you contact. In ordinary waking consciousness, you touch your finger to a rose and feel it as solid, but in truth one bundle of energy and information—your finger—is contacting another bundle of energy and information—the rose. Your finger and the thing it touches are both just minute outcroppings of the infinite field we call the universe. This truth inspired the ancient sages of India to declare:

> As is the microcosm, so is the macrocosm.
> As is the atom, so is the universe.
> As is the human body, so is the cosmic body.
> As is the human mind, so is the cosmic mind.

These are not just mystical teachings but actual experiences of those who could dislodge their awareness from a state of separation and identify instead with the unity of everything. In unity consciousness, people, things, and events "out there" all become part of your body; in fact, you are only a mirror of relationships centered on these influences. The famous naturalist John Muir declared, "Whenever we try to pick out anything by itself, we find it hitched to everything else in the universe." This shouldn't be a rare experience but the first building block of everything we know.

The possibility of experiencing unity has tremendous implications for aging, because when there is harmonious interaction between you and your extended body, you feel joyful, healthy, and youthful. "Fear is born of separation," the ancient Indian sages maintained; in this statement they probed deep into why we age

Seeing ourselves as separate, we create chaos and disorder between ourselves and things "out there." We war with other people and destroy the environment. Death, the final state of separation, looms as a fearsome unknown; the very prospect of change, which is part of life, creates untold dread because it connotes loss.

Fear inevitably brings violence in its wake. Being separate from other people, things, and events, we want to force them to be what we want. In harmony there is no violence. Instead of futilely trying to control the uncontrollable, a person in unity learns acceptance, not because he has to but because there actually is peace and orderliness in himself and his extended body. The modern sage J. Krishnamurti lived into his nineties with wonderful alertness, wisdom, and undiminished vitality. I remember seeing him bound up the stairs to a lecture podium when he was 85, and I was very moved when a woman who had known him for many years told me, "I have learned one thing about him—he is completely without violence."

The quantum worldview is not a spiritual one in its equations and postulates, but Einstein and his colleagues were united by a mystical reverence for their discoveries. Niels Bohr compared the wave aspect of matter to cosmic mind; Erwin Schrödinger ended his life believing that the universe was itself a living mind (echoing Isaac Newton, who maintained that gravity and all other forces were thoughts in the mind of God). The truth is that probing our own spirit always brings humans to the border of spirit in its larger sense. By putting this encounter into objective terms, the new paradigm allows us actually to cross over the boundary that once divided mind, body, and spirit.

The transformation from separation to unity, from conflict to peace, is the goal of all spiritual traditions. "Don't we live in the same objective world?" a disciple once queried his guru. "Yes," his master replied, "but you see yourself in the world, I see the world in myself. This minor perceptual shift makes all the difference between freedom and bondage."

All of us are in bondage to the disorder we create by seeing ourselves as separate and isolated. The perfect example is the Type A personality with its driven, frustrated behavior, its constant sense of being pressured by deadlines. Unable to relax into any kind of acceptance or flow, such a person nurtures his past hurts as anger; this repressed turmoil gets projected into the environment as hostility, impatience, blame, and unacknowledged panic. Endlessly trying to control others, such a person reacts to minor stresses with harsh criticism of both self and others. In the act of creating so much chaos, the Type A person, particularly in the business world, is deluded into thinking that he or she is competing successfully. In actuality, the level of efficient work is very low, and as frustrations mount, the feedback the Type A personality receives from his or her extended body creates more havoc within the physical body. Cholesterol and blood pressure rise; the heart is subjected to needless stressful arousal, seriously increasing the risk of a fatal heart attack or stroke.

Type A is an extreme example of the harm created by not interacting harmoniously with one's extended body. As we will see, perceived stress in the environment is directly related to most of the age changes that overtake everyone. What makes us old isn't the stress so much as it is the *perception* of stress. Someone who doesn't see the world "out there" as a threat can coexist with the environment, free of the damage created by the stress response. In many ways, the most important thing you can do to experience a world without aging is to nurture the knowledge that the world is you.

8. Time is not absolute. The underlying reality of all things is eternal, and what we call time is really quantified eternity.

Although our bodies, and the whole physical world, are a display of constant change, there is more to reality than process. The universe was born and is evolving. When it was born, time and space came into existence. Before the instant of the Big Bang, time and space didn't exist as we know them. Yet the rational mind finds it nearly impossible to ask questions such as "What came before time?" and "What is bigger than space?" Even Einstein, when he was a young physicist working out quantum principles for the first time, held on to the old notion, embraced by Newton, that the universe existed in a steady state—time and space were eternal constants, never born and never dying.

This steady-state version of reality is still the one our five senses report back to us about. You cannot see or feel time as it speeds up or slows down, even though Einstein proved that time does this; you cannot sense space as it expands or contracts, yet this too is part of a rhythmic universe. To go even further, to imagine those dimensionless regions where time and space are born, requires a radical shift in perception. This shift is forced upon us because the universe had to have some kind of timeless source—and the same holds true for us.

You perceive yourself as existing in time because your body is composed of change; to change, one must have a flow or sequence. In this sequence there is a before and after—before this breath was the last breath, after this heartbeat will be the next heartbeat. But theoretically, if you had the time and the equipment, you could make an EKG of all the heartbeats someone has had in a lifetime, and by holding the printout in your hands, you would have past, present, and future contained in one place. You could look at it upside down or backward; you could fold it in half so that the last heartbeat and the first one were next to each other.

This kind of manipulation is what quantum physics reveals about the most basic space-time events in Nature. As they exchange energy states, two particles can move backward in time as easily as forward; things that happened in the past can be altered by energy events in the future. The whole notion of time as an arrow shooting inexorably forward has been shattered forever in the complex geometries of quantum space, where multidimensional strings and loops carry time in all directions and even bring it to a halt.

The only absolute left to us is the timeless, for now we realize that our entire universe is just one incident springing forth out of a larger reality. What we sense as seconds, minutes, hours, days, and years are cut-up bits of this larger reality. It is up to you, the perceiver, to cut up the timeless any way you like; your awareness creates the time you experience. Someone who experiences time as a scarce commodity that is constantly slipping away is creating a completely different personal reality from someone who perceives that he has all the time in the world. Is your day full of time pressure? Do you suffer the breathless, panicky symptoms of "time sickness," which the body translates into rapid or irregular heartbeat, distorted digestive rhythms, insomnia, and high blood pressure? These individual differences express how we perceive change, for the perception of change creates our experience of time.

When your attention is in the past or the future, you are in the field of time, creating aging. One Indian master who seemed remarkably young for his age explained this by saying, "Most people spend their lives either in the past or the future, but my life is supremely concentrated in the present." When a life is concentrated in the present, it is most real, because the past and future are not impinging upon it. At this instant, where are the past and future? Nowhere. Only the present moment exists; past and future are mental projections. If you can free yourself of these projections, trying neither to relive the past nor to control the future, a space is opened for a completely new experience—the experience of ageless body and timeless mind.

Being able to identify with a reality that is not bounded by time is extremely important; otherwise there is no escape from the decay that time inevitably brings. You can catch a glimpse of timelessness with a simple mind-body exercise: Choose a time of day when you feel relaxed and unpressured. Sit quietly in a comfortable chair and take off your watch, placing it nearby so that you can easily refer to it without having to lift it or move your head very much. Now close your eyes and be aware of your breathing. Let your attention easily follow the stream of breath going in and out of your body. Imagine your whole body rising and falling with the flow of each breath. After a minute or two, you will be aware of warmth and relaxation pervading your muscles.

When you feel very settled and quiet inside, slowly open your eyes and peek at the second hand of your watch. What's it doing? Depending on how relaxed you are, the second hand will behave in different ways. For some people, it will have stopped entirely, and this effect will last anywhere from one to perhaps three seconds. For other people, the second hand will hesitate for half a second, then jump into its normal ticking. Still other people will perceive the second hand moving, but at a slower pace than usual. Unless you have tried this little experiment, it seems very unlikely, but once you have had the experience of seeing a watch stop, you will never again doubt that time is a product of perception. The only time there is is the one you are aware of.

You can learn to take your awareness into the region of time-lessness at will—meditation is the classic technique for mastering this experience. In meditation the active mind is withdrawn to its source; just as this changing universe had to have a source beyond change, your mind, with all its restless activity, arises from a state of awareness beyond thought, sensation, emotion, desire, and memory. This is a profound personal experience. In the state of timeless or transcendent awareness, you have the sensation of fullness. In place of change, loss, and decay, there is steadiness and fulfillment. You sense that the infinite is everywhere. When this experience becomes a reality, the fears associated with change disappear; the fragmentation of eternity into seconds, hours, days, and years becomes secondary, and the perfection of every moment becomes primary.

Now that meditation has entered mainstream Western cultural experience, researchers have applied scientific measurements to the subjective experience of silence, fullness, and eternity. They have discovered that the physiological state of meditators undergoes definite shifts toward more efficient functioning. Hundreds of individual findings show lowered respiration, reduced oxygen consumption, and decreased metabolic rate. In terms of aging, the most significant conclusion is that the hormonal imbalance associated with stress—and known to speed up the aging process—is reversed. This in turn slows or even reverses the aging process, as measured by various biological changes associated with growing old. From my experience with studies on people using Transcendental Meditation, it has been established that long-term meditators can have a biological age between 5 and 12 years younger than their chronological age.

The most fascinating aspect of this research, which has been ongoing for over two decades, is that the biological process of aging itself does not have to be manipulated; the desired results can be achieved through awareness alone. In other words, meditation alters the frame of reference that gives the person his experience of time. At a quantum level, physical events in space-time such as heartbeat and hormone levels can be affected simply by taking the mind to a reality where time does not have such a powerful hold. The new paradigm is showing us that time has many levels and all are available to us in our own consciousness.

9. Everyone inhabits a reality of non-change lying beyond all change. The experience of this reality brings change under our control.

At the moment, the only physiology you can maintain is time-based. However, the fact that time is tied to awareness implies that you could maintain an entirely different style of functioning—the physiology of immortality—which would correspond to the experience of non-change. Non-change can't be created as a product of change. It requires a shift out of time-bound awareness into timeless awareness. There are many gradations to this shift. For example, if you are under extreme time pressure at work, your body's reaction to the pressure is not automatic; some people thrive under time pressure, using it to fuel their creativity and energy, while others are defeated by it, losing incentive and feeling a burden that will bring no satisfaction compared with the stress it creates.

The person who responds with creativity has learned not to identify with the time pressure; he has transcended it at least partially, unlike the person who feels constriction and stress. For him, identification with time has become overwhelming—he cannot escape the ticking of the internal clock, and his body cannot help but mirror his state of mind. In various subtle ways, our cells constantly adjust to our perception of time; a biologist would say that we have entrained, or locked in sequence, a series of processes embracing millions of related mind-body events.

It is all-important to realize that you can reach a state where time-bound processes can be realigned. A simple analogy demonstrates this: Look at your physical body as a printout of signals being sent back and forth between your brain and every cell. The nervous system, which sets up the kinds of messages being sent, functions as the body's software; the myriad different hormones, neurotransmitters, and other messenger molecules are the input being run through the software. All this constitutes the visible programming of your body. But where is the programmer? He is not visible, yet he must exist. Thousands of decisions are being made in the mind-body system every second, countless choices that enable your physiology to adapt to the demands of life.

If I see a cobra on the path in India and jump back in fear, the visible apparatus controlling this event can be seen in the muscle reactions I display, which are triggered by chemical signals from my nervous system. My increased heartbeat and panting breath are other visible signs that the hormone adrenaline has kicked in, secreted by the adrenal cortex in response to a specific brain chemical (ACTH) sent from the pituitary. If a biochemist could track down every single molecule involved in my fear reaction, he would still miss the invisible decision-maker that decided to have the reaction, for even though I reacted in a split second, my body didn't jump back mindlessly. Someone with entirely different programming would exhibit entirely different reactions. A snake collector might bend forward with interest; a Hindu devotee, recognizing a form of Shiva, might kneel in awe.

The fact is that *any* possible reaction might have occurred—panic, rage, hysteria, paralysis, apathy, curiosity, delight, etc. The invisible programmer is unlimited in the ways he can program the visible apparatus of the body. At the moment I stumbled across the snake, all the basic processes of my physiology—breathing, digestion, metabolism, elimination, perception, and thinking—depended on the *meaning* that a cobra held for me personally. One sees the truth in a saying from Aldous Huxley: "Experience is not what happens to you; it is what you do with what happens to you."

Where can you locate a meaning? The quick and easy answer is to say that it is located in the brain, but this organ, like every other, is in constant flux. Like migrating birds, billions of atoms are flying in and out of my brain every second. It swirls with electrical waves that never form the same pattern twice in a lifetime. Its basic chemistry can shift if different kinds of food are eaten for lunch, or if a sudden mood swing is experienced. Yet my memory of the snake doesn't dissolve in this sea of change. My memories are available to the programmer who stands above memory, silently observing my life, taking account of my experiences, always ready to entertain the possibility of new choices. For this programmer is nothing but the awareness of choice. It appreciates change without getting overwhelmed; therefore it escapes the time-bound limitations that arise in the normal cause-and-effect world.

The "me" who is afraid of snakes learned that fear somewhere in the past. All my reactions are part and parcel of the time-bound self and its tendencies. In less than a thousandth of a second, its preprogrammed fear arouses the whole sequence of bodily messages that produce my actions. For most of us no other "me" is apparent, because we haven't learned to identify with the decision-maker, the silent witness, whose awareness isn't defined by the past. Yet in a subtle way, we all sense that something inside us has not changed very much, if at all, since we were infants. When we wake up in the morning there is a second of pure awareness before the old conditioning automatically falls into place; at that moment you are just yourself, not happy or sad, not important or humble, not old or young.

As I wake up in the morning, this "me" dresses itself in the mantle of experience very quickly; in a matter of seconds I remember that I am, for example, a 46-year-old doctor who has a wife, two children, a home outside Boston, and ten minutes to get to the clinic. That identity is the product of change. The "me" who is beyond change could be waking up anywhere—as a 5-year-old in Delhi smelling my grandmother's cooking, as an 80-year-old in Florida listening to the wind rattling the palms. This changeless "me," whom the ancient sages in India simply called the Self, serves as my real reference point for experience. All other reference points are bound by change, decay, and loss; every other sense of "me" is identified with pain or pleasure, poverty or wealth, happiness or sadness, youth or old age—every time-bound condition that the relative world imposes. In unity consciousness, the world can be explained as a flow of Spirit, which is awareness. Our whole goal is to establish an intimate relationship with Self as Spirit. To the extent that we create this intimacy, the experience of ageless body and timeless mind is realized.

10. We are not victims of aging, sickness, and death. These are part of the scenery, not the seer, who is immune to any form of change.

Life at its source is creation. When you get in touch with your own inner intelligence, you get in touch with the creative core of life. In the old paradigm, control of life was assigned to DNA, an enormously complex molecule that has revealed less than 1 percent of its secrets to geneticists. In the new paradigm, control of life belongs to awareness. All the examples cited here—of children who can curtail the secretion of growth hormone, medical students who alter their output of interleukins when they feel anxious, yogis who can manipulate their heartbeat at will—indicate that the most basic bodily processes respond to our state of mind.

The billions of changes occurring in our cells are only the passing scenery of life; behind their mask is the seer, who represents the source of the flow of awareness. Everything I can possibly experience begins and ends with awareness; every thought or emotion that captures my attention is a tiny fragment of awareness; all the goals and expectations I set for myself are organized in awareness. What the ancient sages termed the Self can be defined in modern psychological terms as a continuum of awareness, and the state known as unity consciousness is the state where awareness is complete—the person knows the whole continuum of himself without masks, illusions, gaps, and broken fragments.

Because we don't maintain the continuity of our awareness, all of us fall into gaps of one kind or another. Vast areas of our bodily existence go out of our control, leading to sickness, aging, and death. But this is only to be expected when awareness has become fragmented. In a famous series of experiments at the Menninger clinic in the early 1970s, a noted spiritual adept from India, Swami Rama, demonstrated the ability to raise his heartbeat at will from

70 to 300, a rate far beyond the normal range. Essentially, his heartbeat became a flutter that no longer pumped blood in the normal rhythmic fashion. In an ordinary person, cardiac flutter can cause heart failure and other serious or even fatal problems. Such occurrences afflict thousands of unsuspecting people every year.

However, Swami Rama was unaffected by this cardiac event because it was under the direct control of his awareness. What this implies is that a person who dies in a matter of minutes from a sudden interruption in his normal heartbeat (this category would cover all kinds of arrhythmias, fibrillation, and tachycardia) has actually suffered a loss of awareness. In our materialistic worldview, we localize this loss in the heart muscle, saying that the electro-chemical signals that coordinate a healthy heartbeat have become disordered. Instead of orchestrating their individual twitches into a smooth, unified pulsation throughout the whole heart, billions of heart cells lapse into chaotic, isolated contractions, making the heart look like a bag of writhing snakes.

Yet this horrifying spectacle, which every cardiologist dreads, is secondary; loss of awareness among the heart cells is primary. This loss of awareness isn't local but general. The person himself has lost communication with the deep levels of intelligence that govern and control all his cells—indeed, every cell is nothing but intelligence organized into various layers of visible and invisible patterns. An adept like Swami Rama shows us that our awareness is not meant to be thus fragmented and curtailed. If one knew himself as he really was, he would realize that he is the source, course, and goal of all this flowing intelligence. What the world's religious traditions call Spirit is wholeness, the continuity of awareness that oversees all the bits and pieces of awareness.

We are made victims of sickness, aging, and death by gaps in our self-knowledge. To lose awareness is to lose intelligence; to lose intelligence is to lose control over the end product of intelligence, the human body. Therefore, the most valuable lesson the new paradigm can teach us is this: If you want to change your body, change your awareness first. Everything that happens to you is a result of how you see yourself, to an extent you might consider quite uncanny. In the sea battles of World War I, German sailors were sometimes stranded in lifeboats for days or weeks after their ships were sunk. Invariably, the first men to die were the youngest. This phenomenon remained a mystery until it was realized that the older sailors, who had survived earlier sinkings, knew that the crisis could be weathered; lacking such experience, the young sailors perished because they saw themselves as trapped in a hopeless situation.

Taking a clue from these incidents, animal researchers have been able to induce rapid aging, disease, and early death in laboratory rats and mice by putting them in situations of high stress, such as by throwing them into tanks of water with no escape. Animals that have never met such a situation perceive it as hopeless and quickly give up and die. Animals that have been gradually conditioned to the tanks persevere and survive, swimming for long hours without signs of stress-induced deterioration of their tissues.

Much of the history of human aging has been characterized by hopelessness. Our fearful images of growing old, coupled with high rates of disease and senility among the elderly, resulted in grim, self-fulfilling expectations. Old age was a time of inevitable decline and loss, of increasing feebleness in mind and body. Now our whole society is waking up to a new awareness of aging; people in their sixties and seventies routinely expect to be as vigorous and healthy as they were in their forties and fifties.

But one underlying assumption—that humans *have* to age—has not been radically challenged. Having to age is a fact we inherited from the old paradigm, stubbornly fixed in our worldview until a shift in awareness can bring new facts to light. A worldview is just a way of arranging the infinite energy of the universe into a system that makes sense. Aging made sense in a scheme of Nature where all things change, fade away, and die. It makes much less sense in a world where an endless flow of ever-renewing intelligence is present all around us. Which view you adopt is your choice. You can choose to see the rose bloom and die; you can choose to see the rose as a wave of life that never ends, for next year new roses will spring from the seeds of this one.

Matter is a captive moment in space and time, and by seeing our world and ourselves materialistically, we make the captive aspects of the universe assume too much importance. As this book unfolds,

THE LAND WHERE NO ONE IS OLD   ·39·

I want you to experience just how fluid and effortless existence can be when your worldview shifts. Despite its solid physical appearance, your body is very much like a river, akin to the sacred river so beautifully described by Hermann Hesse in his spiritual novel *Siddhartha*. In that book there comes a point when Siddhartha, the seeker of enlightenment, finally finds his peace. After years of wandering he ends up beside a great river in India, where an inner voice whispers, "Love this river, stay by it, learn from it." To me, this whisper says something about my body, which flows on and on in its life processes. Like a river, my body changes as the moment changes, and if I could do the same, there would be no gaps in my life, no memory of past trauma to trigger new pain, no anticipation of future hurt to make me contract in fear.

Your body is the river of life that sustains you, yet it does so humbly, without asking for recognition. If you sit and listen to it, you will find that a powerful intelligence dwells in and with you. It isn't an intelligence of words, but compared to the millions of years of wisdom woven into one cell, the knowledge of words doesn't seem so grand. Siddhartha wanted to learn from the river and to listen, which is tremendously important. You have to want to rejoin the flow of the body before you can learn from it, and that means you must be willing to open yourself to knowledge that was overlooked in your old way of seeing.

Hesse went on, "It seemed to him that whoever understood this river and its secrets, would understand much more, many secrets, all secrets." All that has ever happened to you is recorded in your body, but, more important, new possibilities are there, too. Aging seems to be something that's happening to you, when in fact it is something your body has largely learned to do. It has learned to carry out the programming fed into it by you, the programmer. Since so much of this programming was unconscious, dictated by beliefs and assumptions you hardly knew you held, it's important to shatter the whole edifice of thought that gave you the material world as you know it.

Now we need to return to the body, for the intimate experience we have of our physical selves contains the most personal truth. Being comfortable with its present-moment feelings allows you to escape the shadow of threat that hangs over everything when order is losing the battle with entropy. Such a world is the one we were taught to believe in. There is another way and another world. This was the greatest lesson Siddhartha learned from the river. At the end of the novel he speaks about it with his oldest friend and companion, Vasudeva:

"Have you also learned that secret for the river; that there is no such thing as time?"

A bright smile spread over Vasudeva's face. "Yes, Siddhartha. Is this what you mean? That the river is everywhere at the same time, at the source and at the mouth, at the waterfall, at the ferry, at the current, in the ocean and in the mountains, everywhere, and that the present only exists for it, not the shadow of the past, nor the shadow of the future?"

"That is it," said Siddhartha, "and when I learned that, I reviewed my life and it was also a river, and Siddhartha the boy, Siddhartha the mature man and Siddhartha the old man, were only separated by shadows, not through reality."

He spoke with delight, but Vasudeva just smiled radiantly at him and nodded his agreement.

The delusion fostered by centuries of materialism is that we can conquer the river and control its flow; if we did, our only achievement would be to die. The truth about each of us is that our life spreads out in larger and larger fields of experience. There is no limit to the energy, information, and intelligence concentrated in one person's existence. In physical form this infinite creativity has been embodied in your cells; in unmanifest form it is expressed in the mind's silence, the void that is actually a fullness of untold possible meanings, possible truths, possible creations. The emptiness at the core of every atom is the womb of the universe; in the flicker of thought when two neurons interact there is an opportunity for a new world to be born. This book is about exploring that silence where time's breath does not wither but only renews. Look to the land where no one is old; it is nowhere but in yourself.

IN PRACTICE:

How to Reinterpret Your Body

The first step toward experiencing your body in a different way is to change your interpretation of it. No two people experience their bodies in exactly the same way, because each of us interprets experience—including the experience of inhabiting a body—according to his own personal beliefs, values, assumptions, and memories. An aging body involves one style of interpretation; an ageless body involves an opposite style.

Try to let go of the assumption that your body is aging because things just are that way. If you feel certain that growing old is natural, inevitable, and normal, I don't want you to erase those assumptions instantly. You couldn't do that if you tried, for the old paradigm has taught all of us to accept these assumptions without question. However, while still honoring your deep belief in aging, sickness, and death, allow yourself to set aside the old paradigm for a moment.

The quantum worldview, or the new paradigm, teaches us that we are constantly making and unmaking our bodies. Behind the illusion of its being a solid, stable object, the body is a process, and as long as that process is directed toward renewal, the cells of the body remain new, no matter how much time passes or how much entropy we are exposed to.

The great enemy of renewal is habit; when frozen interpretations from the past are applied to the present, there will always be a gap, a mismatch between the need of the moment and the solution from the past. To have a renewed body, you must be willing to have new perceptions that give rise to new solutions. The exercises below are designed to help you open up new perceptions. Some are exercises in absorbing the new knowledge of the quantum worldview as it applies to your body. Others are exercises in new experience, gaining an inner feeling for that level inside your body that is ageless. Ideally, as we move on to later exercises, knowledge and experience will begin to fuse—that is the sign that you are fully assimilating this new worldview in place of the old.

Exercise 1: Seeing Through the Mask of Matter

The most important step in gaining the experience of ageless body is to unfreeze the perceptions that have locked you into feelings of isolation, fragmentation, and separateness. These frozen perceptions reinforce the idea that only the reality of the five senses can be believed. So let us see if we can go beyond the senses to find a level of transcendental experience, which is in fact *more real* than the world of the senses.

Look at your hand and examine it closely. Trace its familiar lines and furrows, feel the texture of the skin, the supple flesh cushioning the submerged hardness of bone. This is the hand your senses report to you, a material object composed of flesh and blood. In this first exercise we will attempt to "thaw out" your hand and give you a different experience of it beyond the reach of your senses.

Holding the image of your hand in your mind's eye, imagine that you are examining it through a high-powered microscope whose lens can penetrate the finest fabrics of matter and energy. At the lowest power, you no longer see smooth flesh but a collection of individual cells loosely bound by connective tissue. Each cell is a watery bag of proteins that appear as long chains of smaller molecules held together by invisible bonds. Moving closer, you can see separate atoms of hydrogen, carbon, oxygen, and so on, which have no solidity at all—they are vibrating, ghostly shadows revealed through the microscope as patches of light and dark.

You have arrived at the boundary between matter and energy,

for the subatomic particles making up each atom—whirling electrons dancing around a nuclear core of protons and neutrons—are
not spots and dots of matter. They are more like traces of light left
by a Fourth of July sparkler waved in the dark. At this level you see
that all things you once took to be solid are just energy trails; the
instant you see one trail, the energy has moved elsewhere, leaving
nothing substantial to be touched or seen. Each trail is a quantum
event, fleeting, dying out as soon as it is noticed.

Now you start sinking even deeper into quantum space. All light
disappears, replaced by yawning chasms of black emptiness. Far
away on the horizon of your vision, you see a last flash, like the
farthest, faintest star visible in the night sky. Hold that flash in your
mind, for it is the last remnant of matter or energy detectable by any
scientific instrument. The blackness closes in, and you are in a place
where not just matter and energy are gone, but space and time as
well.

You have left behind your hand as a space-time event. Like all
space-time events, your body has to have an origin beyond the
fourth dimension. There is no such thing as "before" or "after" in
this region, no concept of "big" or "small." Here your hand exists
before the Big Bang and after the universe's end in the "heat death"
of absolute zero. In reality these terms are meaningless, for you have
arrived at the womb of the universe, the pre-quantum region that
has no dimensions and all dimensions. You are everywhere and
nowhere.

Has your hand ceased to exist? No, for in crossing the boundary
of the fourth dimension, you didn't go anywhere; the whole notion
of place and time simply doesn't apply anymore. All the grosser
levels of perception are still available to you; your hand still exists
at all these levels you have traversed—quantum, subatomic, atomic,
molecular, cellular—connected by invisible intelligence to the place
where you now find yourself. Each level is a layer of transformation,
completely different from the one above or below it, but only here,
where there is nothing but pure information, idea, creative potential, are all levels reduced to their common origin.

Ponder this exercise for a moment to absorb its lessons:

- The three-dimensional body reported by the five senses is a mirage.
- Every solid particle of matter is composed of more than 99.999 percent empty space.
- The void between two electrons is proportionately as empty as the space between two galaxies.
- If you go deep enough into the fabric of matter and energy, you arrive at the origin of the universe. All events in space-time have a common source outside the reality we perceive.
- Beyond the quantum, your body exists as pure creative potential, a multilayered process controlled by intelligence.

Now examine your hand with a new understanding—it is the stepping-off point for a dizzying descent into the dance of life, where the dancers disappear if you approach too near and the music fades away into the silence of eternity. The dance is forever, and the dance is you.

Exercise 2: Closing the Gap

Now that we have touched that level of quantum space underlying all physical existence, I want you to become more comfortable there. Ordinarily we think of space as cold and empty, but quantum space is full—it is the continuity that connects everything in the universe. When the quantum field is active, it gives rise to a space-time event; when it is quiet, there is just quantum space. But this doesn't signify that the field has gaps in it—imagine the Earth surrounded by lines of magnetic force radiating out of the north and south magnetic poles. All the separate magnets on the planet participate in this field. They are small, separate outcroppings of magnetism, yet even when a magnet is not in your immediate vicinity, the magnetic field surrounds you. A horseshoe magnet is a local outcropping of the field (a space-time event), while the lines of the magnetism surrounding the Earth are a nonlocal, invisible presence. Both are connected as aspects of one underlying field of energy.

Because your body emanates electromagnetic frequencies, you are yet another expression of the same field. The pulsations of nerve signals racing along your limbs, the electric charge emitted by your heart cells, and the faint field of current surrounding your brain all demonstrate that you are not separate from any form of energy in the universe. Any appearance of separation is only the product of the limitation of your senses, which are not attuned to these energies.

Imagine two candles standing about three feet apart on a table in front of you. To your eyes they appear separate and independent, yet the light they cast fills the room with photons; the entire space between them is bridged by light, and therefore there is no real separation at the quantum level. Now carry one of the candles outside at night and hold it up against a background of stars. The pinpoints of light in the sky may be billions of light-years away, yet at the quantum level each star is just as connected to your candle as the second candle in the room; the vast space between them contains waves of energy that bind them.

As you look at the candle and the distant stars, photons of light from both land on your retina. There they trigger flashes of electro-chemical discharge that belong to a different vibratory frequency from visible light, yet they are part of the same electromagnetic field. Therefore, you are another candle—or star—whose local concentration of matter and energy is one outcropping in the infinite field that surrounds and supports you.

Think about this organic connection between everything in existence. The lessons of this exercise are

- No matter how separate anything appears to the senses, nothing is separate at the quantum level.
- The quantum field exists in, around, and through you. You are not looking at the field—in every wave and particle, the field is your extended body.
- Each of your cells is a local concentration of information

and energy inside the wholeness of information and energy of your body. Likewise, you are a local concentration
of information and energy in the wholeness that is the
body of the universe.

When you begin to own this knowledge, nothing in your environment will feel threatening to you. As a result, the fear of separation will loosen its hold over you, and the unbroken flow of
awareness will counter entropy and aging.

Exercise 3: Breathing the Field

The quantum field transcends everyday reality, yet it is extremely intimate to your experience. To fetch a word from your
memory, to feel an emotion, to grasp a concept—these are events
that change the entire field. The eminent British physicist Sir James
Jeans once remarked, "When an electron vibrates, the universe
shakes." There is no flicker of activity in any of your cells that goes
unnoticed across the entire quantum field.

At its finest level, every physiological process registers in the
fabric of Nature. In other words, the more refined a process is, the
more connected to the basic activity of the cosmos. Here is a simple
breathing exercise that can give you a remarkably vivid experience
of this phenomenon.

Sit comfortably in a chair with your eyes closed. Gently and
slowly inhale through your nostrils, imagining as you do so that you
are drawing the air from a point infinitely far away. See the air
gently coming to you from the edge of the universe. Feel it coolly
suffusing your body.

Now slowly and easily exhale, sending every atom of air back
to its source infinitely far away. It may help if you envision a thread
that extends from you to the far reaches of the cosmos; or you might
visualize a star hovering in front of you that is sending light from
infinitely far away—in either case, imagine the thread or the star as
your source of air. If you aren't a good visualizer, don't worry; just
hold the word *infinite* in your mind as you breathe. Whatever

technique you use, the aim is to *feel* each breath coming to you from the quantum field, which at a subtle level is actually happening. Reestablishing the memory of your connection with the quantum field will awaken the memory of renewal in your body.

Exercise 4: Redefining

Having absorbed the knowledge that your body is not a sculpture isolated in space and time, redefine yourself by repeating the following statements silently to yourself:

I can use the power of my awareness to experience a body that is

Flowing	instead of	solid
Flexible	" "	rigid
Quantum	" "	material
Dynamic	" "	static
Composed of information and energy	" "	random chemical reactions
A network of intelligence	" "	a mindless machine
Fresh and ever-renewing	" "	entropic and aging
Timeless	" "	time-bound

Another good set of redefining statements:

- I am not my atoms, they come and go.
- I am not my thoughts, they come and go.
- I am not my ego, my self-image changes.
- I am above and beyond these; I am the witness, the interpreter, the Self beyond the self-image. This Self is ageless and timeless.

Repeating these statements serves as more than a mental reminder. As a process rather than an object, the human body is constantly filled with messages of every kind; the verbal messages we hear in our heads are just one version of the information being exchanged from cell to cell every second. Because every person's awareness is colored by past experiences, the flow of information inside us is influenced by unconscious imprints we are barely aware of. We will examine in detail how these unconscious imprints break down the smooth flow of messages, creating the loss of intelligence that results in aging.

For the time being, know that you can change these imprints by giving the unconscious new assumptions and beliefs to operate with. Every thought you have activates a messenger molecule in your brain. This means that every mental impulse gets transformed automatically into biological information. By repeating these new statements of belief, affirming to yourself that your body is not defined by the old paradigm, you are allowing new biological information to be produced; and, via the mind-body connection, your redefined sense of yourself is being received by your cells as new programming. Thus, the gap between your old, isolated self and the image of yourself as an ageless, timeless being starts to close.

PART
TWO

Aging and Awareness

AWARENESS HAS THE power to change aging, but awareness is a two-edged sword—it can both heal and destroy. What makes the difference is how your awareness becomes conditioned, or trained, into various attitudes, assumptions, beliefs, and reactions. When these mental patterns are destructive, a person finds himself driven by his mind into destructive behavior; when the mental patterns are constructive, the person is motivated toward self-enhancing behavior. Before it gets trained, awareness is just a field of energy and information; it is the mind's faculty for having thought before thought is actually present. Compared to any single expression of matter and energy, whether one atom or one galaxy, the quantum field is incomparably more powerful, because it has the potential to generate infinite combinations of space-time events that have never occurred before.

Likewise, because it always remains capable of generating new mental impulses, which in turn generate new biological information, your awareness is much more powerful than any single thought you might ever have. Retaining this creative potential is the mark of non-aging; giving it up in favor of habits, rituals, rigid beliefs, and outworn behavior is the mark of aging. In ancient China, the *Tao Te Ching* proclaimed the same truth: "Whatever is flexible and flowing will tend to grow, whatever is rigid and blocked will wither and die."

The impressions of past experience lock our minds into predictable patterns that trigger predictable behavior. Everyone's inner life is complex, swirling with both positive and negative thought patterns, but the fact that awareness can be trained is simple; it is the most fundamental thing that happens to us from birth onward. Like melted wax being imprinted with a signet ring, raw, unformed awareness is able to hold an impression, and once the impression has taken, awareness sets around it.

The Illusion of No Choice

In childhood we were at our most impressionable; our awareness was like soft, fresh wax not yet marred by experience. By old age the same awareness has been conditioned thousands of times over, and like old wax that has been used too many times, the mind becomes brittle and stiff. It is difficult to find even a small corner that is not conditioned by multiple layers of experience. Old bodies reflect this underlying rigidity, which is felt in every cell.

The number of impressions that get laid down inside us is staggering—behavioral psychologists have estimated that just the verbal cues fed to us by our parents in early childhood, which still run inside our heads like muffled tape loops, amount to over twenty-five thousand hours of pure conditioning. For each of us, the learning process that teaches us to age is complex and never-ending. It involves attitudes passed along from family, peers, and society since earliest childhood. What did your mother say when she spotted her first wrinkles? Did she see them as a dreaded symbol of lost youth? Did she still feel pretty and desirable? How did your father feel about retirement? Was it the end of his useful existence or the threshold of a better time? Were your grandparents benign, wise guides or distant, fear-inspiring strangers? Were the signs of old age that they exhibited viewed as senility or simply as change?

The effect of conditioning is always the same: choice becomes restricted. For example, the act of eating is a choice, which most of us freely exercise several times a day. But to someone suffering from the eating disorder of anorexia, the choice has become severely limited. Inside the awareness of anorectics are powerful imprints of low self-esteem, harsh guilt, repressed anger, and defective body images. These imprints can be extraordinarily intricate, but the end result is graphically simple. The person can no longer eat normally. The mere sight of food triggers the submerged conditioning; feelings of revulsion spontaneously well up, killing all appetite. If the disorder has progressed to extremes, anorectics are virtually paralyzed, compelled by their old conditioning to starve, even when abundant food is available.

A physician confronting anyone with an eating disorder hears the same anguished cry: "I have to behave this way; I must do what I'm doing." This conviction is an illusion, for the bonds of conditioning can be broken. As long as it is in force, though, this illusion is overwhelmingly convincing to the mind, and under its influence, the physiological mechanism for hunger is distorted into abnormal responses. The same mechanics apply to our subject, aging. Inside everyone lies the hidden conviction "I must age," which operates so powerfully on us that our bodies conform to it.

Any time choice seems to be cut off, some form of illusion is operating. Thousands of years ago the greatest of Indian sages, Shankara, declared, "People grow old and die because they see others grow old and die." It has taken us centuries even to begin to catch up with this extraordinary insight. As a physical process, aging is universal and, to all appearances, inevitable. A steam locomotive doesn't wear out over time and fall apart because it sees other locomotives doing the same thing. The only conditioning that affects any machine is simple wear and tear; certain parts get worn down faster than others because they absorb the most impact or friction. Our bodies also absorb impact and friction; various organs and tissues wear out before others. This physical picture looks so much like mechanical wear and tear that we are blinded to Shankara's deeper point—the aging body is responding to social conditioning.

There are societies in which people share very different styles of conditioning and therefore very different styles of aging. In recent decades anthropologists have been surprised to discover how many so-called primitive peoples are immune to signs of aging that the West has long accepted. S. Boyd Eaton, co-author of a fascinating book about early man's health, *The Paleolithic Prescription*, points to at least twenty-five traditional societies around the world where heart disease and cancer, two diseases long associated with aging, are almost unknown.

These societies are our best testing ground for the hypothesis that "normal" aging is really a collection of symptoms born from abnormal conditioning. Eaton cites native cultures in many places— Venezuela, the Solomon Islands, Tasmania, and the African desert—whose members all enjoy low blood pressure throughout their lives. This is completely contrary to the trend in the United States and Western Europe, where almost everyone's blood pressure rises by a few points every decade and up to half of the aged population needs to be treated for hypertension.

Growing deaf is yet another marker of senescence that modern societies have long accepted as "normal" and inevitable. The onset of deafness may even be getting earlier here; one study of college freshmen in Tennessee revealed that 60 percent had already suffered significant hearing loss. Approximately 25 million American adults have enough hearing loss to qualify for disability payments. Yet certain Bushman tribes in Botswana and the Maabans of southern Sudan exhibit no significant hearing loss as they grow older.

Similarly, although cholesterol levels tend to rise with age in industrialized countries, such tribes as the Hadzas of Tanzania and the Tarahumara Indians of northern Mexico rarely have cholesterol readings over 150; this level, which is 60 points below the American average, strongly protects these people against premature heart attacks. Again, the low readings persist throughout life, while in our culture everyone's serum cholesterol tends to rise, slowly but surely, as we age. A wide variety of cultures has managed to escape one or more of these "diseases of civilization," a misnomer, for highly civilized societies are also marked by good health. The breast cancer that strikes one in nine American women is extremely rare in both China and Japan; colon cancer, a major threat to American men, is also extremely low there, as it is in many indigenous African tribes.

When Japanese, Taiwanese, or African populations move from their traditional settings to this country, exposure to civilization and its "improved" lifestyle often proves disastrous. Rates of heart attack, colon cancer, and hypertension that were a fraction of ours begin to soar; typically, by the second generation there is no advantage left. But is this change only one of diet and lifestyle? To support this explanation, epidemiologists point to the Japanese who live in Hawaii, which is considered a cultural halfway house between East and West in diet and lifestyle. Because they eat less fat than is consumed on the U.S. mainland but more than is customary in Japan, the Japanese immigrants to Hawaii have heart-attack rates that also stand between the two extremes of Japan and the mainland U.S.

This long-accepted explanation was shaken, however, when some of the data was examined in more detail. As psychologist Robert Ornstein and his co-author David Sobel relate in their book *The Healing Brain,* if one looks at the whole spectrum of Japanese immigrants in California, there was one subgroup who continued to have low rates of heart disease that did not correlate with diet or cholesterol levels in their blood. These were males who retained strong ties to Japanese culture despite their having moved to America. The various ways in which their awareness remained Japanese (by growing up in a Japanese neighborhood, attending school with other Japanese children, speaking their native language, and observing traditional customs and social ties) all contributed to producing healthy hearts, no matter whether their blood cholesterol levels were high or low.

What kept these men healthy was a social bond that is invisible but very powerful. They continued to share in the consciousness of traditional Japan, which is a form of extended mind that cannot help but have physiological effects. Along the same lines, studies of auto workers laid off during hard times in Michigan have revealed that those men who felt strong support from family, relatives, and friends were less likely to develop physical or mental symptoms. Similarly, when pregnant women were asked whether they felt supported by their family and friends, it was found that 91 percent of serious complications during pregnancy occurred among those who said that they led stressful lives and had little social support.

Social support is a complex phenomenon, covering all the interactions of language, customs, family structure, and social tradition that bind people together. The net result is that awareness gets programmed; social binding takes place at the level of mind. You perceive that another person is like you and you believe he sees you the same way. What you share is a larger self, an interconnected psyche that is as sensitive and intricate as an individual psyche.

Hundreds of books have been written about the aging process on the assumption that growing old is something that happens to people. Now, however, we are seeing that it is something that social conditioning taught our bodies to do. This is an extremely important distinction. If aging is something that's happening to you, then basically you're a victim; but if aging is something you learned, you're in a position to unlearn the behavior that's making you age, adopt new beliefs, and be guided into new opportunities.

There's an aphorism made famous by the late Norman Cousins: "Belief creates biology." No truer statement was ever made about aging. Our inherited expectation that the body must wear out over time, coupled with deep beliefs that we are fated to suffer, grow old, and die, creates the biological phenomenon we call aging. Life is awareness in action. Despite the thousands of hours of old tapes that program our responses, we continue to live because awareness finds new ways to flow. The positive side of awareness—its ability to heal—is always available.

LEARNING NOT TO AGE:

The Link Between Belief and Biology

Although awareness gets programmed in thousands of ways, the most convincing are what we call beliefs. A belief is something you hold on to because you think it is true. But unlike a thought, which actively forms words or images in your brain, a belief is generally silent. A person suffering from claustrophobia doesn't need to think, "This room is too small," or, "There are too many people in this crowd." Put into a small, crowded room, his body reacts automatically. Somewhere in his awareness is a hidden belief that generates all the physical symptoms of fear without his having to think about it. The flow of adrenaline that causes his pounding heart, sweaty palms, panting breath, and dizziness is triggered at a level deeper than the thinking mind.

People with phobias struggle desperately to use thoughts to thwart their fear, but to no avail. The habit of fear has sunk so deep that the body remembers to carry it out, even when the mind is resisting with all its might. The thoughts of a claustrophobic—"There's no reason to be afraid"; "Small rooms aren't danger-ous"; "Everyone else looks perfectly normal, why can't I get over this?"—are rational objections, but the body acts on commands that override thought.

Our beliefs in aging hold just this kind of power over us. Let me give an example: For the past twenty years, gerontologists have performed experiments to prove that remaining active throughout life, even up to one's late seventies, would halt the loss of muscle and skeletal tissue. The news spread among retired people that they should continue to walk, jog, swim, and keep up their housework; under the slogan "Use it or lose it," millions of people now expect to remain strong in old age. With this new belief in place, something once considered impossible happened.

Daring gerontologists at Tufts University visited a nursing home, selected a group of the frailest residents, and put them on a weight-training regimen. One might fear that a sudden introduction to exercise would exhaust or kill these fragile people, but in fact they thrived. Within eight weeks, wasted muscles had come back by 300 percent, coordination and balance improved, and overall a sense of active life returned. Some of the subjects who had not been able to walk unaided could now get up and go to the bathroom in the middle of the night by themselves, an act of reclaimed dignity that is by no means trivial. What makes this accomplishment truly wondrous, however, is that the youngest subject in the group was 87 and the oldest 96.

These results were always possible; nothing new was added here to the capacity of the human body. All that happened was that a belief changed, and when that happened, aging changed. If you are 96 years old and afraid to move your body, it will waste away. To go into a weight-training room at that age, you have to believe that it will do your body good; you have to be free of fear; and you have to believe in yourself. When I say that aging is the result of a belief, I'm not implying that a person can simply think aging away. Exactly the opposite—the stronger the belief, the more rooted in the body it is and the more immune to conscious control.

According to the belief system you and I adhere to, Nature has trapped us in bodies that grow old against our will. The tradition of aging extends as far back as recorded history and even prehistory. Animals and plants grow old, fulfilling a universal law of Nature. It is hard to imagine that aging is the result of learned behavior, for biology cannot be denied.

Yet the core belief that aging is a fixed, mechanical process—something that just happens to us—is only a belief. As such, it blinds us to all kinds of facts that don't fit the belief system we cling to. How many of the following statements do you believe are facts?

  a) Aging is natural—all organisms grow old and die.
  b) Aging is inevitable—it can't be prevented.

c) Aging is normal—it affects everyone about the same.

d) Aging is genetic—I'll probably live about as long as my parents and grandparents did.

e) Aging is painful—it causes physical and mental suffering.

f) Aging is universal—the law of entropy makes all orderly systems run down and decay.

g) Aging is fatal—we're all growing old and dying.

If you take any or all of these to be statements of fact, you are under the influence of beliefs that do not match reality. Each statement contains a little objective truth, but each can be refuted, too.

a) Aging *is* natural, but there are organisms that never age, such as one-celled amoebas, algae, and protozoa. Parts of you also do not age—your emotions, ego, personality type, I.Q., and other mental characteristics, for example, as well as vast portions of your DNA. Physically, it makes no sense to say that the water and minerals in your body are aging, for what is "old water" or "old salt"? These components alone make up 70 percent of your body.

b) Aging is inevitable, but the honeybee at certain times of the year can shift its hormones and completely reverse its age. In the human body, shifts in hormones may not be as dramatic, but there is enough latitude so that on any given day your hormonal profile may be younger than the day, month, or year before.

c) Aging is normal; however, there is no normal curve of aging that applies to everyone. Some people entirely escape certain aging symptoms, while others are afflicted with them long before old age sets in.

d) Aging has a genetic component that affects everyone, but not to the degree usually supposed. Having two parents who survived into their eighties adds only about three years to a child's life expectancy; less than 5 percent of the population has such good or bad genes that their life span will turn out to be significantly longer or shorter. By comparison, by adopting a healthy lifestyle, you can delay symptoms of aging by as much as thirty years.

e) Aging is often painful, both physically and mentally, but this is the result not of aging itself but of the many diseases that afflict the elderly; much of that disease can be prevented.

f) Aging seems to be universal, because all orderly systems break down over time, but our bodies resist this decay extremely well. Without negative influences from within and without, our tissues and organs could easily last 115 to 130 years before sheer age caused them to stop functioning.

g) Finally, aging is fatal, because everyone has to die, but in the vast majority of cases, perhaps as much as 99 percent, the cause of death is not old age but cancer, heart attack, stroke, pneumonia, and other illnesses.

It is extremely difficult to ascertain what it would be like to watch the body age per se. Two cars left out in the rain will rust at about the same rate; the process of oxidation attacks them equally, turning their iron and steel into ferrous oxide according to one easily explained law of chemistry. The aging process obeys no such simple laws. For some of us, aging is steady, uniform, and slow, like a tortoise crawling toward its destination. For others, aging is like approaching an unseen cliff—there is a long, secure plateau of health, followed by a sharp decline in the last year or two of life. And for still others, most of the body will remain healthy except for a weak link, such as the heart, which fails much faster than do the other organs. You would have to follow a person for most of his adult life before you figured out how he was aging, and by then it would be too late.

The fact that aging is so personal has proved very frustrating for medicine, which finds it extremely difficult to predict and treat many of the major conditions associated with old age. Two young women can ingest the same amount of calcium, display equally healthy hormone levels, and yet one will develop crippling osteoporosis after menopause while the other won't. Twin brothers with identical genes will go through life with remarkably similar medical histories, yet only one will develop Alzheimer's or arthritis or cancer. Two of the most common conditions in old age, rising blood pressure and elevated cholesterol, are just as unpredictable. The aging body refuses to behave according to mechanical laws and rules.

After decades of intense investigation, there is no adequate theory of human aging. Even our attempts to explain how animals age have resulted in more than three hundred separate theories, many of them contradictory. Our notions of aging have been drastically modified over the last two decades. In the early 1970s, doctors began to notice patients in their sixties and seventies whose bodies still functioned with the vigor and health of middle age. These people ate sensibly and looked after their bodies. Most did not smoke, having given up the habit sometime after the Surgeon General's original warnings about lung cancer in the early 1960s. They had never suffered heart attacks. Although they exhibited some of the accepted signs of old age—higher blood pressure and cholesterol, and tendencies to put on body fat, to become farsighted, and to lose the top range of their hearing—there was nothing elderly about these people. The "new old age," as it came to be called, was born.

The "old old age" had been marked by irreversible declines on all fronts—physical, mental, and social. For untold centuries people expected to reach old age—if they reached it at all—feeble, senile, socially useless, sick, and poor. To reinforce this grim expectation there were grim facts: Only one out of ten people lived to the age of 65 before this century.

For centuries in the past, the human body was exposed to the killing influence of a harsh environment: Inadequate nutrition, a lifetime spent in physical labor, and uncontrollable epidemics of disease created conditions that accelerated aging. Leaf through the accounts of immigrants passing through Ellis Island at the turn of the century; some of the photographs will horrify you. The faces of 40-year-old women look haggard and drawn, literally as if they were 70—and an old 70 at that. Adolescent boys look like battered middle-aged men. Under the surgeon's scalpel their hearts, lungs, kidneys, and livers would have looked identical to those of a modern person twice their age. Aging is the body's response to conditions imposed upon it, both inner and outer. The sands of age shift under our feet, adapting to how we live and who we are.

The new old age arrived on the scene after more than half a century of improved living conditions and intensive medical progress. The average American life span of 49 years in 1900 jumped to 75 in 1990. To put this huge increase in perspective, the years of life we have gained in less than a century are equal to the total life span that individuals enjoyed for more than four thousand years; from prehistoric times to the dawn of the Industrial Revolution, the average life span remained below 45. Only 10 percent of the general population used to make it to 65, but today 80 percent of the population lives at least that long.

The Mystery of Aging

Despite this evidence that aging is a shifting, fluid phenomenon, we still find ourselves operating under the belief that aging can be understood strictly as a biological process. When you look at your body and notice how much it has changed physically since you were young, aging seems an obvious phenomenon. In fact, it is anything but.

Twenty years ago I was a young resident working in a vast and dreary veterans hospital outside Boston. In a typical day I ran physicals on dozens of patients, mostly old soldiers who had served in two world wars. The passing years had taken a toll that was all too obvious. Even when I had my eyes closed, the sound and touch of their bodies were unmistakable. Their hands trembled while I took their pulse, and their lungs wheezed under the stethoscope. The pounding lub-dub of young hearts had given way to feebler, threadier rhythms.

I knew that unseen destruction was taking place beneath the thin veil of their dry, wrinkled skin. Blood vessels were hardening and blood pressure was rising. If I could reach in to touch the three coronary arteries, one or more would almost certainly be engorged with fatty plaque. The body's main artery, the aorta, might have turned as hard as a lead pipe, stiffened by calcium deposits, while the delicate arterioles in the head were likely to be so tissue-thin that the slightest contact would make them crumble, triggering a stroke. Vertebrae and hip bones would be getting thin and brittle too, waiting to crack if the person slipped on the stairs. All over the body, hidden tumors would be held in check only by the slowed metabolism of the elderly, which mercifully retards the spread of cancer.

All this may sound like an accurate, if grim, description of the aging process, but in fact *I wasn't seeing old people at all; I was seeing sick people.* All over America doctors were making the same mistake. Caught up in treating various diseases, we forgot what aging is like when disease is not present. Moreover, the few medical researchers who took an interest in the aging process tended to work in veterans hospitals like the one in which I practiced. By definition, the "normal" aging they observed was abnormal, because a normal person isn't hospitalized. No one would dream of defining childhood by studying patients in a children's hospital ward, yet old age was largely defined that way.

Across the general population, only 5 percent of people over 65 are institutionalized, in either hospitals, nursing homes, or mental institutions. Surprisingly, this figure is not significantly higher than for younger age groups. Obviously, there are many reasons besides old age why someone might wind up in an institution. Such places are dumping grounds for the widowed, homeless, alcoholic, mentally incompetent, and destitute. A doctor can't spend a day in a typical big-city hospital without seeing a police car pull up with a load of hapless derelicts swept off the street to become the faceless statistics that researchers use to define aging.

"Fear old age," Plato cautioned over two thousand years ago, "for it does not come alone." He spoke the truth. As we grow older, the things that bother us most are often not aging itself but the ills that accompany it. In the wild, few animals die simply because they have grown too old. Other factors, such as sickness, starvation, exposure to the elements, and ever-vigilant predators, kill off most creatures long before they reach their potential life span. Gaze at a flock of sparrows outside your window this spring; by next spring, half will have died from various causes. So, for all practical purposes, it is irrelevant that sparrows can live over a decade if kept safe in a cage.

Long life spans are possible among birds (in captivity, eagles can survive for fifty years and parrots for more than seventy years), which seems strange considering their fast metabolisms and racing heartbeat. But very little about the aging process is logical. The evolutionary purpose of aging is itself a puzzle to biologists, given that Nature has so many other ways of ending an animal's life. For example, mortality is built into the system of competition for food. Some animals have to die in order for others to live; otherwise survival of the fittest would have no meaning. Among bears and deer, for example, the males fight for territory during breeding season; when the strongest males win the right to breed with the females, they also win the prime territory—land that is rich in food—while the losers must settle for much poorer foraging grounds, where many struggle on the verge of starvation and quickly die.

If a wild animal is fortunate enough to survive to its natural life span, its body will not just be old, it will be riddled with disease. Cancer, heart disease, hardened arteries, arthritis, and strokes are rampant among old creatures. Aged lions suffer coronaries and old eagles get cataracts. Aging is so mixed in with other factors that it is extremely hard to separate it out.

The same blurring occurs in humans. Although we pride ourselves on having escaped the trials of the wild, modern people still rarely die of old age. In 1938 the British medical journal *The Lancet* carried the report of a senior pathologist who maintained that he had never examined a deceased body that had succumbed to age alone. The closest candidate was a 94-year-old man who had died just by fading away without overt disease. But appearances were deceiving: At autopsy it was found that he had been suffering from an undiagnosed case of lobar pneumonia, one of the most common causes of fatality among old people.

Although it appeals to common sense that we grow old because we simply wear out, no wear-and-tear theory of aging has ever held up under close scrutiny. Aging bodies only seem to wear out like overworked washing machines and tractors. "How's the old ticker?" a doctor will ask an elderly patient, as if her heart were a clock winding down on its spring. Unlike machines, however, which run down with too much use, the human body is capable of getting better the more it is used. A well-exercised bicep doesn't deteriorate; rather, it gets stronger. Leg bones gain mass in proportion to how much weight is put on them, which is why osteoporosis is practically unknown in tribal societies where lifelong physical activity is the norm. Moreover, if wearing out were the true cause of aging, it would be a good strategy to rest in bed all your life. In fact, prolonged rest is disastrous for the physiology—a hospital patient confined to complete bed rest for a few weeks will suffer as much muscle and skeletal wasting as someone who has aged a decade.

Any purely physical theory of aging cannot help but be incomplete. Consider arthritis, one of the most common symptoms of age. In medical school we were taught that common arthritis (or osteoarthritis) is a degenerative disorder. This means that its cause is simple wear and tear. After a lifetime of hard use, the cushioning cartilage in large weight-bearing joints deteriorates, which explains why the knee and hip joints, which carry the burden of supporting the body, tend to be favored sites for arthritis. The synovium, the smooth lining that cushions the bones where they meet, also becomes inflamed or deteriorated, leading to the pain, swelling, and burning of arthritis. Sometimes the synovial fluid dries up, and the bones grind against each other, creating pits or bone spurs. This kind of degeneration has plagued mankind since the Stone Age. The familiar image of prehistoric man walking hunched over from the shoulders is now thought to be a distortion of what healthy cavemen really looked like. Archaeologists, it seems, were misled because so many of the intact skeletons they found in their digs were deformed from arthritis of the spine.

As the cause of arthritis, wear and tear appeals to common sense, but it fails to explain several things. Some people never become arthritic, even though they subject their joints to extreme stress. Other people develop arthritis after a lifetime of sedentary desk work, not to mention that certain favorite spots for the disease, such as the fingers, are not called upon to bear weight at all. Newer theories of arthritis look to hormones, genetics, autoimmune breakdown, diet, and other factors; in the end, no clear cause is known.

However, emotional factors have been strongly linked to another major type of arthritis, rheumatoid arthritis. This disorder seems to favor women who have a marked tendency to repress emotion, who adopt passivity and depression as a mode of coping with stress rather than getting angry or confronting serious emotional issues. The disease can get worse under stress, and, for inexplicable reasons, it can also disappear, perhaps in obedience to a deeper current of change.

Three Ages of Man

The complexity of the forces operating inside an aging body becomes even more obvious when you ask a seemingly easy question: How old are you?

Before you rush to reply, consider that there are three distinct and separate ways to measure someone's age:

> *Chronological age*—how old you are by the calendar
> *Biological age*—how old your body is in terms of critical life
>   signs and cellular processes
> *Psychological age*—how old you feel you are

Only the first of these is fixed, yet chronological age is also the most unreliable of the three. One 50-year-old may be nearly as healthy as he was at 25, while another may already have the body of a 60- or even a 70-year-old. To really know how old you are, the second measure—biological age—comes into play; it tells us how time has affected your organs and tissues compared to other people of your chronological age.

Time doesn't affect your body uniformly, however; practically every cell, tissue, and organ is aging on its own timetable, which makes biological age much more complex than chronological age.

A middle-aged marathon runner may have the leg muscles, heart, and lungs of someone half his age, but his knees and kidneys may be aging rapidly due to excessive stress, and his eyesight and hearing could be declining on their own idiosyncratic paths. You become unique as the years pass. At 20, when muscle development, reflexes, sexual drive, and many other primary functions are reaching their peak, most people look alike to a physiologist. Young hearts, brains, kidneys, and lungs all exhibit healthy color and firmness; evidence of malformed, diseased, or dying tissue is scanty or nonexistent. But by age 70, no two bodies are remotely alike. At that age, your body will be like no one else's in the world; its age changes will mirror your unique life.

Biological age also has its limits as a measurement tool. Considered purely as biology, the aging process moves at such a slow rate that its fatal effects rarely match those of faster-moving diseases. Most critical organs can function well at 30 percent of peak capacity. Thus if our bodies are losing 1 percent of their functioning per year after age 30, it would take 70 years, or age 100, before aging per se threatens a particular organ with imminent breakdown. But social and psychological influences are ever at work, our lifestyles subject us to various conditions, and the differences in how we age show up much earlier in life.

Two stroke patients in their midfifties with identical medical conditions can, and often do, display wildly different outcomes— one may recover from his attack quickly, respond well to physical therapy, and easily regain lost speech and movement, eventually returning to normal life. The other may respond poorly to treatment, be overcome with depression, and give up all active pursuits; in short order he may grow old and die. The determining factor is psychological age, which is the most personal and mysterious of the three measurements but also the one that holds the most promise for reversing the aging process.

Biological age is known to be changeable—regular physical exercise, for example, can reverse ten of the most typical effects of biological age, including high blood pressure, excess body fat, improper sugar balance, and decreased muscle mass. Gerontologists have found that elderly people who agree to adopt better lifestyle habits improve their life expectancy on average by ten years. Thus, the arrow of time can move forward quickly or slowly, stop in its tracks, or even turn around. Your body becomes younger or older biologically depending on how you treat it.

Yet your third age, psychological age, is even more flexible. Like biological age, psychological age is completely personal—no two people have exactly the same psychological age because no two people have exactly the same experiences. Listen to the voice of Anna Lundgren, age 101, who made a very important observation as a child that influenced how she aged for the next eighty or ninety years. "Back in Norway where I was a little girl, when people got to be 55 or 65, they just sat. I never felt that old. *That's* old. I don't feel that old today." How old you feel you are has no boundaries and can reverse in a split second. An old woman recalling her first love can suddenly look and sound as if she has turned 18 again; a middle-aged man who hears that his beloved wife has died can wither into lonely senescence in a matter of weeks.

Instead of coming up with a fixed number to answer the question "How old are you?" we need to arrive at a sliding scale that shows how fast our three ages are moving in relation to one another. Take two 50-year-olds:

A, who was recently divorced, suffers from acute depression, with a history of heart disease and overweight; B, who is happily married, healthy, optimistic, and satisfied with his job.

Because of the various factors at work, the true age of A and B is best expressed by a three-tiered graph:

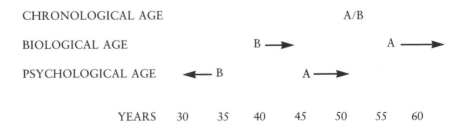

The arrows point in the direction of aging and their length indicates how fast the process is taking place. Although A and B are both chronologically 50, A is under so many negative influences that

his body is 10 years older biologically and is aging quickly; in terms
of psychological age he is about par with his calendar years, but he
is aging fairly rapidly there, too. The picture is very different for B,
who is younger on both the biological and psychological scales. His
good physical and mental health indicate that he is aging slowly
biologically and actually getting younger psychologically.

Overall, A is in much worse shape than B. Depending on how
severe his depression and heart condition are, his composite age
might be as high as 60, but this figure is artificial. It ignores the fact
that all the factors that make him so much older than his chronological age are reversible. Ten years from now, he could be as happy,
optimistic, and fit as B, in which case his composite age would
decline.

When gerontologists try to predict longevity, all of the following
psychosocial factors must be taken into account to accurately determine if the aging process is being accelerated or retarded.

NEGATIVE FACTORS THAT
ACCELERATE AGING

Asterisk (*) denotes major factors

* Depression
  Inability to express emotions
  Feeling helpless to change oneself and others
  Living alone
  Loneliness, absence of close friends
* Lack of regular daily routine
* Lack of regular work routine
* Job dissatisfaction
  Having to work more than 40 hours per week
  Financial burdens, being in debt
  Habitual or excessive worry
  Regret for sacrifices made in the past
  Irritability, getting angry easily, *or* being unable
      to express anger
  Criticism of self and others

POSITIVE FACTORS THAT RETARD AGING

* Happy marriage (or satisfying long-term relationship)
* Job satisfaction
* Feeling of personal happiness
  Ability to laugh easily
  Satisfactory sex life
  Ability to make and keep close friends
* Regular daily routine
* Regular work routine
  Taking at least one week's vacation every year
  Feeling in control of personal life
  Enjoyable leisure time, satisfying hobbies
  Ability to express feelings easily
  Optimistic about the future
  Feeling financially secure, living within means

As you can see, there is much more to psychological age than the cliché "You're only as old as you think you are," and changing your psychological age involves interweaving personal and social factors. Among the major factors are several we have touched upon. The importance of a regular daily and work routine is emphasized by almost every longevity study. Job satisfaction emerges as the most reliable indicator that a person is at low risk for a heart attack, while being dissatisfied with one's job puts one at extremely high risk. Living alone is precarious, while being happily married indicates that one will age slowly.

The combinations of these factors become extremely complex, mirroring the complexity of one's personal life. Gerontologists have gone to great lengths to try to quantify some of these factors, with plausible results. Someone who has lived alone for four years, for example, would have a slightly different psychological age from someone who has lived alone for eight years. The relative value assigned to having a regular daily routine is considered three times

more important than having a satisfying sex life, while being optimistic about the future cancels out, point for point, the negative trait
of not having a hobby.

But I have personal reservations about any attempt to quantify
someone's personal makeup; despite the general accuracy of these
factors, they lose the essence of personal life, which is its ability to
shift and transform itself, to touch many chords both happy and
sad, to undergo sudden reversals and abrupt illuminations. When I
think of myself, my image is not of a fixed collection of attributes—
things are always changing inside, sometimes drastically.

The list cannot quantify intangible qualities such as being able
to give of oneself and having regard for others. In general, this is a
limitation of modern psychology, with its overreliance on numbers
and impersonal data. One unusual study bridged the gap rather
neatly, however. Larry Scherwitz, a University of California psychologist, taped the conversations of nearly six hundred men, a
third of whom were suffering from heart disease, the rest of whom
were healthy. Listening to the tapes, he counted how often each man
used the words *I, me,* and *mine.* Comparing his results with the
frequency of heart disease, Scherwitz found that men who used the
first-person pronoun most often had the highest risk of heart trouble. In addition, by following his subjects for several years, he found
that the more a man habitually talked about himself, the greater the
chance he would actually have a coronary.

Counting the times a person said "I" was an ingenious way to
quantify self-absorption, and to me, there's something very fitting in
the fact that the less you open your heart to others, the more your
heart suffers. The antidote, Scherwitz concluded, was to be more
giving: "Listen with regard when others talk. Give your time and
energy to others; let others have their way; do things for reasons
other than furthering your own needs." In those words, he goes
beyond the quantifiable data to issues of love and compassion,
which appeal very much to our intuitive sense that an open, loving
person should age well.

One thing the quantified research has shown so far is very
valuable: Biological age responds to psychological age. If you look
over the list of positive psychosocial influences, subjective words

such as *happy, satisfied,* and *enjoyable* indicate how completely personal these factors really are. By nurturing your inner life, you are using the power of awareness to defeat aging at its source. On the other hand, changes of awareness in the direction of apathy, helplessness, and dissatisfaction push the body into rapid decline.

The Value of Adaptability

It is very frightening to watch an old person give up his desire for life, and it is extremely difficult to show him what he is doing. When life becomes meaningless, the body's sustaining energy seems to drain silently away like a leaky battery. But if we look closer, we can prove that this draining away of vitality, curiosity, and the will to live is controllable and in fact has nothing to do with normal aging. The body is self-replenishing; it renews its energies automatically after times of depletion. No matter how severe the stress, once the body has responded, it returns to a state of balance. This tendency to remain in balance is completely necessary to life and proves to be a key survival mechanism.

In 1957, Flanders Dunbar, a professor of medicine at Columbia University, reported on a study of centenarians and "nimble nonagenarians." She found that psychological adaptability in the face of stress was dominant among these people. This trait more than any other set them aside from the general population. Although everyone has occasions for grief, shock, sadness, and disappointment, some of us spring back much better than others. Dunbar went on to compile six traits that in her opinion were shared by "precentenarians," people who have the best chance of living to be 100:

1. Responding creatively to change. More than any other, this trait made precentenarians stand out from ordinary people.
2. Freedom from anxiety. Anxiety is a great enemy of our ability to improvise and create.

3. The continued ability to create and invent.
4. High levels of adaptive energy.
5. A capacity to integrate new things into one's existence.
6. Wanting to stay alive.

As with all predictive models, this one is flawed. It must be conceded that some people vegetate and still live to be 100, as do some who are rigid and uncreative, who couldn't care less whether they stay alive. But positive qualities are far more common in centenarians, and as a description of the kind of old age that is most desirable, Dunbar's list is extremely helpful. Her precentenarians are special because they reveal that just as people have strong or weak immune systems, we all vary in how well we adapt mentally. For some, the journey of life, however harsh on the outside, is met with resilience instead of brittleness; they are the reeds who bend in the storm, not the oaks who stand stiff and break.

Adaptability can be most simply defined as freedom from conditioned response. To remain open to change, to accept the new and welcome the unknown, is a choice that involves definite personal skills; for left to inertia, the mind tends to reinforce its old habits and increasingly to fall prey to its conditioning.

ADAPTABILITY QUESTIONNAIRE

If you want to see whether you have learned the skills that make someone adaptable, answer the following questions as they apply to you, assigning the following points:

Almost never applies	0 points
Sometimes applies	1 point
Usually applies	2 points
Almost always applies	3 points

1. When I am first confronted with a problem and have no idea how it can be solved, I take the attitude that the right answer will emerge.
2. Events in my life happen with their own right timing.
3. I feel optimistic about my future.
4. When someone rejects me, I feel hurt, but I accept that the decision was theirs to make.
5. I feel the loss of family and friends who have died, but the grief resolves itself and I move on—I don't try to bring back what cannot be brought back.
6. I feel committed to ideals larger than myself.
7. When I'm arguing with someone, I defend my position, but I also find it easy to acknowledge the rightness in the other side.
8. I vote the man, not the party.
9. I donate time to worthwhile causes, even if they are unpopular.
10. I am considered a good listener. I don't interrupt others when they talk.
11. If someone has a lot of emotion at stake in something, I will hear them out without expressing my views.
12. Given a choice between a high-salaried job that is fairly boring and a job I like doing at half the pay, I'll take the job I love to do.
13. My style of managing other people is to allow them to do what they want rather than try to control them. I interfere as little as possible.
14. I find it easy to trust others.
15. I am not prone to worry; the ups and downs of difficult situations affect me less than most other people.
16. In a competitive situation, I am a good loser—I will say, "Good game," not, "I wasn't at my best."
17. Being right in every situation isn't all that important to me.
18. I feel comfortable playing with young children; I enter their world easily.
19. I don't think about my moods very much.

20. I can easily feel what someone else is feeling.
21. Quiet people make me feel comfortable. Nervous people don't make me nervous.

Total score: _____

Evaluating your score:
50 points or over:

You are an exceptionally adaptable person who has spent a long time on personal growth. Others seek you for guidance and advice. You place a high priority on your ability to remain comfortable under pressure and readily accept new challenges. You pride yourself on being able to resolve conflicts well.

30–40 points:

You are reasonably adaptable to everyday challenges, but the amount of work you have put into this area has probably been limited. You are the kind of person that others consider easygoing, but you are likely to have more worries and regrets that you haven't faced up to. Conflicts upset you, and you tend to fall under the influence of people with stronger emotions than yours.

20–30 points:

You have definite ideas of right and wrong behavior and put a high priority on defending your point of view. Working on personal growth has not been a high priority in your life so far. You are likely to be well organized and decidedly goal oriented. If you find yourself in a situation of conflict or competition, you really want to be on the winning side.

Under 20 points:

Your sense of self needs considerable work. Dominated by one or both parents as a child, you fear rejection and become upset or critical when others disagree with you. You have your way of doing things and do not like surprises.

You are likely to be obsessively orderly, with lots of hidden worry, or else very disorganized, reacting strongly to one external event after another.

———————

The purpose of this test is not to make anyone feel superior or inferior but to spur conscious growth. The common denominator of all adaptable people is that they actually work, on a daily basis, at keeping their awareness open. Most of this book is devoted to that work, and I feel that there is no higher life purpose than trying to open your awareness until the full impact of reality—in all its beauty, truth, wonder, and sacredness—is consciously experienced. Reduced awareness occurs when life is not consciously lived and appreciated. This tendency is often so subtle that it may take months or years before the damaging results are evident, but the trail of clues is very obvious for anyone who cares to look. The age changes that develop in mind and body are the end products of thoughtlessly giving in to rigid assumptions, beliefs, and opinions. Some people, for instance, have absorbed the notion that they are going to lose their memory in old age, an expectation frequently reinforced by those who believe in the "old" old age.

As soon as they are 55 or 60, such people begin to worry about every tiny memory lapse, despite the fact that occasional memory lapses occur to everyone, young and old. Memory is a funny thing. You can't make yourself remember anything, but you can make yourself forget. One way to do this is to block a memory with anxiety. Remember that last time you were in an emergency and had to call home? You rushed to a pay phone in a state of anxiety, and as you picked up the receiver, the thought flashed through your mind, "What's my number? I've forgotten my number!" This thought doesn't go away until you calm down and allow the fog of anxiety to withdraw, which then permits memory to arise spontaneously.

Some people are so anxious about growing old that they cannot help but leak that anxiety into every situation that calls for them to remember something—a friend's name, someone's address, the place where they left their keys. They start trying to monitor their memory ("Okay, am I about to forget this?"), which only makes matters worse, until they get caught up in a vicious circle: They are so persuaded of encroaching senility that they force themselves into memory loss by not allowing enough relaxation for memory to work.

The development of any character trait starts early in life and begins to display itself by middle age. The best way to ensure that you will be adaptable in old age is to work on being that way when you are still young. This was demonstrated in a classic study started fifty years ago by Harvard psychologist George Vaillant. He took 185 young men, students at Harvard during World War II, and monitored their health for almost forty years. Vaillant found that even if someone appeared perfectly healthy in youth, he was very likely to die prematurely if he reacted poorly to stress, fell prey to depression, or was psychologically unstable. Of the men who had the best mental health, only 2 became chronically ill or died by age 53. Of the 48 men with the poorest mental health, however, 18— almost ten times as many—were chronically ill or dead by that age.

Vaillant concluded that early aging—defined as irreversible physical decline—was retarded by good mental health and accelerated by poor mental health. The most formative years for establishing these conditions, he found, were between ages 21 and 46, because those are the years when a person generally succeeds or fails in establishing a secure sense of self, regardless of even the most terrible childhood traumas and abuse. Once the seed is planted, the results of mental health show up physically in one's fifties. Late middle age is the perilous decade often called "the danger zone," because it is then that premature heart attacks, runaway hypertension, and many types of cancer first show up in great number.

To put it more generally, Vaillant found that the aging process is learned. People with good mental health teach their bodies to age well; depressed, insecure, and unhappy people teach their bodies to age badly. Although Vaillant observed that increased stress was often found in the lives of those who became chronically ill and died young, he had the insight to realize that stress doesn't make people sick; giving up their inner adaptability to stress does. The greatest threat to life and health is having nothing to live for. Children display tremendous vitality and rush at each day with open arms. This is natural to them and remains natural unless they learn the dulling habits and attitudes that smother spontaneous curiosity and wonder.

Vaillant was among the first researchers to establish that being depressed often leads to premature aging, chronic illness, and early death. Generally, at the root of depression is a kind of emotional numbness; the person feels he has no laughter or joy inside because these positive emotions have been blocked by unhappy memories. Old traumas lurk inside, and when new feelings try to bubble up, they are filtered through the traumas. Even the most beautiful experience, such as having a baby, cannot survive if it has to be filtered through preexisting hopelessness. Giving birth generates a flood of powerful hormones, generating a surge of energy pouring through the body. In a woman with healthy memories of her early childhood, this surging energy is experienced as a strong bond to her child; at the same time, the body renews its energy after the exhaustion of going into labor. Within a few days, the whole mind-body system has been returned to express the joy and power of motherhood. However, in a woman whose memories associated early childhood with sadness and emotional hurt, the flood of new energy during childbirth triggers the old programming instead. The joy and power are transformed into apathy and fatigue. Postpartum depression is the result of outworn memories seizing a new lease on life.

Although the vast majority of depressed people are treated with antidepressant drugs, such medications do not cure the underlying sadness, trauma, and numbness that are the true cause of the disorder. When the drug is taken away, the depression flowers again. Even though it takes longer and requires more insight and courage, a more effective way to treat depression is through psychotherapy. Classic "couch psychiatry" is often scorned, but counseling a depressed patient, uncovering the inner hurt and releasing it, sometimes accomplishes a lasting cure, which no drug can claim. This implies that premature aging, which Vaillant so closely linked to depression and mental instability, might also be treatable in a similar way. In fact, all of us are learning and unlearning to age, we just haven't looked at ourselves that way.

THE OPENING OF
AWARENESS

While I was writing this section of the book, my family received a visit from my wife's uncle, Prem, who flew in from New Delhi. Prem Uncle, as he would be called in India, is very dear to us. Now 75 and retired from his corporate job, he bounds up and down the stairs much more agilely than I do. Prem Uncle was a star tennis player in his youth, and he still plays every day. Simple in his pleasures and satisfied with his lot, he looks on life with enviable serenity and happiness.

I set aside my reference books and asked him how he kept so young, and this is what Prem Uncle replied: "Well, you know, I never push to extremes. I was just born that way. I never got in the habit of overeating. This morning I had a banana and cereal, and that is about as much as I ever want. I eat lightly at night and never drink more than a little brandy once in a while.

"Second, I sleep very well. That's due to my diet, because if I eat a big dinner, my sleep is disturbed. Third, I don't bother about trivialities. I leave that to my wife"—he laughs—"you know, whose birthday it is and when we are due someplace. Fourth, I play tennis and love it."

Prem Uncle is living proof of his method, but, more important, he doesn't really have a method. The way he has aged is just the result of who he is. Someone else with utterly different habits but the same easy acceptance of himself would age just as well. In our society we pick up hundreds of external cues about how to live, yet experience teaches us over and over that internal cues are the ones we must heed. Prem Uncle did not derive his lifestyle from an outside authority. He evolved a moderate, sane, healthful way of life on his own. Most people who age successfully do the same: They follow their instincts, finding out what works for them.

The fact that successful survival is so individual is not an incidental factor—it is among the most important. For in a society where we are automatically trained to look to outside authority for expert advice, where inner cues from our bodies are drowned out by a flood of external directives, the isolated individual who beats the system is a rarity. Social scientists have set out to take the measure of such people, and the results disclose some striking similarities. In 1973, at a major gerontology conference at Duke University, three papers were delivered describing the type of person who can expect to live to a healthy old age—between 85 and 100 years old (such people amount to less than 5 percent of the current population). In her psychology research at the University of Chicago, Bernice Neugarten concentrated on "life satisfaction," which entails five factors. The person:

1. Takes pleasure from daily activities
2. Regards his life as meaningful
3. Feels he has achieved his major goals
4. Holds a positive self-image and regards himself as worthwhile
5. Is optimistic

From his research at Harvard, psychologist George Vaillant took a second but similar perspective (as we have seen), that of mental health. The longest-lived individuals, he believed, are also the best adapted in their psychological life, a state characterized by:

1. Having a stable family life
2. Regarding their marriages as satisfying
3. Rarely living alone
4. Continuing to grow in their careers
5. Having no disabling mental illness
6. Not being alcoholic
7. Having fewer chronic illnesses

The third perspective came from Eric Pfeiffer, a psychiatrist at Duke who for many years was project director for a long-term study on older Americans. In keeping with the first two papers, Pfeiffer pointed out that using one's physical and mental abilities to the fullest was the best way to age well. People who age successfully, he found, were those who "stayed in training" throughout their adult lives in three major areas: physical activity, psychological and intellectual activity, and social relationships. If we translate all these findings into larger terms, a profile emerges of people who age well psychologically and therefore biologically.

Growing old happens in the mind; it is therefore uniquely variable in humans. After twenty years, any dog is an old dog; after three, any mouse is an old mouse; after one hundred, any blue whale is a very old blue whale. In all these creatures, biological age is the only number that counts, yet everyone knows people who are young at 80 and others who seem old at 25. The great Renaissance man Sir Francis Bacon held a caustic opinion of old people "who object too much, consult too long, adventure too little, and repent too soon." This is the kind of old age everyone wants to avoid. Fortunately, nothing in our physical makeup forces it upon us. If you don't want to grow old, you can choose not to.

Belinda, an 80-year-old patient of mine, is the product of long New Hampshire winters and rocky farms. She grew up with parents who had no time to grow old and who lived actively into their eighties. They raised their daughter to cherish inner qualities such as self-reliance, trust, faith, honesty, and dedication to family. Belinda has escaped many typical miseries of old age. She isn't on drugs for hypertension, as more than half of old people are (or should be—blood pressure medication, even since "water pills" have been improved, is greatly disliked and often not taken); she hasn't had a single mild stroke or heart attack; there is no sign of diabetes.

As Belinda's doctor, I don't believe any of this is an accident. Today is the youth of your old age, and what you do today affects an outcome thirty or forty years from now. Belinda's good health is the direct result of her lifestyle in the days before she saw the first wrinkle. This is medically confirmed by evidence that old-age diseases like hypertension, heart disease, and atherosclerosis arise from microscopic alterations in our tissues beginning as early as age 10, if not younger.

"Why do you think you've aged so well?" I once asked Belinda.

"I stayed out of trouble," she shot back, "and I worked hard every day of my life."

Many old people have a longevity "secret." Belinda's belief in hard work is shared by many old people, but in truth almost every "secret" of longevity comes down to invisible traits in the person's awareness. Some people are nourished at the most basic level of their awareness, others are not. In purely physical terms, Belinda's life of grueling farm labor out in the sun and rain, enduring the harsh climate of New England, could just as easily have aged her before her time. Some people are worn down by hard work, while others thrive on it. The difference lies in complex social and psychological factors to which our bodies are constantly responding. We need to look deeper into these areas before the three ages of man— chronological, biological, and psychological—fall into a coherent picture.

Awareness as a Field Effect

Because so much of our internal programming is unconscious, we miss the fact that the most powerful influence we have over how we age comes simply from our awareness. To gain control over the aging process, one must first be aware of it, and no two people share the same awareness. What is outside our awareness cannot be controlled, obviously, and because aging happens so slowly, it remains outside most people's awareness except in those isolated moments of recognition when we realize that youth is slipping away: Something jogs our awareness to tell us that we don't feel as vigorous or as strong or as sexually attractive as we once did. However, these distressing moments aren't aging. It is in the absence of being aware, when we don't see anything happening, that physiological processes slip out of our control.

Not being aware doesn't mean that a bodily process has stopped. Your conscious awareness is matched by unconscious awareness—the brain's ability to oversee functions you aren't thinking about at the moment. In Nature's scheme, provisions have been made for our lapses of conscious control. The human nervous systems are designed so that critical functions such as breathing and heartbeat can run by themselves or be controlled voluntarily. I previously mentioned Swami Rama, the Indian adept who displayed remarkable control over bodily functions that were thought to be totally automatic. In one instance, he caused the skin temperature on one side of his right hand to grow warmer while the other side became colder. The rate of change proceeded at about 4 degrees F. per minute, until one side of his hand was flushed red with warmth and the other was pale gray with cold; the total temperature difference was approximately 10 degrees.

What power was being displayed there? In the Indian spiritual tradition there is a branch of esoteric practice called Tantra, which teaches elaborate exercises for controlling involuntary responses. Tibetan Buddhism contains similar teachings; young monks are expected to demonstrate their bodily control by such feats as sitting on a frozen lake and melting the ice around them with the warmth they generate in an intense meditational state. Native Americans, Sufis, and all shamanist cultures around the world contain such practices, yet no matter how esoteric these exercises become, the power being called upon is not mystical: It is the same power of awareness that you use when you decide to switch from involuntary to voluntary breathing, blinking, balancing, or any other autonomic function.

This switch-over happens in your awareness without your having to think about it; therefore, we miss the implicit power being expressed. In fact, as soon as you pay attention to any function, a transformation takes place. For example, if someone puts a five-pound weight in your hand and lifts it up and down for you a hundred times, your arm won't gain any muscle strength. However, if you perform the same action voluntarily, completely different signals are sent from the motor cortex in your brain. Not just your biceps but your heart and lung tissues will receive increased stimulus, as will specific areas of your brain that control motor coordination. The activity of having your arm passively moved is analogous to unconscious, unwilled behavior; the activity of exercising represents conscious, willed behavior. The second mode of activity engages the intricate process called learning, which is at the root of growing, as opposed to growing old. Thus, every time you exercise your biceps, you are *teaching* it to be stronger, and your brain, lungs, heart, endocrine glands, and even immune system are adapting to a new mode of functioning. Conversely, if you move your body without awareness, passivity takes the place of learning. Biceps, heart, lungs, endocrine glands, and immune system eventually lose function instead of gain it.

When you start to assert control over any bodily process, the effect is holistic. The mind-body system reacts to every single stimulus as a global event; i.e., to stimulate one cell is to stimulate all. There is a parallel in quantum terms, since a reaction anywhere in space-time, including past, present, and future, causes a shift in the entire quantum field. As one Nobel laureate put it, "If you tickle the field here, it laughs over there." The fact that awareness behaves like a field is now deemed crucial to understanding aging.

On a wider scale, Walter M. Boritz, a senior Stanford physician who specializes in aging, has coined the term *disuse syndrome* to describe how negligence in paying attention to the body's basic needs, particularly the need for physical activity, can destroy health and lead to rapid premature aging. It is a well-known principle in physiology that any part of the body that falls into disuse will begin to atrophy and wither away.

Boritz took the next step and discovered that this effect was body-wide, spreading beyond the cardiovascular system. When a person decides to give up physical activity, he essentially invites his entire physiology to atrophy. As a result, a constellation of problems appears: (1) heart, arteries, and other parts of the cardiovascular system become more vulnerable; (2) muscles and skeleton become more fragile; (3) obesity becomes a high risk; (4) depression sets in; and (5) signs of premature aging indicate that the body is biologically older than its calendar years. These are the five components of Boritz's disuse syndrome, which can be observed in countless older people today.

The physical deteriorations on this list are not surprising, but it seems unusual that being inactive, in and of itself, would lead to depression, long considered a disorder of mood or personality. However, studies from the Russian space program have found that young cosmonauts subjected to the forced inactivity of space flight fall prey to depression; when put on a schedule of regular exercise, this depression is avoided. The brain mechanism that controls depression appears to lie with a class of neurochemicals called catecholamines. In depressed patients, whose levels of catecholamines are abnormally low, healthy levels can be restored by giving antidepressant drugs, but the natural way to accomplish this is through regular exercise.

Being holistic, exercise sends chemical messages back and forth between the brain and various muscle groups; part of this flow of biochemical information stimulates the production of catecholamines. Thus, whenever a doctor writes a prescription for an antidepressant, Boritz declares, he is handing out a proxy for the body's own inner prescription, which is filled by exercise. The news that exercise offsets aging has been well publicized, although its preventive effect on depression may not be as well known. What is far more fascinating, however, is that the underlying logic—function precedes structure—can be extended to say that awareness precedes function. In other words, the parts of the body that age (losing structure) are not just the ones that are not being used enough (losing function); the person has also withdrawn his awareness from them.

The Man Who Learned to Age

Let me show how the learned and the biological components of aging form a personal pattern that defines how a person will age. A patient of mine named Perry, age 67, is a retired realtor whose wife became worried when he began to seem "different from his usual self." When she brought him in for examination, Perry was listless and unresponsive to questions. His wife commented that when she came home late from shopping or visiting a friend, she often found her husband staring at the television, barely noticing that she had walked into the room.

When I asked Perry how he felt, he was noncommittal. "I'm just getting old," he said. "There's nothing wrong with me that being twenty years younger wouldn't fix." But in fact the Perry of twenty years ago was already cultivating the seeds of habit and belief that grew into what he is today. Like many people of his generation, Perry has outlived both his parents, who died at 70 and 72 respectively after a lifetime of hard work in Boston shoe factories. His expectations for himself are probably strongly marked by having seen them age. His father was "put on the shelf" at 65 and retired to a rocking chair. Taking little interest in making a new life for himself, he gained weight, drank a little more than before, and read newspapers. Within three years of getting his gold watch he suffered a heart attack. His doctors advised him to give up all activity, resigning him to an invalid's life. Within a year, however, a second coronary followed, this one fatal.

Perry's mother, on the other hand, remained active all her life. Like many working women in the past, she also took care of her husband and family, doing all the cooking, housework, and laundry while at the same time holding down an accounting job. Whatever else can be said about such a life, it kept her in much better physical condition than her husband; she had no heart or blood pressure problems and was fortunate not to smoke (a habit she considered unladylike). However, she drifted into apathy and loneliness after her husband's death and seemed to lose her purpose in life. With no one to care for and not wanting to be a burden to her children, she became semireclusive. Eventually she died after a series of strokes.

Perry's outlook on aging had been programmed by these two life stories, and although he probably did not consciously see himself winding up like his parents, he appeared to be on the threshold of duplicating how they aged by unconsciously adopting their beliefs. He had lost control of the aging process by losing touch with his own awareness.

Because my medical specialty is endocrinology, Perry and his wife sought my advice in case he had a thyroid condition; among the disorders that can mimic aging is thyroid deficiency (hypothyroidism), which causes an abnormal decrease in metabolism, making its victims slow and dull, their hair gray and skin wrinkled. This imitation of natural aging disappears once normal levels of the missing hormone, thyroxin, are supplied. Perry exhibited adequate thyroid levels, however, throwing the burden of explanation back upon other influences.

Whenever anyone seems to be aging so badly that signs of senility, feebleness, and disability are present, it's important to investigate his lifestyle. Problems crop up in a person's daily routine that are too often ignored, especially when he is only "showing his age." It is estimated that between a third and half of senility cases result from the following treatable factors:

Malnutrition
Side effects from drugs
Smoking
Alcohol abuse
Dehydration
Depression
Inactivity

All these factors begin in awareness, stemming either from neglect or from habit. Alone or in combination, any of these factors can dramatically affect how a person looks and acts. In the "old" old age of Perry's parents, most people would have paid scant attention to the destructiveness of these factors. Elderly people forgot to eat well, neglected fluids, took up smoking and drinking to assuage their loneliness, and sat around in withdrawn silence because that was what being old meant.

Doctors once routinely prescribed blood pressure medication, sleeping pills, and tranquilizers in combination to old patients, knowing full well that most of them were probably mixing these drugs with alcohol or taking wrong doses. Smoking was medically condoned (or even recommended; a man recently told me that when he was a child, his grandmother went to her family doctor with sinus congestion and was advised to smoke menthol cigarettes! Dutifully following doctor's orders, she smoked her first cigarette at 60 and remained addicted until her death fifteen years later.). Giving nutritional advice did not fall under the scope of a doctors' work, and older patients had to be seriously malnourished or dehydrated, sometimes to the point of coma, before medical intervention was sought. Even today, when it is known that lack of essential vitamins can create symptoms of senility, particularly lack of vitamin B_{12}, this information is not relayed to many of the elderly.

Now consider Perry's condition with the above list in mind. Since his wife had already told me that he sat around the house most of the day, physical inactivity was already a given. On being questioned, Perry revealed that he had started drinking more since his retirement and often began early in the day. When he worked he had set himself a rule never to pour a drink before five, but, as he ruefully said, "My self-discipline is shot. I guess it happens."

Being borderline hypertensive, he was taking blood pressure medication, exactly what kind he wasn't sure (it turned out to be a beta blocker); he had not had the dosage changed in two years. "I try not to take the pills unless my pressure's gone up," he confided. I asked how he knew when his blood pressure was up. "You know, if I feel tense, or the wife is nagging me," he replied. In fact, hypertension, despite its name, does not coincide with being tense and indeed has no overt symptoms; and medication, in order to be effective, must be taken every day. This is particularly true of beta blockers, which require a break-in period while the body adjusts to them.

A huge number of preventable aging problems can be traced to the indiscriminate use of prescription drugs. Unless one is alert to this danger, mixing medications becomes a growing habit with many people as they age. Sleeping pills and diuretics (widely prescribed for high blood pressure) are among the most common drugs used by older people. Tranquilizers are also extremely common, along with aspirin and assorted other painkillers taken for arthritis.

Besides abusing these drugs by taking too many too often, older people often become careless about having their dosages monitored regularly by a doctor; many tend to forget when to discontinue a medication and which drug is meant for which condition. Many older Americans drink, and the combination of drugs and alcohol is almost always dangerous. Therefore, a person's medication should always be thoroughly reviewed at the first sign of physical or mental symptoms of abuse or misuse.

In Perry's case I also strongly suspected hidden low-level depression—someone who watches television all day and pays no attention when his wife walks into the room could easily be mildly or clinically depressed. The typical old person sitting quietly in his corner, once accepted as an image of normal aging, was probably depressed. To become silent, withdrawn, apathetic, anxious, and childishly helpless are common signs of this condition. Chronic fatigue is often a physical outcome of depression, accounting for up to 50 percent of cases. Certain severe depressions (called involutional depression) specifically afflict older people, for reasons not yet known. However, many cases of depression can be linked directly to social and personal problems. A person who feels useless, discarded, uncared for, or burdensome to his family can hardly help but fall into depression.

In these cases, the ultimate solution doesn't lie with medicine but with personal change. Harvard psychologist Ellen Langer has demonstrated that people in nursing homes improve remarkably after altering their lives in the simplest ways—giving them a potted plant to tend, allowing them to make up their own menus and take charge of tidying their rooms. Instead of being passive, lonely dependents playing the role of "old folks in a nursing home," these people regained a sense of usefulness and worth.

For Perry, the last hidden factor in his condition could be dehydration, which starts to impair a person's judgment before he realizes that there is a problem. Not drinking enough water every day is one of the commonest conditions in old age, and although it has received almost no publicity, chronic dehydration is a major cause of preventable aging. Some authorities go so far as to count dehydration among the leading causes of death in old age. It is certainly an avoidable complication that leads to many problems.

When body fluids fall below a certain level, the physiology begins to enter a toxic state; vital electrolyte balance is thrown off, and eventually so is the balance of brain chemistry. A host of difficulties can result—literally anything from kidney failure and heart attack to blackouts, dizziness, lethargy, and full-blown senile dementia. As the person becomes less alert and more forgetful about drinking water, a vicious circle gets set up. The same is true for almost all these causes of false senility—the longer they go over-looked, the harder it is for the person to see the problem.

But Perry's wife was concerned, even if he wasn't, and she promised to remind him about these things. Some would be easier than others: Since she did all the cooking, she could be more careful with his diet (adding a multiple vitamin pill can't hurt and on the off chance might help); she could see that he drank more water and used his medications properly. This extra attention could help lift his spirits, too, but I was most concerned about the alcohol and the depression. In my mind, Perry was walking a thin line. His prevail-ing self-image was contained in two disquieting words: "I'm old." It would be hard to imagine a phrase that is more crippling, or more likely to lead someone into the escape of alcohol or the dead end of depression.

Aging as a whole is a vicious circle. When someone expects to be withdrawn, isolated, and useless after a certain age, he creates the very conditions that justify his beliefs. Our deepest assumptions are the triggers for physical changes. It would be naïve, then, to think that just listing a few preventable causes for aging could actually prevent it. What good does it do to tell someone like Perry to quit drinking if he feels despair? The whole business of growing old is a morass of hidden feelings that people find too difficult to face—if anything, drinking is a merciful anesthetic compared to living with dread and lost hope. It is far easier to follow one's internal program-ming than to break through into new territory. But, over time, our hidden programming robs us of choice more and more, making it harder to break the bonds of self-destructive behavior. In this regard aging is much like addiction: The person feels that he is still in control when in fact the behavior is controlling him. From the outside, I could see this in Perry. He was transforming himself into a dying man before my eyes, and the tragedy was that he could not see that he was doing it to himself. Awareness, once it becomes conditioned, assumes the shape of habit; unconscious repetition reinforces the destructive patterns, and unless new learning takes place, inertia will carry the body downhill year after year.

Awareness and the Reversal of Aging

The bright side of Perry's case was that almost everything happening to him could be corrected by creating a new mode of awareness. To do that, we take advantage of the fact that awareness is always generating biological information. With even the slightest change of awareness, energy and information move in new patterns. The reason old habits are so destructive is that new patterns aren't allowed to spring into existence—conditioned awareness is therefore synonymous with slow dying.

On the other hand, by increasing someone's awareness, bringing it into a new focus and breaking out of old patterns, you can alter aging. A brilliant demonstration of this was offered in 1979 by psychologist Ellen Langer and her colleagues at Harvard, who effectively reversed the biological age of a group of old men by a simple but ingenious shift in awareness. The subjects, all 75 or older and in good health, were asked to meet for a week's retreat at a country resort. They were informed in advance that they would be given a battery of physical and mental exams, but in addition one unusual stipulation was placed upon them: They were not allowed to bring any newspapers, magazines, books, or family photos dated later than 1959.

The purpose of this odd request became clear when they arrived—the resort had been set up to duplicate life as it was twenty years earlier. Instead of magazines from 1979, the reading tables held issues of *Life* and the *Saturday Evening Post* from 1959. The only music played was twenty years old, and, in keeping with this flashback, the men were asked to behave entirely as if the year were 1959. All talk had to refer to events and people of that year. Every detail of their week in the country was geared to make each subject feel, look, talk, and behave as he had in his midfifties.

During this period, Langer's team made extensive measurements of the subjects' biological age. Gerontologists have not been able to fix the precise markers that define biological age, as I noted earlier, but a general profile was compiled for each man using measurements of physical strength, posture, perception, cognition, and short-term memory, along with thresholds of hearing, sight, and taste.

The Harvard team wanted to change the context in which these men saw themselves. The premise of their experiment was that seeing oneself as old or young directly influences the aging process itself. To shift their context back to 1959, the experimenters had their subjects wear I.D. photos taken twenty years before—the group learned to identify one another through these pictures rather than present appearance; they were instructed to talk exclusively in the present tense of 1959 ("I wonder if President Eisenhower will go with Nixon next election?"); their wives and children were referred to as if they were also twenty years younger; although all the men were retired, they talked about their careers as if they were still in full swing.

The results of this play-acting were remarkable. Compared to a control group that went on the retreat but continued to live in the world of 1979, the make-believe group improved in memory and manual dexterity. They were more active and self-sufficient about such things as taking their own food at meals and cleaning up their rooms, behaving much more like 55-year-olds than 75-year-olds (many had become dependent on younger family members to perform everyday tasks for them).

Perhaps the most remarkable change had to do with aspects of aging that were considered irreversible. Impartial judges who were asked to study before-and-after pictures of the men detected that their faces looked visibly younger by an average of three years. Measurements of finger length, which tends to shorten with age, indicated that their fingers had lengthened; stiffened joints were more flexible, and posture had started to straighten as it had in younger years. Muscle strength, as measured by hand grip, improved, as did hearing and vision. The control group also showed some improvements (Langer explained this by the fact that going on a trip and being treated specially made them feel younger, too). But the control group actually declined in certain markers such as manual dexterity and finger length. Intelligence is considered fixed in adults, yet over half of the experimental group showed increased intelligence over the five days of their return to 1959, while a quarter of the control group declined in I.Q. test scores.

Professor Langer's study was a landmark in proving that so-called irreversible signs of aging could be reversed using psychological intervention. She attributed this success to three factors: (1) The men were asked to behave as if they were younger; (2) They were treated as if they had the intelligence and independence of younger people (unlike the way they were often treated at home—for example, their opinions were elicited with respect and actually listened to); (3) They were asked to follow complex instructions about their daily routine. Because all three factors overlapped, Langer ultimately was not certain which of them was the most important. She speculated that a similar reversal of aging might have resulted if the men had been given any complex task to perform, such as composing an opera—a task Verdi set for himself in his late seventies.

I have been pondering Professor Langer's results for several years, ever since I first wrote about it in the context of personal time. The old paradigm tells us that time is objective, but in fact our bodies respond to subjective time, as recorded in memories and internal feelings. Langer enabled these men to be inner time travelers; they journeyed back twenty years psychologically, and their bodies followed. The simplest way I can explain this is that two aspects of awareness were being shifted: attention and intention. Awareness always has these two components. Attention focuses awareness to a local perception. Intention brings about a change in that localization. In Langer's experiment, the subjects had their attention sharply localized on the context of the year 1959; this started a new flow of biological information, because everything they saw, heard, or talked about had to relate to that one specific

localization. At the same time, they had to act on an intention—
intending to be just as they were twenty years earlier. There is no
magic in either factor; we all pay attention to various things
throughout the day; we all carry out various desires and intentions.

The magic is in how the body follows this change of awareness
across the barrier of time. It's not feasible or realistic to try to live
in the past, but there are valuable clues that can be followed here:
Again we see that *the quality of one's life depends on the quality of
attention.* Whatever you pay attention to will grow more important
in your life. There is no limit to the kinds of changes that awareness
can produce. In our society, we do not use the flow of attention to
produce results; we are not clued in to the energy and information
that starts to be generated inside us anytime we experience a change
of awareness. In the following exercises, we will explore how to
consciously call upon the power of awareness and use it to our
benefit, for if we do not use it consciously, our awareness will be
trapped in the old conditioning that creates the aging process.

IN PRACTICE:

Using the Power of Awareness

The exercises below are designed to prove that you can consciously direct the flow of energy and information in your body. There are major benefits to be gained once you begin to consciously use your awareness:

- You can tap into subtler levels of information in the form of bodily cues you have been ignoring. Your body will tell you what it needs when it needs it—this is the exact opposite of being driven by habit, which will never precisely fit the body's actual wants.
- You can focus attention on parts of the body that are expressing discomfort. Simply by localizing your awareness on a source of pain, you can cause healing to begin, for the body naturally sends healing energy wherever attention is drawn.
- You can activate desires and intentions to fulfill them more efficiently. An intention is basically a disguised need, and the mind-body system is set up to meet all needs directly and spontaneously. (This is very different from the addictive or compulsive desires that our old programming has built into us.)

When all three of these areas are operating properly, conditioning starts to dissolve at the deepest cellular levels; this has to happen to prevent the body from growing old. There are numerous spiritual teachings in all areas related to the power of awareness, and the techniques of Native American shamans might differ extremely from those of Tibetan monks or Hindu yogis. In general, however, awareness is used as a healing power: It restores balance wherever it is allowed to flow freely.

Bringing awareness into contact with frozen patterns of old conditioning starts to melt those patterns, for ultimately everything we can sense or think about is simply an aspect of our awareness. The discomfort the body manifests as pain, numbness, spasm, inflexibility, and trauma are all knots that awareness can undo by itself. Through practice and dedication, you can heal any imbalance in the mind-body system through awareness, once the appropriate techniques of relaxation, release, and insight are learned.

Below are some beginning procedures for localizing attention and fulfilling intentions. We will progress to deeper, more powerful techniques in later sections, but even at these stages, the connections being forged between mind and body are extremely helpful for breaking out of the old pathways that create aging.

Exercise 1: Paying Attention to Your Body

Although we all know how to pay attention to something outside ourselves, and we all feel our attention drawn to a pain in the body, such as a toothache or muscle spasm, there are many subtle cues that escape us in everyday life. Awareness has many levels, and it must be allowed to flow from one to the other, for flow is its natural state. In this first exercise, you are asked to easily direct your attention to each area of the body; as this happens, the act of paying attention releases deep-stored stresses. Like a child, your body wants attention and feels comforted when it receives it.

Sit with your eyes closed in a comfortable chair or lie down. (Choose a quiet room that is free of distracting noises.) Place your attention on the toes of your right foot. Curl them down until they feel tense, then release the tension and feel the sense of relaxation that flows into them. Don't rush either the tensing or the relaxing; take time to feel what is happening. Now let out a long, deep sigh as if you are breathing out of your toes, letting all stored fatigue and tension flow away with your breath. Don't puff or blow; just let the sigh release itself in one long exhalation, like a sigh of relief, without holding back. If you let out a moan or groan, all the better—that is a sign of deep release.

Now repeat this procedure with the top of your right foot, first placing your attention on it, then tensing the muscles (by arching your foot backward), and finally relaxing them. When the top of your foot feels relaxed, let out a sigh as if you are breathing out through your toes.

Once you have this basic technique down, take your attention to all parts of the body in the following order. Remember that this is not just a muscle relaxation technique; your attention needs to linger comfortably at each bodily location.

Right foot: toes, top of foot, sole of foot, ankle (two stages: flexing back, then flexing forward)

Left foot: toes, top of foot, sole of foot, ankle (two stages: flexing back, then flexing forward)

Right buttock and upper thigh

Left buttock and upper thigh

Abdominal muscles (diaphragm)

Lower back, upper back

Right hand: fingers, wrist (two stages: flexing back, then flexing forward)

Left hand: fingers, wrist (two stages: flexing back, then flexing forward)

Shoulders (two stages: flexing forward, then flexing upward toward neck)

Neck (two stages: flexing forward, then flexing backward)

Face (two stages: screwing face into tight grimace, then tensing brow and forehead)

This exercise sounds rather complicated when described verbally, but flexing various body parts simply follows the natural way the joints and muscles move. After one session, you will be able to feel your way around your body effortlessly.

Short version: A complete circuit of the body as described above takes about fifteen minutes. If you are pressed for time, a short version involves only the toes, diaphragm, fingers, shoulders, neck, and face.

Exercise 2: Focused Intention

This exercise demonstrates that having an intention is enough to accomplish a result. When properly focused—which means easily and without strain—awareness has the ability to carry out quite specific commands. An intention doesn't have to be a verbally expressed thought; in fact, our deepest intentions are body-centered. Our most fundamental needs—for love, understanding, encouragement, support—permeate every cell. The desires that arise in your mind are often clouded by ego motives, which are not true needs; people get caught up in the pursuit of money, career goals, and political ambitions in ways that are disconnected from the fundamental need for comfort and well-being that every healthy organism must fulfill. Many of us are so alienated from our basic needs, so programmed to run after what the ego wants, that we have to relearn the basic mechanics of how attention and intention actually work.

There are many ways to get fulfillment besides the outward-oriented ones our culture teaches us. The most valuable lesson in this regard is that *intentions automatically seek their fulfillment if left alone.* Every cell in your body is seeking fulfillment through joy, beauty, love, and appreciation. This is hard to realize when the mind sets up its own separate agenda for fulfilling other kinds of desires, ones that are loveless, without joy or satisfaction. Yet millions of people have programmed themselves to reach only such goals.

In the three related procedures given here, you will experience the effortless way that intentions can get fulfilled, bypassing the ego and the rational mind (for best results, do exercise 1 as a warm-up, in order to bring your body into a receptive state). Even though the intentions being carried out are simple, they give you confidence in your ability to direct your awareness, which is critical if you want to change the deep-rooted patterns of aging, for aging itself is an intention that your cells are obeying without your control.

1. Take a piece of string about twelve inches long and tie a small weight at the end to form a pendulum (a lead fishing weight, household washer, or one-inch bolt will work well). Hold the string in your right hand and brace your elbow on a table or the arm of your chair so that you can hold the pendulum steady. Sit comfortably and make sure that the pendulum is not moving.

Now look at the weight and project the intention that the pendulum move from side to side. The simplest form of intention is to visualize how you want the weight to move, but you can verbalize the words *side to side* if you wish. Keep your attention on the pendulum and keep the intention firmly in mind, but make sure you hold your arm steady. In a few seconds you will be surprised to see the pendulum start to move of its own accord. If it moves erratically at first, don't try to correct its swing—just wait until the desired motion is found automatically.

Now change your intention to direct the pendulum back and forth instead of side to side. Again see this motion in your mind's eye and easily hold it there. Typically, your pendulum will hesitate for a few seconds, move erratically, then take up the desired direction.

After watching it for a few seconds, intend for the pendulum to swing in a circle. Again it will pause, move erratically for a second or two, then move exactly as you visualized. The harder you try to hold your arm rigidly still, the faster the pendulum will move. Curiously, doing this exercise in a group produces the greatest effect; I have observed several hundred people sitting mesmerized while their pendulums instantly changed direction at the touch of an intention, often moving in wide, fast arcs. Although this exercise is very simple, the effect can be quite uncanny.

2. Sitting comfortably, hold your right hand open, palm upward. Have the intention that your palm should get warmer. To aid in this, imagine that your hand is touching a red-hot stove or

burning coal. Hold the image in your mind. Within a few seconds the sensation of warmth will start to appear. Now hold up your left hand and aim the fingers of your right hand at it, fingers out stiff and close together. Intend for the warmth to shoot out of your right hand into the palm of the left. To aid in this, sweep your right hand back and forth, as if painting your other hand with warmth (but don't let the two hands touch). Most people will feel warmth broadcast from one hand to the other; others will feel a mild tingling or ticklish sensation in the left palm.

This exercise is most effective if you guide someone else through it. If you are doing it alone, familiarize yourself with the instructions first so that you can try the experiment without interruption.

3. Sit comfortably and hold an ordinary thermometer between the thumb and forefinger of your right hand. Close your eyes and pay attention to your breathing for a moment. As your body relaxes, continue to easily follow your breath, then note the temperature on the thermometer. You are going to change it through intention alone.

The intention of cold. Breathing through your mouth, feel the cool air in your throat as it moves in and out. Think the word *cool* as you do this. Now imagine that the thermometer is a piece of ice that you can barely hold between your fingers. After a minute or so, look at the temperature on the thermometer—it will likely have dropped from two to five degrees. If you notice no change, resume the exercise for another minute or two before checking again.

The intention of warmth. Breathing through your nose, feel the warmth in the center of your chest for a moment. Now think the word *hot* and imagine that the thermometer is a glowing red ember you can barely hold. After a minute or so, look at the thermometer—it will likely have risen from two to five degrees. If you notice no change, resume the exercise for another minute or two before checking again.

The last two exercises are based on classic experiments performed over fifty years ago by the pioneer Russian neurologist A. R. Luria. Luria's most famous subject was a journalist he simply called S., a man who was gifted with an almost flawless photographic memory. S. could attend a press conference without taking notes and afterward recount every word spoken by any number of speakers; he could memorize long strings of random numbers and recall the details of any scene in which he had been present down to the most minute detail.

In addition, S. could use simple visualizations to change all kinds of involuntary functions. If he imagined himself staring at the sun, his pupils would contract; if he imagined himself sitting in the dark, his pupils would dilate. He could raise and lower the temperature of his hands using the procedure described above. Once you have mastered that, you can try his method for changing his heartbeat. If he wanted his heart to beat faster, S. saw himself running after a train as it pulled out of a station; if he wanted to slow down his heart, S. saw himself lying in bed taking a nap.

Luria considered these achievements remarkable, just as future researchers did a generation later when they observed Swami Rama performing the same feats. However, in both cases what was being demonstrated was biofeedback without machines. Instead of needing an oscilloscope or a beep to indicate that an intention was being carried out, S. and Swami Rama relied on their bodies' own feedback loops.

Although we are not ordinarily aware of it, the body is constantly regulating temperature, heart rate, and other autonomic functions by listening in to its own internal messages. The slightest change in any function registers, however faintly, in the awareness of the nervous system. As these exercises demonstrate, such silent signals can be consciously tapped. Awareness is a field, and by sending an intention into that field, you shift the flow of biological information. This registers in the conscious mind as a faint sensation, intuition, or just a silent knowing. The response varies from person to person, but with practice one's sensitivity to one's own awareness becomes stronger.

As applied to aging, this sensitivity is necessary, because the new paradigm tells us that aging begins as a distortion in the field of awareness. The smooth flow of information in the body becomes blocked by stresses, memories, past trauma, and random mistakes.

Although such breakdowns are subtle, they are not lost to awareness; the heart, liver, kidneys, and every other organ *know* when they are malfunctioning. Disturbances in cellular intelligence eventually register in the mind as discomfort or pain or just being out of sorts. What we are learning to do here is to refine such perceptions so that they register at an earlier stage. The earlier it is detected, the more easily a distorted function can be corrected using awareness alone. Full-blown aging is a very gross sign that the body has suffered a loss of energy and information at some vital point, usually in the brain, immune system, or endocrine glands.

Cancer, diabetes, and senility are typical late-stage manifestations of dysfunction. There are rare cases in which patients have used the power of awareness to cure themselves of even the most serious disorders, yet it is far simpler to correct the underlying problem at an earlier stage. The very first stage of any physiological disruption takes place in awareness itself; quite naturally, the best way to move these disruptions back into balance is also by using attention.

Exercise 3: A Trigger for Transformation

Every intention is a trigger for transformation. As soon as you decide that you want something, your nervous system responds to reach your desired goal. This holds true for simple intentions, such as the intention to get up and get a glass of water, as well as for complex intentions, such as winning a game of tennis or playing a Mozart sonata. In either case, the conscious mind doesn't have to direct every neuronal signal and muscle movement to achieve its goal. The intention is inserted into the field of awareness, triggering the appropriate response.

When I go to sleep, my intention to sleep triggers a complex series of biochemical and neurological processes. Medical science cannot duplicate this connection; it is controlled at the level of intelligence. The connection can be crudely manipulated only from the molecular level (for example, I can go to sleep by taking a sleeping pill, but the kind of sleep that results will not be natural;

there will be disruptions in the normal sequence of sleep stages, particularly REM or dream sleep).

When you have an intention, your brain can supply only the reactions it has learned; if you are a good tennis player or pianist, your trained response will produce very different results from those achieved by someone less skilled than you. Yet the deepest skill resides in managing intention itself. The people who succeed best at any endeavor are generally following a pattern of handling their desires without undue struggle with their environment—they are in the flow. If you review the section on adaptability (p. 72) you will find a good description of how the most successful people solve problems—they allow the solution to present itself, trusting their own abilities to cope with difficult challenges. By creating a minimum of anxiety, conflict, worry, and false expectation, they promote highly efficient use of their mental and physical energies. The resulting ease of mind-body functioning is directly correlated to aging well—the more naturally you exist in the flow of your awareness, the less wear and tear on your body.

As is true of all abilities, people vary enormously in their use of intention. When Professor Ellen Langer and her colleagues provided a group of elderly men with the challenge of acting twenty years younger (p. 92), the researchers gave their subjects a common focus of intention. The key to reversing the age of these men was that their bodies responded to external cues from the past.

In the following exercise, you are asked to participate in a kind of internal time travel using a visual image from your past; the purpose is to experience how quickly your body adapts to this intention with feelings of renewed youthfulness.

Sit comfortably or lie down with your eyes closed. Pay attention for a moment to your breathing, easily following the rise and fall of your chest, feeling the air as it passes in and out of your nostrils. Feel your arms getting heavy at your sides. When you are relaxed, conjure up in your mind's eye one of the most wonderful moments from your childhood. It should be a vivid scene of joy, and preferably you should be the center of some activity.

For example, one such scene for me took place while playing cricket when I was a child. In summer my father took us to the hill stations in northern India, and I vividly remember one of these, named Shillong, nestled in the cool green mountains. I can see the flat meadow ringed by hills where we played our games. There was one instance where I made a winning run, and this is the moment I choose to relive in memory. I feel the weight of the bat in my hands and the hard smack when I hit the ball. I see it soaring high, against the green and red roofs of distant cottages. I feel the cool air and the excitement in my body as I start to run. My heart is pounding, my legs straining with all their might. In my mind's eye I swing my arms open wide, embracing this victorious moment. With every fiber I am participating in it, not just recalling it, and the intensity of desiring to be back there in my youth makes me feel light, expanded, happy, absorbed in an experience so fulfilling that it stops time.

Find your own moment and see how powerful it is for you. Details are important; for that reason, intensely physical experiences are the easiest to use. Feel the air and sunlight on your skin; sense whether you were hot or cold. Observe colors, textures, faces. Name the locale and the people in your scene. Notice how everyone was dressed and acted. But most important, recapture the feeling in your body as you rose up to blend into and become that moment. By rejoining the flow of one magical instant, you trigger a transformation in your body. Signals being sent from your brain are activated just as easily by memories and visual images as by actual sights and sounds. The more vivid your participation, the closer you will come to duplicating the body chemistry of that youthful moment. The old channels are never closed, they are only unused. Therefore, by changing the context of your inner experience, you can go back in time using the biochemistry of memory as your vehicle.

Exercise 4: Intentions and the Field

The new paradigm tells us that our underlying reality, the field, is continuous and therefore equally present at all points in space-time. Your awareness and every intention that springs from your awareness are enmeshed in this continuity. This means that when you have a desire, you are actually sending a message into the entire field—your slightest intention is rippling across the universe at the quantum level. We have already seen that when you have an intention related to your body, it gets carried out automatically. The same thing should occur, then, with intentions you send outside your body—the field has the organizing power to automatically bring fulfillment to any intention.

Everyone notices occasional instances when a desire unexpectedly comes true, when something you wished for appears out of nowhere—a call from an old friend, unexpected money or job offer, a new relationship. These are the times when your connection to the field is clear. When your desires don't come true, your awareness has suffered some block or disconnection from its source in the field. *It is normal to have all desires be fulfilled if your awareness is open and clear.* It takes no special act of providence to fulfill desires; the universal field of existence has been designed to operate for that purpose; if it were not so designed, you couldn't wiggle your toes, blink your eyes, or carry out any mind-body command. Every voluntary action depends on the invisible transformation of an abstract intention into a material result.

Your body is the material result of all the intentions you have ever had. In the last exercise, we called back a moment from the past, using intention to create a certain mind-body response. If you imagined your experience vividly enough, all kinds of involuntary reactions—blood pressure, heartbeat, respiration, body temperature, and so forth—started to conform exactly to how you felt in the past. You were reliving not just a visual image but the entire physiological response that went with the image. Millions of such holistic responses went into creating the physiology you now experience. But since you did not possess the skill consciously to use these intentions for your benefit, your body contains stored impressions of traumas and stresses that contribute to the aging process.

In the next section I will describe how to remove these old impressions, but here it is important to learn the mechanics of intention that prevent aging in the first place. An intention is a signal sent from you to the field, and *the result you get back from the field is the highest fulfillment that can be delivered to your particular nervous system.* When two people want the same thing, they don't always get the same result; this is because the quality of intention changes as it is sent into the field and then reflected back as a result. For example, if you have a strong desire to be loved, the love you want and will receive is highly conditioned by your experience: The love of Saint Paul is totally different from the love known to an abused child. Nevertheless, whenever a desire comes true, the mechanics have certain similarities for every person:

1. A certain outcome is intended.

2. The intention is specific and definite; the person is certain about what he or she wants.

3. Little or no attention is paid to the details of the physiological processes involved. Indeed, paying attention to the details inhibits the flow of the impulses of intelligence that produce the outcome, slowing down or preventing success. In other words, the person takes an attitude of noninterference.

4. The person expects a result and has confidence in the outcome. There is no anxious attachment to a result, however (if you are anxious about falling asleep, for example, that prevents the very outcome you desire). Worry, uncertainty, and doubt are the three primary obstacles that prevent us from making efficient use of the power contained in every intention. The power is still there, but we turn it against itself. In other words, when you doubt that a desire will come true, essentially you are sending out a self-defeating intention, which the field computes as canceling your first desire.

5. There is a self-referring feedback involved. In other words, every fulfilled intention teaches you how to fulfill the next intention even better. When the result occurs, it confirms the power of intention at a conscious level, increases confidence, and makes success stronger—the

effect is self-reinforcing. This changes doubt to certainty. (People whose desires don't come true also experience feedback, but it reinforces failure.)

6. At the end of the process, there is no doubt that the outcome was obtained by a definite, conscious process that extends beyond the individual to a larger reality— for some this is God or Providence, for others it is the Self or the Absolute. I have been using a more scientific term, the field, but without excluding any of these more traditional spiritual names. In all cases, the material world is an expression of an unmanifest, overriding intelligence that responds to human desire.

These six steps display the most important characteristic of inner intelligence—it has organizing power built in to it. This organizing power is the link that connects intention and result. Without it, there could be no cause and effect. The "quantum soup" would remain chaotic, since without organizing power there can be no patterns, orderliness, natural laws, physical structures, or biochemical processes.

To take advantage of this knowledge, you can use the following exercise with any desire. Do not worry if you have not had much success in fulfilling your intentions in the past. Gaining clarity about the mechanics of intention is the most important step in achieving anything. By going through this exercise, you will be clearing a path for greater success; just have confidence that the field automatically fulfills all impulses sent into it. In some form or other, every desire reaches its goal; it is only your limited perspective in space-time that clouds your perception of the outcome being produced.

1. Sit quietly and use any of the methods already given for relaxing your body and feeling calm inside.
2. Intend the outcome you want. Be specific. You can visualize the outcome or express it to yourself verbally.
3. Don't get bogged down in details. Don't force or concentrate. Your intention should be as natural as intending to lift your arm or get a drink of water.

4. Expect and believe in the outcome. Know that it is certain.

5. Realize that doubt, worry, and attachment will only interfere with success.

6. Let go of the desire. You don't have to mail a letter twice; just know that the message was delivered and your result is on the way.

7. Be open to the feedback that comes to you either inside yourself or from the environment. Realize that any and all feedback was elicited by you.

This last step is extremely important. Being so conditioned by the materialist worldview, all of us tend to look for material results. However, someone who wishes for wealth may actually be desiring the security that he imagines wealth brings, and if that intention is dominant in his awareness, the field might favor an outcome that brought a sense of security rather than material wealth. The feedback produced from an intention is capable of manifesting in unexpected ways, but some result is always produced, however faint.

In regard to aging, most of us want to avoid mental and physical deterioration; we might have a specific intention, such as not to contract Alzheimer's or cancer, but these intentions might not be effective, since they are disguised forms of deeper wishes, such as not wanting to suffer and die. My suggestion is to intend to remain at the most youthful level of functioning possible. You can also intend, in both mental and physical function, to improve every day, and to reinforce the results of that intention, you can resolve to take notice of anything you are able to do better every day. Do not set any restrictive expectations—perhaps one day all you will notice is that you did the laundry more cheerfully or appreciated a sunset. Awareness branches in a thousand directions, and keeping every channel open is valuable.

Here is one form your intention might take:

Today I intend to experience
1. More energy
2. More alertness

3. More youthful enthusiasm
4. More creativity
5. Continued improvement in physical and mental capacity
   on all levels

The following intention can be added as an all-encompassing wish:

I intend that my inner creative intelligence will spontaneously orchestrate and guide my behavior, my feelings, and my response to every situation in such a way that all five of the above intentions will automatically be carried out.

Finally, it is helpful to remind yourself that you can rely on this approach because you are tapping into the fundamental nature of your physiology as it operates all the time: "My internal cues are my best feedback, and the more I respond to them, the more I will amplify the force of my intention to get the outcome I want."

PART THREE

Defeating Entropy

THE BASIC MATERIAL of the human body is extremely fragile. If you isolate a single cell and leave it outside on a balmy June day, it will wither and die in a matter of minutes. Inside each cell is a microscopic wisp of genetic material, your DNA, which is even less sturdy. Despite the fact that they are secreted away in the nuclei of the cells, your genes are damaged every day by radioactivity, ultraviolet light, chemical toxins and pollution, random mutations, X rays, and even the process of life itself. Highly reactive oxygen atoms called free radicals are released when food is metabolized in the cells, and among the many chemicals they bond to and damage is DNA.

The world is a dangerous place for life to survive in, and if we look beyond the localized dangers of our planet, a cosmic force stands ever ready to destroy life. It is called entropy, the universal tendency for order to break down into disorder. Entropy came into existence at the instant of the Big Bang; starting with the creation of the universe, heat, light, and all other forms of energy have been dissipating, spreading out over time as the universe expands. This tendency to spread out, moving energy to less concentrated areas, is entropy. Entropy is a one-way arrow. When an old car starts to rust and decompose, the process can't reverse itself automatically. By the same token, an aged body doesn't automatically turn young again.

Whenever matter and energy collect into orderly patterns, entropy is defied, but physics has always held that these "islands of negative entropy" are temporary, even though some of them—planets, stars, galaxies—endure a very long time. Eventually stars burn out, planets lose their orbital momentum, galaxies dissipate.

The planet Earth is an island of negative entropy that feeds off the borrowed energy of sunlight; when the sunlight is no more, we will succumb to entropy, growing cold and lifeless. Entropy is dragging the entire cosmos down to its end, when all energy will be evenly distributed across the vastness of space. This ultimate "heat death" lies billions of years in the future, but every molecule is being pushed toward it. Some of the most fundamental building blocks of matter, such as the proton, are so long-lived that it takes aeons for them to decay, while other exotic subatomic particles, such as the meson, flash into physical existence for a few millionths of a second before winking out of sight again. The breakdown of orderliness is inherent in the physical makeup of the universe, and it is at the core of the reason why our bodies deteriorate and age over time. If we want to defeat aging, we must first learn how to defeat entropy.

Opposed to Chaos

The human body exists in utter defiance of entropy, since it is incredibly orderly and capable of adding to its order with even more complexity. Why, then, are we alive to begin with? What force works against chaos to assert higher and higher complexities of order? The creation of human DNA, with its billions of precisely coded chemical bases, depended on the ability of less complex chemicals (amino acids and sugar) to remain intact over billions of years and to persist in building more and more complex chains of molecules. At any time these structures could have collapsed and dissolved back into the quantum soup. The force of entropy does not make exceptions; it is pushing all things into dissolution and chaos.

In purely material terms, physics doesn't describe a force working against entropy. Yet it is obvious that the universe hasn't just expanded after the Big Bang; it has evolved. The primordial hydrogen atoms that came into existence soon after the Big Bang were not content with their simple lives; they increased in complexity to form helium atoms, whose orderliness remained stable and then led to ever more complex atoms, all the way up to superheavy uranium and plutonium. Evolution, or growth, creates more complex structures from less complex ones.

However, a huge hole was punched in the theory of evolution by scientific insistence that the entire chain of evolution, beginning with simplest one-called algae and bacteria and extending to the most complex organ in nature, the human brain, came about randomly. Although it may be true that animal survival depends on random selection, the deeper flaws in this explanation are obvious. Whenever a baby is conceived, the fertilized egg duplicates the process of cell division that has produced billions of babies before it. The growth of one cell into two, two into four, four into eight, and so forth, is evolution in action. There is nothing random about it; therefore, why do we say that the process which created birth was random? Clearly, there is a counterforce pushing evolution along, creating life, fending off the threat of entropy.

The counterforce is intelligence, which at the quantum level is far more than a mental phenomenon. Intelligence holds together the blueprint of each cell in its DNA, and many scientists now believe the same holds true of the entire universe. In his book *The Cosmic Blueprint,* British physicist Paul Davies summons many theoretical findings to support the new view that the universe organizes itself and reacts to its own internal events much as our cells do. The cosmos is not just expanding like a balloon but growing like a living entity. "The universe is revealed in a new, more inspiring light," Davies writes, "unfolding from its primitive beginnings and progressing step by step to ever more elaborate and complex states." Something that progresses is showing signs of intelligence, however reluctant mainstream science may be about using the term.

Intelligence is a synonym for creative power. It reaches out into chaos and from the quantum soup forms beautiful symmetries. It infuses dead molecules with life and breath. When entropy gains an upper hand, intelligence must wane. The two forces are in constant battle. Since both have existed since the Big Bang, what determines the outcome of their clash? A human baby is born, which is a monumental victory for intelligence, but the baby one day starts to age, which is a victory for entropy. It isn't accurate to equate aging with entropy—there is a subtle but necessary distinction to be made here. Creation and destruction coexist. In every cell some chemical reactions are creative—producing new proteins, for example, from building blocks of amino acids—while others are destructive—for instance, the process of digestion, which breaks down complex foods into simpler compounds, or the process of metabolism, which burns sugar and releases its stored energy.

Without destruction, life couldn't exist. Therefore, aging isn't simply the destruction of the body. This is an extremely important point missed by those who equate life with nothing but the play of random material forces. Entropy is actually on the side of life; it performs as one player in a complex balance of forces. Without intelligence, the balance would immediately be thrown off.

For instance, there is a terrible endocrine disorder called progeria, which is caused by a deformation in just one of the hundred thousand genes in a newborn baby. An extremely rare disease, progeria leads to rapidly accelerated aging. Wrinkles, baldness, wasting of muscles, and hardening of the arteries begin to appear in early childhood. By age 12, a child with progeria may have suffered massive strokes or become a candidate for coronary bypass, and death comes very early, usually before age 20.

Progeria is entropy that has been drastically, horribly sped up, and that happens because one gene, a minute speck of the body's pattern of intelligence, goes awry. Forces of disorder are unleashed by tipping the balance that each cell must maintain to remain alive. The same lesson applies to normal aging. As long as the body can renew itself according to its blueprint of orderliness, entropy is countered. As an old stomach or skin cell breaks down, it gets replaced; whenever a particle of food is metabolized, wastes are excreted and new food arrives.

We can call this balance of creation and destruction *dynamic non-change*. In other words, change takes place within a stable framework. As far as our bodies are concerned, this state of dynamic non-change is crucial. Tipping the balance in either direction spells disaster—lack of change leads to death; too much change leads to wild disorder (as when a cancer cell starts dividing indiscriminately until it eventually takes over vital tissues and causes its own destruction, along with that of the rest of the body).

Every cell knows how to defeat entropy by bringing intelligence to the rescue whenever disorder begins to intrude. The most critical example is provided by DNA itself. Long thought to be an inert chemical that sits unchanged in the cell's nucleus, DNA is now known to have a remarkable capacity for self-repair. Under the assault of free radicals and other damaging influences, at least seven different kinds of mistakes can appear in a strand of DNA. (You can think of DNA as a computer tape whose information gets confused when the tape is broken, twisted, or bunched up.) If your genes passively accepted such damage, as every other chemical would, the information coded on the double helix would get more and more garbled, making orderly life impossible. But DNA has learned to repair itself. It can sense exactly which kind of damage has occurred, and via special enzymes the appropriate missing links are spliced back into place. This astonishing display of intelligence has been linked directly to human aging. If you graph the life expectancy of various animals, starting with short-lived shrews and mice and proceeding through cows, elephants, and man, the resulting curve is almost perfectly matched by how well each animal's DNA can repair itself. The long-tailed shrew, for example, has an extremely short life span, usually less than a year, while humans have the longest life span of any mammal, at a known maximum of between 115 and 120 years.

In the early 1970s, two young gerontologists, Ron Hart and Richard Setlow, exposed the DNA of various animals to ultraviolet light in order to create a specific kind of damage (adjacent molecules on the DNA strand became unnaturally fused). They then measured how much repair took place over a period of an hour, and in fact cells from the shrew repaired themselves more slowly than did cells from a mouse, which lives somewhat longer. The rate of self-repair increased with cows and elephants, culminating with humans, who have the fastest genetic-repair rate known. Later, Dr. Edward Schneider at the National Institutes on Aging verified that older cells repair themselves much less efficiently than do younger ones. The overall conclusion is that aging results from the inability of DNA to keep up with the constant damage being inflicted on it millions of times per year.

If this is how the balance of forces gives way inside us, why does Nature allow it to go on? If a human cell is more than 99 percent efficient at self-repair, why didn't evolution fill in the remaining deficit? This is a perplexing question, for to answer it you must know the secret of life itself. What we can say is that over a lifetime, each of our cells undergoes more damage than it can repair. Aging is the result of this deficit. If a cell repaired itself perfectly every time, every cell would be as new as the day we were born, and we would never grow old. This implies that by preventing as many genetic mistakes as possible, we would be preventing the result of those mistakes—the aging process.

As seen from the level of intelligence, your cells want to be new at every moment. But old cells are littered with past mistakes that have taken physical form as toxic debris, clogged pigments, cross-linked molecules, and damaged DNA. These rigid bits of matter no longer flow and change, which is necessary to life. In this section we will look at the living blueprint of the body, which is made of intelligence, to discover how it allows mistakes to occur. There is no biological necessity for these mistakes, and there are many techniques for correcting and avoiding them.

Unlike the shrew, mouse, cow, or elephant, you are not imprisoned within a fixed genetic-repair rate. According to the new paradigm, your entire body is one field of awareness, and the activity inside your cells is directly influenced by how you think and act. You are talking to your DNA via the chemical messages sent from your brain, and these messages directly affect DNA's output of information. One enduring legacy from the past twenty years of mind-body research is that we have a very precise notion of how the transformation from intelligence to physiology takes place. We are no longer in doubt about the fact that invisible wisps of thought and emotion alter the fundamental chemistry of every cell. This knowledge raises the hope that the mistake of aging can be abolished at its source, in the depths of cellular awareness.

WRINKLES IN THE
QUANTUM FIELD:

The Transformation of Messages into Molecules

To follow the trail of entropy from the visible to the quantum level, we can examine a single symptom of aging: wrinkles. Sometime when you're standing in front of the bathroom mirror, consider the tiny wrinkles that form with age at the corner of your eyes or around your mouth. The lines in your face trace old, familiar emotions, and the map of anxiety, anger, frustration, fulfillment, happiness, and joy gets etched deeper into the skin every year. "Wrinkles should merely indicate where smiles have been," Mark Twain commented; but even if every wrinkle was the trace of a smile, how do they form?

To a cell biologist, the cause of wrinkles lies in the skin's structure. Your skin is composed of many kinds of tissue—blood vessels, nerves, hair follicles, muscles for giving us goose bumps and making our hair stand on end, fat cells, and two layers of skin cells, the dermis and epidermis—all of which is surrounded by water and loose connective tissue. This connective tissue is composed primarily of collagen, a protein that has the extremely useful property of being able to bind with water.

Collagen provides the skin with a soft, moist webbed cushion, giving it plumpness as well as the ability to stretch and fold as your body moves. Collagen itself isn't made of cells, but nearby cells produce and repair it. The state of this connective tissue is therefore under the supervision of DNA. As people age, their collagen undergoes change, becoming stiffer and less moist. As it loses resilience, collagen no longer snaps back when it is stretched or folded. It starts holding creases, and once a crease is permanent, a wrinkle has formed.

The Free-Radical Theory

Many physical influences can hasten the aging of collagen: smoking, excessive exposure to sunlight, vitamin deficiency, malnutrition, dehydration, underactive thyroid, and genetic predisposition, to name but a few. Yet there is no clear division between these influences and psychological factors. A widow grieving for her husband can become worn and wrinkled very quickly. The skin of a cancer patient undergoing chemotherapy can age prematurely, both from the side effects of the drugs and his state of emotional turmoil.

What these diverse influences have in common is that all can promote a specific kind of mistake in the molecular structure of collagen. Separate collagen molecules get attached to one another through a process known as cross-linkage, a chemical reaction that permanently locks up the outer atomic shells of the collagen. The cause of cross-linkage lies in the destructive tendency of free radicals, the highly unstable oxygen atoms that bind indiscriminately with many vital molecules in the body, including DNA. In the mid-1950s, Dr. Denham Harman of the University of Nebraska was the first researcher to theorize that free radicals are an important if not primary cause of aging at the cellular level.

Cross-linkage is only one example of the damage free radicals can inflict. They can also split up nearby molecules, break off pieces of molecules, garble information in various parts of cells, clog cell membranes, promote cancerous mutations, and impair the functioning of mitochondria (the energy factories inside each cell). Some cholesterol researchers believe that free radicals are responsible for the harm that cholesterol does to our bodies. In laboratory settings it is next to impossible to get cells to take up cholesterol in its normal form, but once free radicals react with cholesterol, causing it to oxidize (the same process that turns fat rancid), cells readily absorb it. Like sharks roaming the cell, free radicals will attack almost any molecule; the extent of the damage they do is so wide that the free-radical theory of aging has grown in popularity with each passing decade.

Free radicals provide an excellent example of entropy at work, for the changes they produce tend to be one way, irreversible, and permanent. Wrinkled skin is less orderly than unwrinkled skin, and normally it does not repair itself. Likewise, when you break a dish, the damage to the plate is irreversible. This is because entropy follows the arrow of time. Once something orderly breaks apart, the dispersed matter and energy won't automatically come back together again. The future holds only more disorder: The bits of broken crockery will eventually get broken into smaller bits, and the aging skin will eventually wither and die.

Paradoxically, free radicals are necessary to life. Chemically the body's free radicals are mostly unstable variations of the oxygen atom (hydrogen peroxide and hydroxyl are two common examples) that vary from their stable parent by having an extra electric charge in the outer electron shell. This apparently minor change makes free radicals want to bind instantly with nearby molecules in order to offset the extra charge and become stable. Thus a free radical is really a temporary stopping-point leading from one stable molecule to another. The normal life span of such unstable particles can be measured in thousandths of a second; millions of these fleeting molecules are emitted in every cell as it processes life-giving oxygen through the metabolism of food.

If free radicals are so pernicious, why does the body produce them? Far from being loose bullets careening around the cell, free radicals fit into the body's overall balance. In some instances, they are extremely good to have: white cells in the immune system use free radicals to bond with invading bacteria and viruses and kill these invaders. In that role, the free radical's tendency to latch onto anything in sight saves your life.

To protect itself from damage, every cell produces enzymes to degrade, neutralize, and detoxify free radicals. These "free-radical scavengers" include various antioxidants (such as superoxide dismutase and catalase) that can bond to highly reactive oxygen ions and render them harmless before they attack a vulnerable molecule. Once again, the balance of creation and destruction is the real issue, not the molecules or the chemical reactions involved. At the very origin of life, with the appearance of simple bacteria, Nature had already figured out how to counter free radicals by generating antioxidant enzymes. If this provision hadn't been made, the oxygen in our atmosphere could easily have destroyed the chances of life on Earth; instead, thanks to the cellular intelligence that pushes against entropy, oxygen made life possible.

Millions of people have become acquainted with the free-radical theory of aging thanks to the success of the 1983 book *Life Extension* by Durk Pearson and Sandy Shaw. The premise of their approach is that free radicals are the body's enemy, and readers are therefore urged to dose themselves with a wide variety of antioxidants. However, the eminent Japanese medical investigator Dr. Yukie Niwa, himself a staunch proponent of the free-radical theory, has demonstrated in the laboratory that dosing a culture of cells with antioxidants usually does little to decrease free-radical production. It would be still less effective for a person to swallow these antioxidants. Many would be nullified by digestive juices in the mouth, stomach, and intestines long before they got to the cells they were meant to protect.

Even so, life extenders swallow all manner of antioxidants in the form of vitamins, food additives, and prescription drugs. Among the most touted are vitamins C and E (two substances Dr. Niwa found particularly unsuccessful when he applied them to test-tube cells). Ironically, life extenders tend to be highly health-conscious people, the sort who used to believe that food additives should be banned from bread, crackers, cookies, cereals, and other processed foods. Now, to follow the dictates of life extension, the same people find themselves taking food preservatives such as BHT and BHA in massive amounts compared to the few parts per million needed to keep a loaf of bread from going stale on the grocery shelf.

More exotic prescription drugs with antioxidant properties include Hydergine, L-dopa, and bromocriptine, none of which was originally intended to be taken for antiaging purposes. Each of these is a potent drug rife with side effects; each can cause permanent damage if taken in overdoses or for too long. The life-extension pharmacy hardly stops there. Throw in some other favorite antiaging supplements—beta carotene, the whole vitamin B complex, zinc, and selenium—and you are supposed to have armed yourself with the best, scientifically validated defense against the body's self-destruction through free radicals.

But why should we believe that the body is self-destructive to begin with? The whole life-extension enterprise, I believe, misses the point. The damage caused by free radicals is secondary, not causal, just as the bullet fired from a gun cannot take responsibility for pulling the trigger. In its normal state, the body controls free radicals as a matter of course.

Your body is not blindly fighting for its life against "bad" chemicals; such a notion is far too simplistic. If you could view a cell as it produces its myriad free radicals and myriad antioxidants at the same time, you would see the two floating around in the same environment, not like loose cannons on the deck but closely monitored and controlled by DNA's superlative intelligence. Both are kept in balance and used as they need to be. The main reason why free radicals hold such a strong appeal for scientists is that they are *things;* they fill our need for physical objects that can be weighed, measured, labeled.

There is no denying that free-radical damage occurs and is suspiciously linked with aging, along with cancer and heart disease, the two leading causes of death. Yet it has not been shown that older people necessarily have higher levels of free radicals in their cells or lower levels of antioxidants. What I'd like to suggest is that free-radical damage is but one type of imbalance that can occur at the level of cellular intelligence when the balance tips toward entropy. If the body's intelligence is at full strength, disorder and chaos do not attack a cell. The basic tenet of life extension—preventing free-radical damage before it occurs—is sound. To do that, however, we need to understand how to influence a cell's intelligence directly.

Exercise: Working Against Entropy

One of the simplest ways to prevent entropy is to give the body something to do. In physics, entropy is opposed by work, which is defined as the orderly application of energy. Without work, energy simply dissipates. We have already seen that mental and physical neglect (the "disuse syndrome") promotes premature aging. No group is at higher risk for depression, disease, and early death than people who are completely sedentary, and by now the value of regular exercise for all age groups has been well documented. Physiologists used to believe that exercise primarily benefits us at young ages, when muscles are in their prime developmental stage. However, research with the elderly has conclusively demonstrated that someone who takes up exercise at any age, including centenarians, will receive the same increase in strength, stamina, and muscle mass. (This is true for both men and women, by the way; in the past most exercise research was conducted on men, but now it has been established that women need to be just as active at every age.)

One special advantage exercise delivers is that it can reverse the previous effects of entropy. Researchers at Tufts University, where the federal government sponsors a major center for the study of human aging, have demonstrated that the major symptoms of biological aging can be improved through increased activity (the effect is boosted with secondary emphasis on improved diet). Two Tufts scientists, William Evans and Brian Rosenberg, have outlined these findings in their book *Biomarkers*. The title refers to the ten markers for age that are now considered reversible:

> Lean body (muscle) mass
> Strength
> Basal metabolic rate
> Body fat
> Aerobic capacity

> Blood pressure
> Blood-sugar tolerance
> Cholesterol/HDL ratio
> Bone density
> Body temperature regulation

These markers typically grow worse as people age. There are many variations from individual to individual; yet before the Tufts findings emerged, normal aging was defined to include the following:

1. *Muscle mass.* The average American loses 6.6 pounds of muscle with each decade after young adulthood; the rate of loss increases after age 45.

2. *Strength.* Older people are less strong because bundles of muscles and motor nerves (called "motor units") have been deteriorating. Between the ages of 30 and 70, the average person loses 20 percent of the motor units in the thighs, with similar losses in all the large and small muscle groups elsewhere in the body.

3. *Basal metabolic rate.* The body's metabolic rate—how many calories it needs to sustain itself—declines by 2 percent per decade after age 20.

4. *Body fat.* Between the ages of 20 and 65, the average person doubles his or her ratio of fat to muscle. Sedentary lifestyle and overeating can raise this ratio even more.

5. *Aerobic capacity.* By age 65, the body's ability to use oxygen efficiently declines by 30 to 40 percent.

6. *Blood pressure.* The majority of Americans show a steady increase of blood pressure with age.

7. *Blood-sugar tolerance.* The body's ability to use glucose in the bloodstream declines with age, raising the risk for type II diabetes.

8. *Cholesterol/HDL ratio.* Total cholesterol tends to rise in both men and women until around age 50, and the "good" HDL cholesterol that protects the body against

heart disease loses ground to the "bad" LDL cholesterol that increases heart-attack risk.

9. *Bone density.* Calcium tends to be lost from bones with
age, making the skeleton weaker, less dense, and more
brittle. This tendency, if it goes too far, becomes the
disease osteoporosis.

10. *Body temperature regulation.* The body's ability to
maintain a steady internal temperature of 98.6 degrees
F. declines with age, making old people more vulnerable to both hot and cold weather.

When the Tufts team discovered that all ten biomarkers could
be reversed in older people, they delivered a sweeping endorsement
of the benefits of exercise. Evans and Rosenberg feel that the first
two markers—muscle mass and strength—are the most important,
because the body's tendency to double its fat and lose half its muscle
mass by age 65 or 70 creates many of the other problems of metabolism. Traditionally, one of the classic markers of growing old has
been a decline in lean-body mass, a medical term for all tissues that
are not fat—i.e., bones, muscles, and vital organs.

With each decade of life after young adulthood, the average
American loses 6.6 pounds of lean-body mass. Many people who
become increasingly overweight after middle age assume that their
problem is too much fat. To the Tufts researchers, the actual problem is a combination of too much fat and too little lean-body mass,
particularly muscles. Fat and muscle tissue do not share the same
metabolism; comparatively, fat is much more inactive. It serves as
an energy-storage tissue, while muscle is an energy-spending tissue.

If you were a member of prehistoric hunter-gatherer society,
having a thick layer of body fat would be useful. Stored energy gives
the body a fuel reserve for times of famine, and its insulating capacity preserves body warmth in winter. Because it is much less active
biologically, fat suits modern life poorly, however; it requires many
fewer calories than muscle tissue to maintain itself (this is also true
of the other components of lean-body mass, bones and vital organs,
but to a lesser degree). Someone with more muscle than fat will have

a faster metabolic rate and thus can eat larger meals without gaining weight.

Gerontologists have found that muscle is much more responsible for the body's overall vitality than most people, including most doctors, ever supposed. Based on their research, Evans and Rosenberg hold that muscle mass, along with strength, is critical—that by building muscles late in life, old people can significantly rejuvenate their whole physiology. Since the rate at which you lose lean-body mass accelerates after age 45, the Tufts team concentrates on full-scale exercise programs for the 45 + age groups, reversing our social programming, which says that vigorous physical activity belongs to the young.

Previously, a decline in muscle strength was considered inevitable with increasing age. Bundles of muscles thoughout our bodies are connected to the central nervous system by motor nerves. Together, nerves and muscles make up "motor units," and by looking at cross-sections of muscle tissue, physiologists determined that motor units are lost with age.

The Tufts group conclusively proved that this trend can be reversed. Twelve men between the ages of 60 and 72 were put on regular supervised weight-training sessions three times a week for three months. They were asked to train at 80 percent of their "repetition maximum," the heaviest weight they could lift at one try. At the end of the experiment, the men's strength had increased dramatically, the size of their quadriceps had more than doubled, and their hamstrings had more than tripled. By the end of the program, these older men could lift heavier boxes than could the 25-year-olds working in the laboratory. Milder weight-training programs for people over age 95 proved equally successful.

The clear implication is that our notions about "taking it easy" as we age need to be reexamined. The same exercise regimen that builds muscles has a holistic effect, helping to bring the other biomarkers into line. Blood pressure and blood-sugar tolerance improved, the typical metabolic decline of old age was reversed, and the body's ability to regulate its internal temperature stabilized. Physical fitness is also intimately linked to one's general well-being;

although it wasn't their primary goal, the Tufts team was gratified to find that their subjects felt much younger and much better about themselves than they had in years.

How much exercise is needed to attain these benefits? In the laboratory, the kind of activity varied widely depending on what was being studied: As little as twenty minutes of walking three times a week improved the cholesterol/HDL ratio, but to be most effective, exercise has to be tailored to the individual, taking weight, age, and fitness into account. If we look back in history, the benefits of lifelong physical activity were evident even in ancient times. Ancestral humans in hunter-gatherer societies stood tall and erect. They had excellent bones and muscles, which they preserved at all ages (the widespread incidence of arthritis is one glaring exception to this; osteoporosis, however, was virtually unknown). Everyone remained fit and physically active throughout their lives. Compare this with modern America, where health promoters boost the concept of being "fit for life," while statistics reveal that 40 percent of American adults are completely sedentary (the percentage is much higher for the elderly) and only 20 percent can be considered active in any reasonable sense.

The Value of Balance

Before you decide that hard work is the way to prevent aging, consider that "work" as defined by physics is not synonymous with sweat and strain. Work is needed to create orderliness and oppose the force of entropy. Exercise has a quantum effect, regardless of how much or little you do, by giving the body a chance to restore subtle patterns of functioning. The quantum nature of exercise has emerged slowly, through bits and pieces of research. In the 1960s a Swedish physiologist named Bengt Saltin wanted to observe the effects of complete bed rest on the human body. The standard advice to seriously ill patients had always been to recuperate in bed, yet there was some doubt about whether this advice was sound. Saltin asked five young men, ranging in condition from extremely fit to sedentary, to remain lying in bed twenty-four hours a day for three weeks. At the end of that time he was astonished to discover that all his subjects, regardless of their physical condition previously, suffered a decrease in aerobic capacity that was equal to twenty years of aging.

This was a striking finding, but the most fascinating part is that when each subject was allowed to stand up out of bed for five minutes a day, almost the entire loss of function was prevented. They did not have to move around or in any way use their muscles. The simple exposure to a quantum force—gravity—allowed their bodies to remain normal. In a later U.S. study, female runners were tested to see if hard physical exercise helped prevent osteoporosis. The best protection against the disease, some experts feel, is not supplemental calcium or estrogen replacement but building up good bone density in younger years. Since bones get stronger as more weight is brought to bear upon them, long-distance running should increase bone density in the legs by a considerable amount. The application to aging goes beyond osteoporosis, which is an extreme form of bone thinning. Short of acquiring this disorder, old age brings thinner bones in most people, and among the very elderly, hip fractures strike one out of three women and one out of six men.

At the Tufts aging center, the bone density of a group of young women runners was compared with that of women who did no regular exercise. Even though they were 20 percent lighter than the nonrunners, the runners still had stronger leg bones. This made sense considering that the runners' leg bones were doing more work and bearing more weight, but the researchers were startled to find that the runners' forearm bones were also denser, despite the fact that these bones received no extra weight at all. Somehow the whole skeleton shared the message to deposit more calcium into the bone tissue, thanks to chemical signals (probably in the form of hormones) that were triggered at the quantum level. The whole body *knew* that exercise was being taken.

In quantum terms, whatever promotes orderliness is beneficial in opposing entropy. The entire physiology is an island of negative entropy; therefore our efforts need to be directed holistically to preserving orderliness in every aspect. Because the body uses both creation and destruction to keep its vital processes going, doing constant work is not the answer. Exercise has to be balanced by rest, because there is extensive muscle destruction during exercise that needs to be restored in periods of rest. In every area of life the key is balance, a very general term that can be broken down into four headings:

MODERATION

REGULARITY
                    =   BALANCE
REST

ACTIVITY

Moderation means not going to extremes. Regularity means following a consistent routine. Rest means rest. Activity means activity. These four things sound simple, but, being the only species gifted with self-awareness, only humans have conscious control over them. The cycle of rest and activity in lower animals is dictated by instinct, which humans are free to override. If we override it in the wrong direction, then we actually hasten entropy. This has become apparent in the worst aspects of modern life, which paradoxically blends increased creature comfort with mounting disorder.

A striking example of how our bodies reflect the imbalance of our lifestyle is heart disease, the major affliction of the elderly in our society and the cause of more deaths than all other diseases combined. In the 1920s, cardiology emerged as a flourishing specialty in direct response to the alarming epidemic of heart attacks that was mysteriously sweeping through our society. The epidemic worsened without check for another fifty years, and when it finally abated sometime in the late 1960s, there was little agreement over what had happened. We are still asking ourselves why Americans, second only to the Finns, suffer more coronaries than any other people in the world.

William Osler, a founder of Johns Hopkins Medical School and the most famous physician in America at the turn of the century, noted that in ten years of practice at one hospital he saw no cases of angina pectoris, the typical chest pain that indicates the presence of heart disease. In seven years at Johns Hopkins, Osler saw a total of four angina cases. Today, every cardiologist sees that number in an hour. The incidence of heart attacks doubled in this country every two decades after 1900. Dr. Paul Dudley White, the most eminent cardiologist in the generation after Osler's, believed that the epidemic was due primarily to two changes that had taken place in America during this century—the enormous acceleration in the pace of everyday life and a "general enrichment of the diet."

"Enrichment" basically means more fat. In the 1920s and afterward, foods such as butter, cream, and beefsteak became available not just to the wealthy but to everyone. The quickening pace of life was due to the increasing use of the automobile, which vastly accelerated the time in which people reached their destinations and thus gave another impetus to "the disease of being in a hurry." Clearly, these two great changes fitted people's desires for a materially better life. An Irish immigrant who could put steak on the table in place of cabbage and potatoes thought he was improving his family's lot; to replace the horse and buggy with a Model T was a goal everyone shared.

Our increased consumption of red meat and other foods high in saturated fats, such as milk, cheese, ice cream, and eggs, has been particularly unbalanced. If you plot the incidence of heart attacks, arteriosclerosis, breast cancer, and colon cancer in the countries of the world, you will see that certain countries will tend to fall to the bottom end for nearly every disease—Japan, Taiwan, Thailand, El Salvador, Sri Lanka—while others rise to the top—the United States, Canada, Australia, Germany. Now, if you graph the countries of the world according to how much milk, red meat, eggs, and cheese they consume, the same distribution will occur. The nations with low disease rates turn out to be those where there is very little consumption of high-fat foods, while the societies with the richest diets have catastrophic rates of heart attacks, hardening of the arteries, and cancer.

Achieving cardiovascular fitness also became much more difficult in our leisure society, where pleasures such as radio, television, and movies are more enticing, at least superficially, than exercise.

To begin with, exercise is artificial. Until the twentieth century, people were intensely active whether they liked it or not. Before America became a mechanized society, the concept of exercise for its own sake was all but unknown, since everyday life contained an enormous amount of physical activity. Advising a farmer's wife to take up aerobics would have been laughable. As late as 1900, human labor accounted for 80 percent of the total calories expended to work the land, despite the fact that tractors and combines were already in widespread use. Today, when nearly all agriculture is mechanized, human labor accounts for only 1 percent of the total calories expended. To resume the normal activity the body needs, we all must consciously oppose the trend toward increased physical leisure.

Other, more intangible changes stand out equally. Before 1920, half of Americans lived in small towns, chiefly on farms; after that date, the majority lived in cities. (The migration to urban areas continues, although there is some indication of a backlash with the movement of middle- to upper-class families back to rural areas. They are not going back to work the farm, however, but for cleaner air and less noise than they found in the city.) People's lives are no longer paced by the rising and setting of the sun. We get up and go to bed when we like; we work in offices, out of contact with the open air. If we wish, we can work all night. More important, we do not labor for ourselves but are frequently tied to someone else's goals. Corporations set timetables and deadlines, assign job tasks and descriptions, and effectively keep decision-making in the hands of the privileged few.

The fact that modern life tends to be so unbalanced, in defiance of the body's innate needs, is not lost on the physiology. Your body sends unmistakable messages whenever its needs aren't being met. The stomach says it's too full; muscles tremble when pushed beyond their strength. People who pay attention to the instincts of their bodies, who try to flow with daily activity rather than push and rush, have a better chance of setting a natural rhythm, despite to modern life's few physical requirements.

The overall benefit of a balanced lifestyle emerged in 1965, when a Southern California research team headed by Nadia Belloc and

Lester Breslow, now dean of public health at UCLA, decided to follow the aging patterns of people in Alameda County. A twenty-three-page lifestyle questionnaire was handed out to almost seven thousand subjects asking them in great detail about their health status and lifestyle.

After five and a half years, 371 subjects had died. By looking back at the original response to these questionnaires, researchers discovered that the most important distinguishing feature of those who survived was not their income, physical condition, or genetic inheritance, but a handful of extremely simple lifestyle habits:

1. Sleeping seven or eight hours a night
2. Eating breakfast almost every day
3. Not eating between meals
4. Normal weight—i.e., not more than 5 percent under-weight, and no more than 10 to 20 percent overweight (the lower number was for women, the higher for men)
5. Regular physical activity—i.e., engaging often in active sports, long walks, gardening, or other exercise
6. Moderate drinking—i.e., taking no more than two alcoholic drinks a day
7. Never smoking cigarettes

This is a very brief list of balanced habits, the kind children learn at their mother's knee, yet they led to dramatic conclusions. Analyzing the statistics, Belloc found that a 45-year-old man who observed from zero to three healthy habits could expect on average to live another 21.6 years, while someone who followed six or seven good habits could expect to live 33 more years. In other words, doing something as simple as eating breakfast, no matter what kind of breakfast, and getting enough sleep added more than 11 years to a man's life (by comparison, having both sets of parents and grand-parents live to age 80 increases one's life expectancy by only about 3 years).

The cumulative results were not quite as dramatic for women, but the same pattern was observed at all age levels. A 45-year-old woman who followed at least six good habits could expect to live

7.2 years longer than a woman who followed fewer than four; this increased to 7.8 years by age 55. As impressive as these figures are, they become much more so when we look beyond survival to overall health. A person in late middle age (55 to 64) who practiced all seven good habits was found to be as healthy as young adults 25 to 34 years old who followed only one or two.

The trend held good for older age groups as well. If someone followed all seven good habits, his health at age 75 was comparable to that of someone in his thirties or forties who neglected good habits. What seems to pay off is sheer regularity—the *kind* of diet or physical activity being followed was not taken into consideration. (By comparison, similar population studies from Southern California have shown that people over age 65 who take large doses of vitamins and adhere to strict health-food diets did not gain any significant advantage in life expectancy.)

The UCLA researchers further noted that older subjects in general followed a healthier lifestyle, implying that those who didn't had already died at younger ages. This is consistent with the Surgeon General's estimate that two-thirds of the illness suffered in old age is preventable. At the top of the list for those who died earliest in the study were sedentary lifestyle and smoking.

Overall, the study showed that as people with good habits moved through life, they could expect to enjoy an advantage in health of thirty years over those who had bad habits. Almost three decades after the UCLA study, no one has challenged its major conclusion: A balanced lifestyle is one of the most important steps toward retarding the aging process. What we want to do now is to probe into the deeper mechanics of balance to see if this beneficial effect can be improved. The human body thrives on orderliness, but the ultimate responsibility for creating order out of disorder rests with each cell. The secret of keeping destruction at bay is revealed only at the invisible level where intelligence is constantly preserving the balance of life.

THE FLOW OF
INTELLIGENCE:

Preserving the Balance of Life

By themselves, the body's molecules have no intelligence. There is nothing "smarter" about oxygen or hydrogen just because it is being cycled through a human cell. The same sugar molecules that sit inertly in a sugar cube are found, with minor variations, inside DNA, but in us, sugar comes alive. The basic fuel of the body is glucose, or blood sugar, which is the brain's only food. Burning a sugar cube over a gas flame yields a flash of light and heat and a greasy lump of carbon, but the same sugar burned in the brain produces all the thoughts and emotions we have. The Sistine Chapel, *Paradise Lost,* and Beethoven's Ninth are all accomplishments of burning sugar; so is this book and your ability to read it.

Beginning with DNA, RNA, and the enzymes they produce, our cells teem with molecules that react with precise orderliness, but this fact is misleading—the real decisions are made by the body's intelligence, which is invisible. It acts as the choreographer who invents every step of the dance but prefers not to appear center stage. Since all cells in the body are made up of molecules that found their place because DNA directed them there, it could be said that physiology is nothing but intelligence at work, and that every process under way in every cell is essentially intelligence talking to itself.

A polygraph expert named Cleve Backster has performed hundreds of astonishing experiments that verify this theory. The basis of the polygraph, or lie detector, is that it measures small changes in the skin's galvanic response—its ability to conduct electricity— which provides an indirect measure of whether a person's body is tense (associated with lying) or relaxed (associated with telling the truth).

However, the same differences in electrical charge occur when threat or arousal is present. The polygraph will jump if a person looks at an erotic picture or relives a past trauma. Amazingly, Backster found that even cells removed from the body and placed in another room react to these stimuli when the person does. If a few cells scraped from the inside of someone's mouth are connected to a polygraph in one room while he sits in another, their electrical discharge will remain even and flat while he is sitting still and spike wildly when he looks at erotic pictures; at the moment when he stops looking, his polygraph calms down again and so does the polygraph of his cells in the other room.

This uncanny result does not appear to be affected by distance. In one experiment, Backster asked a World War II Navy veteran to watch films of the battles in the Pacific. As soon as the man saw footage of a fighter going down in flames, his polygraph displayed heightened galvanic response. At the same moment, viewed through simultaneous video pickup, there was sudden activity on a polygraph connected to his mouth cells *seven miles away*. Significantly, this man had been in battle himself and had witnessed planes being downed by enemy-aircraft gunnery. His memory of threat was triggered, and every cell of his body knew it.

Being abstract and invisible, intelligence has to react before it can make itself known. Your brain makes its intelligence known by producing words and concepts; your body makes its intelligence known by producing molecules that can carry messages. It is fascinating to observe how these two types of intelligence meld into each other. The whole operation takes place at the quantum level, where the line between the abstract and the concrete blurs. At the source of intelligence there is very little difference between thoughts and molecules, as a simple example will demonstrate.

The Body as Information

If you bite into a lemon, the juice instantly makes your mouth water as salivary glands under your tongue start secreting two digestive enzymes called salivary amylase and maltase. These enzymes begin digesting the fruit sugar found in the lemon juice before passing it along to the more complex gastric juices in the stomach. There is little mystery involved; the presence of food in our mouths automatically triggers digestion.

But what happens if you merely visualize a lemon or think the word *lemon* three times to yourself? Again your mouth waters and the same salivary enzymes are produced, even though there is nothing to digest. The message sent from the brain is more important than the presence of actual food. Words and images function just as well as "real" molecules to trigger the ongoing process of life.

We can diagram the process as a circle that constantly renews itself:

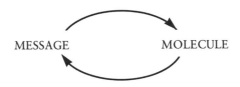

MESSAGE   MOLECULE

A message is not a thing, yet your body turns it into a thing. This is how nature operates behind the illusion of physical reality. Our materialistic bias forces us to keep looking at molecules as the source of life (disregarding the obvious fact that a newly deceased body contains precisely the same molecules as it did before it died, including a full complement of DNA). We assume that lemon juice is the real thing, while the word *lemon* is a fake. Saliva does not digest words, after all. But we in fact are digesting messages all the time. The molecules of lemon juice trigger salivation by fitting into receptors on the taste buds, which send a message to the brain, activating return messages to the salivary glands.

Nothing in nature is more miraculous than this transformation. Turning lead into gold is trivial by comparison, for lead and gold are just minor reshufflings of a few protons, neutrons, and electrons. If you hear the words *I love you* and your heart starts to pound, a much more astonishing metamorphosis has taken place. An emotion in another person's mind has been transformed into molecules of adrenaline rushing through your bloodstream. These, in turn, activate receptors situated on the outside of your heart cells, which in turn tell each cell that the appropriate response to love is to twitch faster than normal. More important, the body feels transformed—knowing that you are loved, you feel a sense of lightness and joy, the world appears more vivid, and everyday problems seem to vanish.

Why are these appropriate responses? How did the body ever learn that the word *love,* and not *glove* or *above,* is the trigger for bounding joy in the heart? This mystery defies the most complex knowledge of biology, medicine, psychology, chemistry, and physics, yet it is vitally important. The heart is kept physically intact by a stream of messages from the genes, and these in turn are formed from subatomic messages, weaving in and out of the quantum dance.

By implication, the language we use to refer to ourselves is of tremendous importance. Child psychologists have found that young children are much more deeply influenced by ascriptive statements from their parents (e.g., "You're a bad boy"; "You're a liar"; "You're not as smart as your sister") than by prescriptive statements (e.g., "Always wash your hands before eating"; "Don't put your toys in your mouth"; "Be on time for school"). In other words, telling a child *what he is* makes a much deeper impression than telling him *what to do.* The mind-body system actually organizes itself around such verbal experiences, and the wounds delivered in words can create far more permanent effects than physical trauma, for we literally create ourselves out of words.

This is particularly important when we look at those two potent words *young* and *old.* There is an enormous difference between saying "I'm too tired to do that" and "I'm too old to do that." The first statement delivers a subliminal message that things will improve; if you are too tired now, your energy will come back and you won't be too tired later. Being too old sounds much more final, because in our culture, old is defined by the passage of linear time; old things don't become young again.

Words have the power to program awareness; it is therefore important to avoid passively accepting the negative connotations that the word *old* carries. Because they expect to accumulate more problems and grievances in old age, many people glorify youth, not

for its specialness but because *it came before all the trouble began.*
In *Age Wave,* an insightful book on aging in America, Ken Dychtwald cites a birthday card that reads:

(FRONT) Don't feel old. We have a friend your age . . .

(INSIDE) . . . and on good days he can still feed himself.

This type of black humor makes people laugh by exposing just
a bit of the anxiety that could be overwhelming if confronted in full.
But whether funny or just morbid, the joke implies a complaint that
another birthday card states baldly: "You have just turned 30. You
will never have fun again for the rest of your life." What this
message says directly is that aging is deeply resented; what is left
unsaid is that there is nothing we can do about it. The sad fact is that
our society, lacking good models of aging, has loaded the very word
with layers of prejudice.

Dychtwald spells out the implications of putting old and young
at opposite poles:

- If young is good, old must be bad.
- If the young have it all, then the old must be losing it.
- If young is creative and dynamic, old must be dull and
  staid.
- If young is beautiful, old must be unattractive.
- If it's exciting to be young, it must be boring to be old.
- If the young are full of passion, the old must be beyond
  caring.
- If children are our tomorrow, then old people must be our
  yesterday.

The typical American way of handling this polarity is to fixate
on being young forever. Young, beautiful bodies fill the pages of
magazines and television screens. To judge by mass advertising,
America is a paradise inhabited by people under 30 with perpetually
tanned skin, sleek muscles, and ecstatic smiles. But the image of
America as the land of eternal youth is grossly at odds with reality:
as of July 1983, there were more people over 65 in this country than
there were teenagers, meaning that we officially ceased to be young
a decade ago.

This fact is difficult to reconcile with a value system in which the words *young* and *old* are polarized, and the positive pole is youth. Elevating youth as the ideal of life is one side of the coin; the other is the denial that old age exists. On television only 3 percent of the characters are over 65, compared to 16 percent in the general population. Old people are rarely used as models in advertising. In social situations, asking people their age is considered rude, and if people answer, many will subtract a few years (unlike in China and other countries where old age is valued—there, people will tend to add a few years).

Dychtwald points out that while people over age 65 now enter into maturity healthier than ever, "the image of youth as vigorous and powerful and sexy still has as its shadow an image of older people as incompetent, inflexible, wedded to the past, desexed, uncreative, poor, sick, and slow." For someone who accepts that these degrading terms apply to old age, their ascriptive power is just as strong as the ones from childhood that make us feel guilty, ashamed, and unworthy for years afterward. Words are more than symbols; they are triggers of biological information. If we look at it closely, the word *young* is a code for many things that actually have nothing to do with youth. The highest rates of crime, drug abuse, alcoholism, suicide, schizophrenia, and social unrest occur among the young. Nevertheless, youth is a symbolic ideal that almost everyone responds to positively.

If we wanted to, we could transfer the same positive value to age. An Old Testament verse dating back to the reign of Solomon declares:

> Gladness of heart is life to a man,
> joy is what gives him length of days.

The belief that long life represents maximum joy is echoed in other cultures, particularly in those where reaching great age is esteemed and every added year holds more value. Hokusai, the great Japanese woodblock artist, began life as a prodigy—he could draw proficiently from the age of 6—but he tells us that he was not satisfied with his skill until he turned 70. Looking further ahead, he predicted that "at 80 I shall have considerable talent, at 100 I shall be sublime, and at 110 I shall render life to a single line, a single point." Hokusai did not live to be 110—he died in 1849 as he was turning 90—but however old he was, he believed that the best was yet to come.

In our society, the word *old* implies increasing disorder and frailty, but in truth disorder, being the result of imbalance, can occur at any age: A 70-year-old jogger is likely to have an immune system superior to that of a sedentary 45-year-old. Despite our fears that the aging brain must fall prey to senility, the vast majority of old people retain their faculties intact, and many creative abilities ripen toward the very end of life. In 1992, a marvelous 99-year-old pianist, Mieczyslaw Horszowski, announced his 100th birthday concert in Carnegie Hall, following a long tradition of masterful musicians who performed into their eighties and nineties, including Toscanini, Horowitz, Rubinstein, and Serkin. Although we identify creative genius with child prodigies such as Mozart, researchers in creativity point out that the careers that last longest are often those that began late.

If we look beyond the false duality of "old" and "young," what we find is a different reality: The body is a network of messages constantly being transmitted and received. Some of these messages nourish and sustain us, while others lead to disorder and breakdown. Life-nourishing experiences go far beyond cell biology. The tenderness of a mother watching her toddler walk for the first time feeds the baby's body (witness how a baby languishes when motherly love is withdrawn, even for a day). To a growing child, the sensitive encouragement of a teacher is as important as a hot lunch. What makes for a straighter spine, vitamin-D milk or self-esteem?

Once we reach adulthood, gaining the wholehearted respect of co-workers wards off heart disease as effectively (and much more naturally) as counting milligrams of cholesterol. Respect makes the heart feel trusting and confident, two ingredients that belong inside any healthy body. The decisions we make in terms of our basic happiness and fulfillment are therefore exactly the ones that determine how we age.

It has dawned on medicine that nurturing is immensely valuable physiologically. If newborns are touched and caressed, their levels of growth hormone increase, and the protective coating of the motor nerves, myelin, becomes thicker. A mother's loving urge to cuddle her baby translates directly into life-sustaining biochemical reactions. Babies deprived of loving attention can become emotionally stunted or dysfunctional. In experiments with rhesus monkeys, newborns were taken away from their mothers and provided with a choice of two artificial substitutes—either a cold, wire-mesh model with a bottle sticking out of its middle or a plush, warm, terrycloth model that was not affixed with a bottle and had no milk to offer. In every case, the baby monkeys chose to cling to the warm, soft "mother" even though it did not give food. The instinct for emotional nourishment proved more powerful than did that for physical nourishment.

The Music of the Body

How can a person sustain a nurturing life? This is a broad, daunting question, given the harsh conditions of our environment. No two people lead identical lives or contain the same information inside their mind-body systems. Nevertheless, there are some basic rules governing everyone's inner intelligence:

1. Intelligence is meant to flow.
2. Every impulse of intelligence has a physical correlate.
3. The body keeps in balance through complex rhythms and cycles—these biorhythms are our connecting link to the larger rhythms of Nature.
4. When the body is in balance, it sends out signals of comfort; when it is out of balance, it sends out signals of discomfort. Comfort indicates that a person is in harmonious relationship to his environment; discomfort indicates that some kind of disharmony has arisen.
5. Living in harmony with the body's rhythms overcomes entropy by allowing a frictionless flow of biological information. Living in opposition to the body's rhythms produces an increase in entropy, leading to disorder.

If my intention is to live in harmony with my environment, my single best indicator of success is my body's feelings of comfort. We go through so many experiences in life that it is difficult to be aware of the actual basis for comfort; many psychological and physical factors are blended into every moment of existence. But Nature has programmed us biologically with rhythms and cycles that remain strikingly similar for most people. A new science called chronobiology (the biology of time) has studied the effects of these cycles on everyday life. Founded and named by Dr. Franz Halberg, professor of medicine at the University of Minnesota, chronobiology asserts that our bodies have an internal music that we can—and should—tune in to.

In order for you to move your eye from my last word to this one, for example, a dozen activities have to mesh with total precision. Each retinal cell and brain neuron pulsates hundreds of times per second with electrical charges created by the pumping of potassium and sodium ions across the cell membrane; the synapses, or gaps, between neurons fire bursts of neurotransmitters to send signals down the optic nerve and throughout the visual cortex; the minute muscles that move the eye twitch continually like an idling engine throbbing with chemical discharges; all of this cellular pulsation in turn depends on incredibly rapid vibrations of atomic "clocks" at the quantum level.

Biorhythms have many medical implications: Everyone's body temperature has a daily cycle, and hormones move in complexly interwoven cycles, with daily rhythms enmeshed in larger monthly and seasonal cycles. (Growth hormone, for example, changes daily, while a woman's menstrual cycle reflects monthly hormonal rhythms.) Rheumatoid arthritis hurts most in the morning, when the body's natural inflammatory agents appear to be low; this is the best time to take aspirin or other painkilling drugs. Blood pressure and adrenaline peak in the morning, which may explain why so many heart attacks and strokes occur at 9:00 A.M. In asthmatics, bronchial tubes are more constricted in late evening than in morning. By studying patients' individual cycles, we may be able to prevent disease. Some babies may show blood pressure cycles that predict hypertension in adulthood, for example, and heat fluctuations in the breast may predict tumors.

Dr. Halberg has made fascinating findings about how the timing of surgery and chemotherapy can significantly alter a patient's outcome. For instance, women who underwent breast cancer surgery in the week before and around the time of their period were four times more likely to suffer a recurrence of their disease and to die within ten years than were women who had surgery between day 7 and day 20 of their monthly cycle (this finding is according to a preliminary study at New York's Albany Medical Center). The reason may be that the hormones released around a woman's menstrual period suppress the immune system. At midcycle, however, scavenging immune cells may be present in force and destroy stray malignant cells that were missed by surgery.

Timing chemotherapy to match the body's biorhythms has also helped patients with bladder, colo-rectal, pancreatic, and ovarian cancer, according to researchers at the University of Texas at Houston. Since cancer cells have different activity patterns from normal cells, it is best to give drugs when the cancer cells are active and the normal cells inactive; thus, lower doses can be given and toxicity reduced.

After extensive testing of many critical functions at various times of day, chronobiologists have derived a timetable for peak efficiency:

Morning	Alertness gets increasingly sharp
	Short-term memory is at its best
	Sensitivity to allergens dips
	Sex hormones peak
Noon	Body temperature peaks, heightening vigilance and alertness
	Mood is at its best
	Sight is sharpest
Afternoon	Manual dexterity peaks
	Flexibility is at its height
	Long-term memory is at its best

Late afternoon/early evening	Best time for easy repetitive tasks
	Best time for physical workout
	Taste and smell are at their sharpest
	Worst time for allergies
Evening	Worst time to eat large meal if you want to lose weight; metabolism at its lowest
Midnight to dawn	Alertness at worst between 3:00 and 6:00 A.M.
	Most accident-prone period
	Most common time to give birth

Whether it is advisable to try to live according to these precise times is debatable. The fact that the body, if left to itself, naturally wakes and sleeps on a twenty-five-hour cycle (known as the circadian rhythm) does not prevent us from waking and sleeping on a twenty-four-hour cycle without harm. On the other hand, studies of night-shift workers have demonstrated that their bodies never completely adjust to the reversal of the wake-sleep cycle. Night workers suffer a higher incidence of colds and depression than day workers and tend to have chronically weakened immune systems.

What is fundamentally important about biorhythms, I believe, is that they provide the basis for the state of dynamic non-change. I used this phrase to describe the balance of opposites that must be maintained in order for the body to resist disorder. It is necessary that we think, feel, and move in balanced cycles. If you decided to run in a marathon and your body insisted on keeping to its "normal" levels of functioning, you would quickly collapse. A faster heartbeat, higher body temperature, and elevated blood pressure have to kick in for you to be able to run. Medically speaking, a runner has gone into mild fever, tachycardia, and hypertension, but these are perfectly normal under running conditions, assuming that they are kept within a healthy range and return to their balance point when the runner comes to rest again.

We are awash in a tide of balance and imbalance surging back and forth. Dozens of bodily functions are disturbed every second, meaning that any fixed definition of health becomes meaningless— one might as easily try to define a symphony by stopping the orchestra on one chord. Food, water, and air flow through us in rhythmic patterns determined by dozens of variables, and residues of experience are built up like shifting sand dunes. Structure and motion, the fixed and the changing, both count. Your doctor may tell you that you have a resting pulse of 80, blood pressure of 120/70, and body temperature of 98.6 degrees F., all of which are considered normal. Yet this assessment is purely for convenience. Such measurements are good only for the moment they are taken, for each dances around its balance point, creating the music of the living body.

When the Music Dies

Aging is marked by a loss of many of the body's key balance points. Elderly people often find that their body temperature recovers more slowly from extremes of heat and cold; their sense of balance is impaired, making walking difficult; blood sugar, hormone levels, and metabolic rate are thrown off. To understand why this happens, we can turn to one of the worst imbalances of aging, high blood pressure. Left untreated, high blood pressure cuts life short by an average of twenty years, making it far more lethal than any single disease. Hypertension is not a disease but a skewed cycle in the body's natural rhythms. Blood pressure is controlled by the brain, which sets up a cycle that rises and falls throughout the day, responding to all sorts of inner and outer cues. Taking a blood pressure reading is therefore like taking one snapshot of a roller coaster—you need at least three widely separated readings to glimpse the peaks and valleys of your blood pressure cycle, which sometimes takes several days to complete.

Blood pressure rises and falls in everyone, but for some people the fall will not return to its former level; elevated pressure begins to creep in, and, over time, the cyclic swing will become skewed toward hypertension. This tendency is so common as people age that it follows a predictable general pattern. Here is the chart for males between the ages of 20 and 70:

AVERAGE MALE BLOOD PRESSURE

Age 20   122/76
Age 30   125/76
Age 40   129/81
Age 50   134/83
Age 60   140/83
Age 70   148/81

The chart shows a steady increase in both the lower (diastolic) and upper (systolic) readings, but at different rates, with the diastolic or resting blood pressure moving half as fast. (The same tendency holds for women, although the rise in pressure is generally slower.) This rise is not normal; to remain healthy, the body needs to maintain readings in the range of 120/80, although higher levels may be acceptable for a while.

Since clinical hypertension is usually defined as readings higher than 140/90, the average male seems safe until after age 70, but in reality 60 million Americans (approximately one-third of all adults) have already crossed the threshold into hypertension. Even a small encroachment can be dangerous. Half the deaths associated with high blood pressure occur among "borderline" patients whose pressures are in the range of 130/90. Many males in their thirties are already in this range. Compared to a healthy person, someone with hypertension is at twice the risk for dying in the next year, three times the risk for dying of a heart attack, four times the risk for having heart failure, and seven times the risk for having a stroke. The price of losing one's internal balance is very high.

The list of influences that can raise blood pressure is long and wide-ranging. If you work the body hard, blood pressure rises. Emotional stress and anxiety can cause the same result. Even without any outside influence, time of day has an effect (one of the complications that can make it difficult to diagnose hypertension is that some people experience their peak readings at night). But 90 percent of high-blood-pressure patients are classified as "essential" hypertensives, meaning that there is no identifiable cause for their condition.

Researchers have put portable monitors on secretaries, nurses, and Wall Street brokers who have normal blood pressure. The monitor is able to send electronically a continuous reading of how the events of a typical day alter normal blood pressure. These researchers found that "normal" is a fiction in terms of any fixed number; when the secretary was yelled at, or the nurse attended to an emergency gunshot wound, or the stockbroker traded in the bidding frenzy of a sliding market, blood pressure skyrocketed. How much elevation occurred depended on the person and the stress; people also varied in terms of how long the elevation lasted. The nurse might still have high blood pressure six hours after the emergency, when she was at home apparently relaxing over a quiet dinner. As far as her body was concerned, the memory of stress was just as real as the stress itself.

This gives us a valuable clue—the body's memory of stress causes normal cycles to be thrown out of balance. Instead of returning to their original position, they drift slightly. Over time, the net result is a state of dynamic imbalance. The back-and-forth dance continues but slightly out of line. As applied to aging, this can be portrayed with a simple diagram:

```
 •   •   •        •    •    •       •    •    •

 •   •   •        •    •    •       •    •    •

 •   •   •        •    •    •       •    •    •

RESTING STATE         STRESS         RESTING STATE
```

Each dot represents one of the many balance points for blood pressure, body temperature, endocrine levels, etc., that the body's intelligence keeps in balance. Under stress, all shift together, only to regain their original position when the body returns to its resting state. Let's say that the above is you at age 20. When you are 60, the picture will be skewed toward stress even while you aren't under stress:

THE   AGING   PROCESS

. . .   .

. . .   .

. . .   .

RESTING STATE   STRESS   RESTING STATE

The difference between the resting state and stress is now much greater, and when the stress is over, the body still feels the effect. The balance points have shifted as a result of remembering too much of the stress. (In physical terms, stress hormones have damaged various tissues; in subjective terms, the person feels less energy, and a vague sense of impairment begins gradually to increase over time.) The skewed dots on the right remind me of how old people walk bent over, their pitched-forward posture denoting the imbalances that are ravaging their physiology. Finally, balance collapses at the point of death.

APPROACHING   DEATH

. . .   . .   .

. . .   .   . .

. . .   . . .

RESTING STATE   STRESS   DEATH

The scattered dots represent balance points that stray from orderliness, meaning that the body's intelligence no longer controls them sufficiently, if at all. Near death, the body is so close to total imbalance that adding extra stress, in the form of disease, emotional shock, or simple daily challenges, places too great a strain on the weakened information network that is the blueprint of life. The balance points start to unravel in some critical area—heartbeat flutters erratically, the immune system collapses, an ulcer perforates. The state of dynamic non-change loses its coherence, and in death, balance points scatter into disorder. Entropy has triumphed.

The best defense against this catastrophe is to preserve and renew the body's instinct for balance. The fact that blood pressure is controlled by the autonomic (involuntary) nervous system once convinced doctors that it was beyond conscious control. However, three decades of research with biofeedback, meditation, hypnosis, and other mind-body techniques have shown that the mind is capable of taking control of involuntary functions. The deeper question has been whether controlling one stray rhythm such as blood pressure meant that a much broader effect such as aging could also be controlled. You cannot hook someone up to a biofeedback machine that beeps whenever he is getting older. Fortunately, there is a very broad-based cycle in the body that directly reflects the aging process, the cycle of hormones. These messenger molecules carry an enormous amount of the information circulating inside us. If hormonal balance can be preserved, we will have a reliable indicator that the flow of intelligence is also balanced. It is likely that many of the most important age changes are mediated by hormones triggered by stress and can be prevented by controlling stress. This is the possibility we will investigate next.

THE INVISIBLE THREAT:

Aging, Stress, and Body Rhythms

For more than fifty years physiologists have known that putting stress on an animal causes it to age very quickly. When you place a mouse on an electric grid and administer shocks to it, you need not raise the shocks to a lethal level to kill the mouse. Simply by giving very mild shocks at random intervals, you will arouse the mouse's stress response. Each time this happens, its body breaks down a little bit. After a few days of such stress, the mouse will die, and on autopsy its tissues will display many signs of accelerated aging. Since the shocks themselves were mild, the cause of death was not the external stress but the mouse's reaction—its body killed itself.

Similarly, humans can withstand extraordinary stresses from the environment, but if we are pushed too far, our stress response turns on our own bodies and begins to create breakdowns both mentally and physically. In war, which is a state of extremely heightened, continual stress, every front-line soldier will eventually go into shell shock or battle fatigue if kept under fire too long; both syndromes are signs from the body that it is exceeding its own coping mechanisms.

The human brain retains a primitive memory that is programmed to cope with every stress in basically the same way as our ancestors coped with saber-toothed tigers. If someone points a gun at you and threatens to shoot, you instantly make a dramatic shift into a state of heightened arousal. A full-blown fight-or-flight response explodes throughout your body, preparing you for action. A message of alarm from the brain releases a flood of adrenaline from the adrenal cortex, which races through the bloodstream and completely overturns the usual business of the body.

Most of the time, your cells are occupied with renewal—
roughly 90 percent of a cell's energy normally goes to building new
proteins and manufacturing new DNA and RNA. When the brain
perceives threat, however, the process of building is set aside. Whatever you decide to do in fight-or-flight situations, your body needs
a massive burst of energy to propel your muscles. To allow this, the
normal style of metabolism that builds the body, called anabolic
metabolism, converts to its opposite, catabolic metabolism, which
breaks down tissues.

Adrenaline launches a cascade of responses—blood pressure
rises, muscles tense, breathing becomes shallow and rapid, sexual
desire and hunger are suppressed, digestion stops, the brain becomes
hyperalert and the senses uncannily clear (in times of intense fear,
such as in battle, soldiers hear themselves breathing as loud as
bellows, and the eyes of an approaching enemy loom as large as
saucers). As a temporary expedient, the stress response is vital, but
if it is not terminated in time, the effects of catabolic metabolism are
disastrous. Every aspect of stress arousal leads to its own specific
disorder under prolonged situations:

RESPONSE	DISEASE RESULT
Mobilized energy	Fatigue, muscle destruction, diabetes
Increased cardiovascular activity	Stress-induced hypertension
Suppressed digestion	Ulceration
Suppressed growth	Psychogenic dwarfism
Suppressed reproduction	Impotence, loss of libido, interruption of menstruation
Suppression of immune response	Increased risk of disease
Sharpening of thought and perception	Neuron damage or death

What is so striking about these long-term consequences of stress is that taken all together they look very much like growing old. Hypertension, ulcers, impotence, wasted muscles, and diabetes are common signs of aging. The elderly have lower disease resistance, and senility seems directly connected to lost or damaged neurons in the brain. On the surface these appear to be unrelated symptoms, but they become unified as extreme results of the stress response. Stress researchers have shown that arousal occurs only at the onset of stress. If the exposure to threat is not removed, arousal turns to exhaustion, because the body finds itself unable to return to the normal anabolic metabolism that builds reserves of tissue and energy. Old people, then, appear like shell-shock victims, exhausted by overlong exposure to the struggle of life.

A steady decline in the stress response is universal as aging proceeds. Older people take longer to recover from stress, and they become less tolerant of strong stresses (for example, it is extremely rare for a young person to die of grief, an event that becomes more likely with age). This decline is more than a straight-line drop. It doubles exponentially, meaning that one year of old age produces as much deterioration in the stress response as two years of middle age. For very old people, it may take only six months; eventually, the instinct to come back into balance breaks down completely, and even mild stresses—a bout of flu, a minor fall, losing a small amount of money—become extremely difficult to cope with.

Whenever stress is blamed for an ailment, people jump to the conclusion that the problem is too much stress, but in fact the fault lies with the body's coping mechanism. The mice who die from too many shocks serve as a good example—if their bodies were given time to recover between shocks, the animals wouldn't be harmed. But the frequency of the shocks overtaxes the physiology, eventually exhausting its ability to spring back to normal.

When Hans Selye introduced the concept of stress in the 1930s, he assumed that a powerful outside stressor, such as physical injury, starvation, exposure to heat or cold, or sleep deprivation, would call forth much the same stress response every time. But this did not prove true. When two monkeys are deprived of food for a long period of time, their bodies react by releasing glucocorticoids, the stress hormones we are now familiar with. On the verge of starvation, the monkeys' bodies have to start breaking down their muscles in order to survive. But if one monkey is fed artificially sweetened water, which has absolutely no nutritional value, its levels of glucocorticoids do not rise, despite the fact that it has received no real nourishment. The monkey *perceives* that its situation has improved, and that is enough to signal its body that the threat of starvation has passed.

In many ways stress research has not recovered from this shocking finding. How can a mirage of food substitute for the real thing? The only viable answer, I think, is that the monkey felt nourished from within, and its perception of satisfaction was accepted as food by its body. The theory of stress has to be modified to include the mind-body connection, for such invisible elements as interpretation, belief, and attitude count enormously in the actual workings of the stress response.

Stages of Stress

Whenever you experience a stress, there are three phases to your response: (1) the stressful event; (2) your inner appraisal of it; (3) your body's reaction. What makes the stress response so difficult to handle is that once it begins, the mind has no control over it. In totally inappropriate situations, such as sitting in a traffic jam or being criticized at work, the stress response can be triggered with no hope that its intended purpose—fighting or running away—can be carried out.

Modern life is full of external stressors that cannot be avoided. A city is essentially a monolithic stress machine, cranking out noise and air pollution, along with excessive speed, overcrowding, crime, and rudeness. In relation to just one ever-prevalent stress, noise pollution, studies have suggested many damaging effects: The incidence of mental disorders rises under the flight paths near airports; children who live near the Los Angeles airport have higher than average blood pressure; sleep disturbances continue in the vicinity of uncontrollable noise long after a person thinks he has adapted to it; outbreaks of violence and a breakdown of courteous behavior occur more frequently in noisy work environments. A noise doesn't have to be loud to be damaging. The stressful effects come about if any irritating noise is repeated over and over, out of your control.

This places the burden of dealing with stress on phase 2, appraisal. Although you may not be able to control the stressful event or your body's reaction to it, your appraisal, the vital link that bridges the event and the reaction, is up to you. Any situation that appears the same on the outside can turn into a powerful stress once the interpretation of it changes. A policeman appearing at the scene of a crime evokes tremendous fear in the criminal but great relief in the victim. A diagnosis of cancer sends the patient into wild stress but not the doctor.

The totally personal way in which we filter all events determines how stressful they are. External stressors are basically triggers. If you don't feel triggered, there is no stress. A prevailing myth has arisen that some people thrive on stress. They perform best under high-pressure deadlines and blossom in the heat of competition. What's really happening is that they aren't being triggered physiologically. Nobody can thrive when the body keeps secreting cortisol and adrenaline; as we saw, these hormones function to break down tissue, and extended release of them leads to disease.

Management of stress therefore turns out to be much more complicated than is generally supposed, because a person's interpretation of any situation is basically projected from his memory—our reactions to new situations are always colored by our experiences in the past. Instead of appraising each new situation afresh, we slip it into old categories; this happens instantaneously and is beyond our conscious control. If you hate raw oysters, just the sight of them can make you gag. If you feel outraged by an acrimonious divorce, your rage will reemerge when you run into your former spouse on the street. Neutralizing these old impressions is essential, for otherwise you have no control over stress—the stressful event will trigger your response automatically, making you its prisoner.

This unfortunate state has been extensively researched as that of "hopelessness/helplessness." Since growing old brings deep feelings of both kinds, this research has been extremely valuable. A classic experiment in physiology is to yoke two mice together so that only one is free to eat, sleep, walk around, and engage in activity, while the other is passively dragged along. In short order the two will look remarkably different; the animal who has freedom of choice will continue to be robust and healthy, while the one who suffers loss of autonomy will be apathetic, disease-prone, and old before its time.

The dragged-along mouse has suffered no physical abuse, but losing its freedom of choice is stressful enough to trigger massive destructive reactions in its body. In experiments involving similar techniques, laboratory animals can be induced to develop practically any disease, or if a disease has been introduced, such as a chemically generated tumor, it can be made to advance much faster. When rats are crowded together like tenants in a tenement project, their immune systems decline and signs of hypertension, neurosis, apathy, and depression appear. When baby monkeys are separated from their mothers at birth and deprived of nurturing, they exhibit disorientation, hyperactivity, introversion, and various learning disabilities. Induced stress in general has been found to hasten the spread of cancer in rats, rabbits, and mice, and to promote heart attacks.

The Critical Factor: Interpretation

Everyone has a different level of stress tolerance, but what seems to produce the greatest perceived threat in a given situation are the following:

> Lack of predictability
> Lack of control
> Lack of outlets for frustration

When these elements are present, innocuous situations can turn stressful, sometimes far out of proportion to their actual stimulus. Driving behind a weaving car on the highway is nerve-racking because you cannot foresee what will happen next; so is being told that your airline flight has been delayed indefinitely. Both situations contain the element of unpredictability. If you are locked out of your car accidentally, having to wait for an hour until the locksmith comes is extremely frustrating, even though you know you will get back in; you usually expect your car to be under your control, but now suddenly it's not. Engaging in a heated argument and then having the other person abruptly concede your point is maddening; even though you have won the argument, you have suddenly lost your outlet for anger.

Needless to say, everyday life is full of such situations, and as they build up, we internalize the memory of them, reinforcing our conditioned responses. In a series of precise experiments, stress researchers have shown that it takes no outside stress event but just the mere *perception* of unpredictability, lack of control, and lack of outlets for frustration to create the stress response. The experiments involve rats that are put into small cages and administered electric shocks under varying conditions.

Unpredictability: If the rats are provided with a red light to warn them in advance that a shock is coming, they will display a decreased stress response compared to rats that are given no warning. The signal allows the animals to predict the shock, and with their anxiety thus removed, their bodies can relax. Rats subjected to unpredictable shocks must remain vigilant all the time, and the vigilant state triggers stress.

Lack of control: Two rats are subjected to equal shocks, but one can press a lever to decrease the rate of shock, while the other simply receives a shock whenever the first animal does. Because it has no control over the situation, the second rat will display a higher stress response, despite the fact that the shocks are equal for both. In a fascinating variation on the same theme, a rat is given a lever to push to avoid being shocked. If it is prevented from doing this, it will have a stress reaction *even if no shock is administered.* Just remembering that it once had control creates a stressful situation.

Lack of outlets for frustration: When rats are being given shocks, they will display less stress if they can gnaw on a piece of wood or attack another rat. The same reduction occurs if they are given something to eat or drink or a wheel to play on.

For millions of people, life is so frustrating that their only hope of relieving stress is by overeating and drinking, while whole societies try to escape their miseries by attacking other countries. Strife breaks out over issues that seem trivial to an outsider, but frustration and lack of control are enormously painful conditions to live under. When someone close to you suddenly dies, the unbearable heartache of grief is tied up in potent intangibles: You couldn't have predicted the death, you couldn't have stopped it, and in many cases there seems no way to express enough of the pent-up feelings of loss and abandonment. This becomes particularly painful if the person to whom you need to express your feelings is the one who died.

In medical terms, the toll in sickness due to these elements is great. Dr. George Eagle, a psychiatrist at the University of Rochester, investigated 160 cases of sudden death that had no physical explanation: 58 percent took place at a time of bereavement or loss and 35 percent at a time of threat; only 6 percent coincided with a time of pleasure. It is not the stress itself that is fatal, since the same losses and threats are survived by other people. The ability to withstand the stress is lacking. This vulnerability overrides physical factors. When someone under 50 dies of a heart attack, for example, half the time none of the classic risk factors for heart disease—hypertension, elevated cholesterol, and smoking—are present. The leading cancer in America, lung cancer, is directly tied to smoking, a habit that for most people is purely an outlet for frustrated emotion, a pleasure seized upon the way a caged rat seizes a piece of wood to gnaw on.

In the laboratory, animals that are less evolved than rats (frogs, for example) do not respond to intangible stressors. The key factor is memory. If an animal has only a primitive memory, it won't recognize the difference between one situation and the next. Rats remember the unpleasant sensation of being shocked, and therefore they can be trained to press a lever to avoid repeating the sensation. When the lever is taken away, their memory is also good enough to anticipate the next shock—they have expectations. This is like the nervous patient in the dentist's chair who jumps as soon as he hears the drill; the mere sound triggers an expectation of pain that in turn activates the pain response.

In either case the expectation *is* the stressor. This has enormous implications for aging, because all of us carry around a world inside ourselves—the world of our past. We generate our own stresses by referring to this world and the traumas imprinted on it. There would be no stress without the memory of stress, for our memories dictate what frightens us or makes us angry. We feel out of control and frustrated whenever a situation reminds us too closely of earlier times when we were out of control and frustrated. The curse of memory is that it ages us from the inside; our inner world is getting older, shutting us out from reality, which is never old.

The perfection of human memory is astounding. In the early days of psychoanalysis, Freud was amazed by the accuracy of his patients' unconscious retention of the past. He might lead a depressed patient back to a trauma that occurred at age 2, such as being left overnight in the hospital by his mother for a tonsil operation. At first Freud found that the memory would not allow itself to be revealed at all clearly. Blankets of numbness and denial covered over the original feeling of being abandoned, and yet if the patient was courageous enough, those cloaks could gradually be peeled back.

With the utmost clarity, the patient would recall exactly what had happened that night in the hospital, not just every nuance of feeling but the minutest physical details—the time on the clock, the number of steps leading to the operating room, the color of the nurse's hair. But why shouldn't we recall such details? They have been imprinted onto us like microchips, adding their output to all future events.

There are few if any simple stresses in human life, because as soon as a new event occurs, the imprint of old memories becomes activated, triggering the kind of stress we anticipate. Thus, stress becomes a self-fulfilling prophecy: Our reactions fit our expectations. The fact that every event cannot help but get imprinted with an interpretation gives memory its treacherous power.

The Hormone Connection

The stress reaction involves the release of powerful chemicals that the body, as I've described, must cut off before damage is done to itself. Endocrinologists classify stress hormones as glucocorticoids, which are hormones secreted by the adrenal glands as part of the heightened arousal demanded of the body under stress. The function of glucocorticoids is to activate the shift from anabolic to catabolic metabolism. Specifically, glucocorticoids break down glucagon in the liver, a form of stored energy that the body can use as needed; when the glucagon is used up, the same glucocorticoids go on to break down proteins. Under extreme conditions, such as times of famine, the body must fend off starvation by starting to consume its own muscles in order to keep up blood sugar, and again the chemicals responsible are glucocorticoids.

The best known of the glucocorticoids is cortisol, which plays a hidden role in the aging of certain animals, specifically the Pacific salmon. After hatching, young salmon spend their first four years at sea before they are mysteriously guided thousands of miles to the exact freshwater lakes where they were born. After a heroic journey upstream over rapids and man-made dams, mature salmon spawn and almost immediately die.

What causes the fish to age overnight into feeble, spent creatures is not sheer exhaustion but an internal "aging clock," built in to their DNA, that bides its time until spawning, then releases a rush of corticoid hormone in massive amounts from the adrenal glands. Cortisol is a potent stress hormone in all animals; in salmon it is a death hormone. Its fatal release occurs even if a fish is taken out of the water before its grueling migration and allowed to spawn in peak physical condition.

Aging clocks obey their own timetable, having no regard for the environment. Taking a salmon upstream by hand, giving it adequate food, and protecting it from all stress will not save it; after spawning, the fish's biological clock knows that the appropriate time for death is at hand. "Appropriate" is a very flexible term in Nature. A mayfly that lives only one day and a giant clam that survives over one hundred years each have an "appropriate" life span. Nature balances many ingredients to arrive at the life span of a creature. Size, weight, metabolic rate, food supply, predators, breeding age, and number of offspring, among other factors, influence when aging will begin.

A mouse might live a year or less in the wild, but within that year the creature matures, breeds, bears a number of young, and keeps its species going. In the balance of Nature, that is sufficient; if a species can keep its population going before it ages and dies, its purpose has been fulfilled.

In animals the onset of aging is tied to physical evolution. Each animal has evolved to a given life span that accords best with its survival. If mice lived to be 100 and continued to have dozens of offspring every year, the world would be overrun by mice and the predators that eat them. Nature does not allow such gross imbalances to persist, however; all the species fit in to their own niche of life span and follow their own specific aging patterns. Sometimes Nature's specific intent is hard to decipher—why, for example, do tiny brown bats live for twelve years or more while field mice, who weigh the same and share the same fast metabolism, struggle to survive for only a season or two? The factors that influence the life spans of different animals are so complex and subtle that explaining how animals age is difficult—more than three hundred theories currently vie for an answer.

Aging clocks are disturbing to the imagination because they are time bombs that animals unwittingly carry around inside them, the instruments of their own destruction. Many biologists speculate that human DNA contains an aging clock; if it does, it must be much more variable than that in salmon, for humans die at extremely wide-ranging ages. In the Roman empire average life expectancy was around 28 years; today it has risen to 75 years in America and 82.5 years for women in Japan, the longest-lived group in the world. This increase was achieved by the trait that sets us apart from lower animals—free will. Our moment of death is not determined at birth;

humans defy fate by building shelters against the elements, planting crops against starvation, inventing cures for disease.

Yet the biochemical inheritance that we carry within us poses a constant threat. Like Pacific salmon, our bodies have the ability to release large doses of hormones outside our voluntary control. For example, a small, nonlethal dose of cortisol is released every time we are in a threatening situation. To many physiologists, this implies that our bodies are not well adapted to modern life. Also beyond our conscious control is the effect of glucocorticoids in a host of other destructive processes: muscle wasting, diabetes, fatigue, osteoporosis, thinning of skin, redistribution of body fat, fragility of blood vessels, hypertension, fluid retention, suppression of immune function, and impaired mental function.

The above are signs of steroid poisoning, which looms as a danger if patients are kept too long on large doses of steroid medications. In situations where a person cannot terminate the stress response or act it out, his own body administers a tiny dose of steroid poisoning. The danger of repeated inappropriate stress is much greater, then, than any single catastrophic stress.

Meditation Lowers Biological Age

The connection between aging and stress hormones has been strongly demonstrated, but the problem of how to control these hormones remains. Because the stress reaction can be triggered in a split second and without warning, it is impossible for us to control the molecules themselves. However, there is one mind-body technique that goes directly to the root of the stress response by releasing the remembered stresses that trigger new stress: meditation. Levels of cortisol and adrenaline are often found to be lower in long-term meditators, and their coping mechanisms almost always tend to be stronger than average.

Before the early 1970s, these benefits were not even suspected. Meditation held little appeal for Western medicine until a young

UCLA physiologist named R. Keith Wallace proved that besides its spiritual implications, meditation had profound effects on the body. In a series of experiments begun in the late 1960s as part of his doctoral work, Wallace took groups of mostly college-aged volunteers who practiced Transcendental Meditation (TM) and hooked them up to monitors to test critical bodily functions while they were in meditation. Subjectively these young volunteers reported a sense of increasing calm and inner silence. Although it had been previously thought that it took years of practice to attain a deep meditational state, the TM technique very quickly produced profound relaxation and significant changes in breathing, heartbeat, and blood pressure.

TM is based on the silent repetition of a specific Sanskrit word, or mantra, whose sound vibrations gradually lead the mind out of its normal thinking process and into the silence that underlies thought. As such, a mantra is a very specific message inserted into the nervous system. Since mantras have been in use for thousands of years in India, their precise effect on the physiology is well known as part of the science of Yoga, or union. The aim of Yoga is to unite the thinking mind with its source in pure awareness. In modern terms, "pure awareness" means quantum space, the silent, empty void that is the womb of all matter and energy. Pure awareness exists in the gap between thoughts; it is the unchanging background against which all mental activity takes place. We would not ordinarily suspect that such a state exists because our minds are so preoccupied with the stream of thoughts, wishes, dreams, fantasies, and sensations that fill waking consciousness. That is why the ancient Indian sages had to devise the specific technique of meditation, in order to show the mind its own origins in the quantum depths.*

*The description of TM in this text necessarily falls short of actually teaching the reader how to meditate. The technique of TM can be described verbally or in print, but to learn it properly, one should receive personal instruction from a trained TM teacher. Thousands of people begin meditation only to give it up prematurely; this is because nothing is more challenging than the intimate relationship with oneself that meditation opens up. Picking up meditation casually almost always leads to failure, and since the benefits are too profound

When Wallace initiated his research, the mechanics of meditation were poorly understood in scientific terms. He was the first to show that sitting in meditation with the eyes closed induces the nervous system to enter a state of "restful alertness"—i.e., the mind remains awake while the body goes into a deeply relaxed state. (In the jargon of physiology, Wallace called this state "hypometabolic wakefulness" to indicate that the subject's metabolism had decreased while he retained wakeful consciousness.) When first discovered, the state of restful alertness generated considerable curiosity in the medical profession, because rest and alertness had previously been considered opposites. Sleep is a hypometabolic state in which oxygen consumption decreases, heartbeat slows, and consciousness blanks out. The waking state, on the other hand, is marked by higher oxygen consumption, a faster heartbeat, and an alert mind.

Wallace found that these opposites were united in meditation; while remaining alert enough to push a button every time they transcended (i.e., felt the experience of pure awareness), his TM subjects went into a state of rest twice as deep as deep sleep. Moreover, they did so very quickly, usually within ten minutes after shutting their eyes, compared to the four to six hours it takes us to reach our deepest relaxation in sleep.

Beginning in 1978, Wallace researched the effects of meditation on human aging. He used three markers for biological aging as shorthand for the aging process as a whole: blood pressure, near-point vision, and hearing threshold, all of which typically decline as people grow older. He was able to show that all these markers improved with long-term practice of TM, indicating that biological age was actually being reversed. Meditators who had been practicing the TM technique regularly for fewer than five years had an average biological age five years younger than their chronological age; those who had been meditating longer than five years had an

---

to throw away so lightly, I have decided, albeit reluctantly, not to tell my readers how to meditate. Fewer people may start as a result, but the purity and value of the teaching will be preserved, making it all the better for those who start properly.

average biological age twelve years younger than their chronological age.

These results held good for both younger and older subjects. Later research on the overall health status of two thousand meditators in a group-insurance plan confirmed that they had remarkably good health in all age groups. TM meditators visited doctors and entered hospitals only half as often as did those in the control group. Across-the-board reductions were seen in thirteen major health categories, including more than 80 percent less heart disease and more than 50 percent less cancer than in the controls. Significantly, the meditators in age groups 65 and over showed the most improvement.

A decade later I was able to play a part in proving that these benefits were linked to exactly the kinds of hormones I have been discussing as prime markers for aging. As a physician I had been prescribing TM since 1980 as well as practicing it myself. In the late 1980s a colleague of mine, Dr. Jay Glaser, invited me to join his research on a very intriguing steroid called DHEA (dehydroepiandrosterone). DHEA is a plentiful but only vaguely understood substance secreted by the adrenal cortex; it circulates in the bloodstream in quantities thousands of times greater than either sex hormone, estrogen and testosterone, yet pinning DHEA down to a specific role in the body has proved elusive.

Glaser decided to follow up one property of DHEA, which is that it is the only hormone that declines in a straight line with age. Levels of DHEA peak around age 25, fall off at an increasing rate after menopause, and dwindle to 5 percent of their maximum by the last year of life. It was known that DHEA is a precursor of stress hormones such as adrenaline and cortisol, which means that every time the body makes these hormones, it has to use up some of the reservoir of DHEA that we are provided with at birth. That would account for why DHEA declines over time; however, this decrease is not the cause of aging but mirrors stress as it continues to build up over a lifetime.

Great excitement had been generated in the late 1980s when Arthur Schwartz, a biochemist at Temple University, administered

DHEA to mice and observed a remarkable reversal of aging: Old mice regained youthful vigor, and their coats resumed their former sleek and glossy texture; incipient cancers, whether naturally occurring or induced by artificial means, disappeared; obese animals returned to normal weight; immune response increased; and animals with diabetes improved drastically. The race to patent a version of the DHEA molecule began, although, as with all hormones, the risk of serious side effects was worrisome and taking DHEA orally was of little use, since it gets broken down in the digestive tract.

But Glaser felt, as I do, that DHEA is a marker for the body's exposure to stress. We know that with accelerated stress glucocorticoids increase, lowering the reservoir of DHEA at the same time. On the other hand, high DHEA levels are associated with reduced incidence of coronary artery disease, breast cancer, and osteoporosis. This makes sense because all these disorders of aging could be associated with excessive stress response. Higher DHEA is also associated with longer survival and decreased death from all diseases in older men.

As further evidence in the case, it was also found that cortisol levels go up markedly in patients awaiting surgery; it stays up the day after surgery, with a slight elevation in DHEA. Two weeks later, cortisol is still up, but DHEA has fallen, supporting the theory that the DHEA reservoir was depleted by stress.

The logical conclusion from this evidence is that if someone can keep up his DHEA levels, his body must be resisting stress, and with fewer stress reactions, aging should be retarded. Was that a clue as to why TM meditators showed less biological aging? Apparently so—Glaser took 328 experienced meditators and compared their levels of DHEA to those of 1,462 nonmeditators (to be precise, he looked at the closely related DHEAS, or dehydroepiandrosterone sulfate).

His subjects were divided by age and sex. In all the women's groups, the levels of DHEA were higher among meditators; the same was true for eight out of the eleven men's groups. Since higher DHEA appears in younger people, Glaser took this as proof that biological aging was decreased as a result of practicing TM. Interestingly, the biggest differences showed up in the older subjects. The meditating men over the age of 45 had 23 percent more DHEA, the women 47 percent more. This impressive result was independent of factors such as diet, exercise, alcohol consumption, and weight. Overall, Glaser estimated that the meditators' DHEA levels were equivalent to those of people five to ten years younger.

Connecting Mind, Body, and Spirit

Whether DHEA turns out to be as significant as it now appears, this connection between antiaging and meditation is very important. But the implications go even deeper. Meditation is a spiritual practice. That is its purpose in India and throughout the East. Millions of Westerners wrongly assume that this makes meditation nonphysical, something you do in your head. In truth, nothing is just in the head or just in the body. When I first met His Holiness Maharishi Mahesh Yogi, who brought TM to the West, he made a deep impression on me with one overriding point: Spirituality is not meant to be separate from the body. Sickness and aging represent the body's inability to reach its natural goal, which is to join the mind in perfection and fulfillment.

At every stage of spiritual growth, the greatest ally you have is your body. Is this statement surprising to you? Most of us assume that body and spirit stand at opposite ends of the spectrum. When we feel sensations that are body-centered, such as hunger and thirst, pain and pleasure, we do not regard them as spiritual experiences. Sensuousness, which encompasses the whole range of physical delight, is often considered low compared to the heights the soul can reach. But spirituality must also be sensuous, because a spiritual person is one who lives fully in the present moment, which means living fully in the body. Maharishi inspired me to see that using meditation as a way to defeat aging was a legitimate spiritual goal.

Unfortunately, our culture has made the mistake of deciding that the human body is a machine, an inert lump of matter that works without any intelligence of its own. This misconception led to a second mistake—that the most spiritual people must be those who renounce the body, deny its passions, or at the very least attempt to control its desires.

This kind of prejudice against the body runs contrary to the way that Nature fashioned us. Nature balanced mind, body, and spirit as co-creators of our personal reality. You cannot do a single thing, from falling in love to uttering a prayer to metabolizing a molecule of sucrose, without affecting everything that you are. The body is the platform that allows any experience to emerge and see the light of day; it is a 3-D projection of billions of separate processes going on at any moment, including a process as profound as coming to know the reality of God.

In our society people suffer from a sense that spirit is basically separate from them. Our bodies process food, air, and water perfectly well without spirit; our minds effectively think about a million things without touching upon spirit. We find it easy to set aside spiritual life, waiting for the day when some as-yet-impossible leap takes us out of everyday life into a more exalted realm.

Every aspect of reality is one piece of a mystery, a facet of overarching wholeness, the totality of what is. Atoms, molecules, rocks, stars, and the human body are material expressions of what is. Pain and pleasure are psychological expressions of what is. Compassion and love are spiritual expressions of what is. When the material, psychological, and spiritual dimensions are brought into balance, life becomes whole, and this union brings feelings of comfort and security. Only if you feel sure of your place in the universe can you begin to face the fact that you are surrounded by creation and destruction as they constantly play themselves out. You cannot defeat entropy as a physical force, but you can rise to a level of realization that is not touched by entropy. At the deepest level, intelligence is immune to decay. Your cells come and go, yet your body's knowledge of how to make a cell survives and gets passed on generation after generation. The evolutionary intelligence that DNA embodies has many levels, and our task as humans is to experience every level and make each a part of ourselves.

In the midst of change, there are five realizations that entropy cannot touch. They are expressed in every spiritual tradition and form the core of personal evolution age after age:

1. I am Spirit.
2. This moment is as it should be.
3. Uncertainty is part of the overall order of things.
4. Change is infused with non-change.
5. Entropy holds no threat because it is under the control of infinite organizing power.

These realizations are crucial because they allow a person to rise above the world of duality, which is inevitably caught up in the battle of creation and destruction. There is a perspective that the New Testament calls "seeing with one eye," a state of unity in which all events, however painful or distressing at the moment, serve one end, which is intelligent, loving, and well ordered. This unified perspective cannot be forced on anyone until his or her consciousness is prepared to accept it. If you are caught up in your own pain and convinced by your own life drama, that is your perspective, and you have a right to it. But everyone wants an end to pain and suffering, and at a certain point in your personal evolution these five realizations will form the trail that leads the mind out of suffering. Let me translate each point in terms of the new paradigm.

1. I am Spirit.

Although my physical existence is confined to space and time, my awareness is not limited to that. I am aware of the whole field as a play of creation and destruction. Matter and energy come and go, flickering in and out of existence like fireflies, yet all events are held together and made orderly by the deep intelligence that runs through all things. I am one aspect of that intelligence. I am the field unfolding itself in local events. My spirit is experiencing the material world through the lens of perception, but even if I see and hear nothing, I am still myself, an eternal presence of awareness.

In practical terms, this realization becomes real when no outside event can shake your sense of self. A person who knows himself as spirit never loses sight of the experiencer in the midst of experience. His inner truth says, "I carry the consciousness of immortality in the midst of mortality."

2. *This moment is as it should be.*

This present moment is a space-time event within the eternal continuum. Since that continuum is me, nothing that can happen is outside myself; therefore, everything is acceptable as part of my larger identity. Just as every cell reflects the overall process of the body, each moment reflects all other moments, past, present, and future. This realization is born when a person gives up his need to control reality. That need is a natural response to past pain and frustration, since it is the memory of old traumas that drives us to manipulate the present and anticipate the future.

In unity, every moment is as it should be. The shadow of the past does not spoil the fullness that is possible only in present time; therefore, each moment is like a clear window letting in the possibility of equal joy, equal appreciation of what is unfolding in front of you. The voice of inner truth says, "My desires are part of this moment, and what I need is provided here and now."

3. *Uncertainty is part of the overall order of things.*

Certainty and uncertainty are two aspects of your nature. At one level, things have to be certain or order couldn't exist. At another level, things have to be uncertain or there would be no newness. Evolution moves forward by surprising events; the healthiest attitude is to realize that *the unknown* is just another term for "creation." This realization saves a person from fear, which will always arise if uncertainty is resisted.

In unity, a person sees the wisdom of uncertainty. He realizes that his very next breath, next heartbeat, or next thought is totally unpredictable, and yet out of this total openness, order is still maintained. Opposites can and must coexist. In reality, you embrace all opposites in yourself, just as the quantum field embraces the two greatest opposites, entropy and evolution. The uncertainty of things holds no fear for someone in unity consciousness, because he is certain of himself. The voice of inner truth says, "I embrace the unknown because it allows me to see new aspects of myself."

4. Change is infused with non-change.

Life is an eternal dance. The movements of the dance are choreographed through your awareness. Your desires and attentions guide the path of your growth. Because attention is always flowing, the dance never ends. This is the essence of living. Every movement is part of the dance; therefore, every space-time event is meaningful and necessary. It is the order within the chaos.

When you realize that you are held securely within this unchanging framework, the joy of free will arises. You cannot exercise free will if you fear that it will bring uncertainty, accidents, and calamity. To someone in unity, however, each choice is accepted within the overall pattern. If you choose A, the field will bend to accommodate you; if you choose B, the field will accommodate that, even if B is the exact opposite of A. All possibilities are acceptable to the field, since by definition the field *is* a state of all possibilities. The voice of inner truth says, "I am getting to know the Absolute by playing here in the relative."

5. Entropy holds no threat because it is under the control of infinite organizing power.

Your body reflects the simultaneity of order and chaos. The molecules of food, air, and water swirling through your blood move chaotically, but when they enter a cell, they are used with precise orderliness. The neurons firing in your brain produce a chaotic storm of electrical signals, yet what emerges are meaningful thoughts. Chaos, then, is just a point of view. Things that appear random to a limited awareness fit into place perfectly when awareness is expanded. In unity, you realize that every step into decay, dissolution, and destruction is being used to organize new patterns of order. When your perception can see the birth that springs from decay, the inner voice of truth says, "Through alternating steps of loss and gain, silence and activity, birth and death, I walk the path of immortality."

These are descriptions only; no words on a page can substitute for the personal realization (what I have called the inner voice) as it unfolds for every individual. But we all intuitively want to get rid of discomfort, and it takes satisfying answers about who you are and why you are here to bring inner discontent to an end. In its true nature, life is comfortable, easy, unforced, and intuitively right.

This means that the self-realized state is the most natural one; the accumulation of stress, along with the aging that it produces, indicates that strain and discomfort are still present. While we are still unrealized, life is a struggle. We are constantly trying to relieve old hurts, escape old fears, and impose control over the uncontrollable. The following "In Practice" section is devoted to ending this struggle by the technique that finally works—learning to accept your life not as a series of random events but as a path of awakening whose purpose is maximum joy and fulfillment.

IN PRACTICE:

The Wisdom of Uncertainty

Life's uncertainty makes constant demands on everyone's coping mechanisms. There are basically two ways to cope with uncertainty—acceptance and resistance. Acceptance means that you allow events to unfold around you and react to them spontaneously, without suppression. Resistance means that you try to change events from what they really are and react to them with familiar, safe responses. Acceptance is healthy because it permits you to clear any stress as soon as it occurs; resistance is unhealthy because it builds up residues of frustration, false expectations, and unfulfilled desires.

In his book *Emotionally Free,* the noted psychiatrist David Viscott refers to the state of having stored-up feelings as emotional debt, which he links directly to aging: "Sorrow ages you prematurely. When you're in emotional debt, you're pessimistic about the future and, even in your green years, long to return to the past to remedy the shortfalls of love and opportunity you suffered. Sometimes you yearn for more caring, for more time with someone who is no longer here, for a chance to speak your mind and release your emotional burden, or just to resolve your confusion by finally discovering what really happened to you."

Untold numbers of people find themselves in emotional debt that grows larger with the passing years. Growing old is a psychological state in which emotional debt increases until the body's coping mechanisms can no longer deal adequately with present stress. The result is infirmity, sickness, and death. It takes conscious work not to fall into this trap. Although every new moment is unknown and therefore potentially threatening, there is no real security in resorting to the past. As Viscott writes, "You can speculate, you can lament, you can yearn, but as much as you may wish to return and round off your emotional experience, you can never go home again. Your real home is in this place, at this time. The present is for action, for doing, for becoming, and for growing."

Biologically, your body is perfectly set up to live in the present and acquires its greatest joy and satisfaction there. Your body never knows what its blood pressure will be the next second, so it has a built-in flexibility to allow a wide range of pressures; the same flexibility is built in to every other involuntary response. This is the wisdom of uncertainty, which permits the unknown to take place and welcomes it as a source of growth and understanding. We see this wisdom expressed in the spontaneity of every cell and organ. The pattern of electrical firings in your brain is never the same twice in a lifetime, yet this radical uncertainty allows you to have new, original thoughts. Every minute nearly 300 million cells die, never to be seen again, and this stream of death is assimilated into the vaster stream of life that keeps your body functioning.

The mind, however, finds it much harder to accept uncertainty. It fears change, loss, and death. This is the source of resistance, which the body translates into stress. By imposing mental resistance, you create a threat your body has to cope with. Some people riding a roller coaster are screaming from excitement, others from terror. The ride is the same, but the ones who hold back and tense their bodies, generating a flood of stress hormones, experience terror. The ones who let go and allow themselves to be carried by the ride experience exhilaration.

In the following exercises you will learn how to restore your awareness to a state of acceptance, so that living in the present is as fulfilling as it can possibly be. First, however, you need to get a sense of how much resistance you are now in. Our psychological defenses are extremely good at hiding this from us; by definition, stored-up emotions are the ones we can't feel. However, resistance gives rise to a telltale behavior pattern—control. Having to be in control is a compulsion rooted in fear and threat. Even if you cannot get at the threat, your controlling behavior gives away its presence.

CONTROL QUESTIONNAIRE

Put a check beside the following statements if they apply to you *frequently, most of the time, or almost always*. Some of the statements do not sound very flattering, but try to be as candid and honest about yourself as you can.

1. I like to be in control of work situations and am much happier working alone than with others.
2. When I'm under pressure, the easiest emotion for me to show is anger or irritability.
3. I rarely tell anyone that I need them.
4. I tend to harbor old hurts. Rather than telling someone that he hurt me, I would rather fantasize about getting even.
5. I have quite a few resentments about the way my brothers and sisters relate to me.
6. The more money I spend on someone, the more that means I love them.
7. I keep to myself how unfairly others treat me.
8. If a relationship starts to go bad, I secretly wish I could take back everything I bought for that person.
9. If it's my house, the people in it should follow my rules.
10. I find it hard to admit being vulnerable. I don't often say "I'm wrong" and mean it.
11. It's better to nurse my wounds than to show someone that I'm weak.
12. I'm a better talker than listener.
13. What I have to say is usually important.
14. I secretly think others don't take my opinions as seriously as they should.
15. I have a pretty good sense of what's good for people.

16. At least once in my life I got caught opening someone else's mail.
17. People have called me cynical or negative.
18. I have high standards, which others sometimes mistake for criticism.
19. I tend to be a perfectionist. It bothers me to let a sloppy job go out.
20. I feel uncomfortable if someone gets too close to me emotionally.
21. After a relationship breaks up, I look back and think I was mostly in the right.
22. I'm neat and orderly. I like my way of doing things and find it hard to live with someone who is sloppy.
23. I'm good at scheduling my day and put a high value on punctuality.
24. I'm good at caring for other people's needs, but then I get disappointed when they don't think as much about mine.
25. I have a logical explanation for the way I act, even if others can't always accept it.
26. I don't care that much if other people don't like me.
27. In my opinion, most people don't usually express their true motives for the way they behave.
28. I'm not good at handling noisy or rambunctious children.
29. I still blame my parents for a lot of my problems, but I haven't told them so.
30. When I get into an argument with my spouse or lover, I can't resist bringing up old grievances.

Total score _____

Evaluating your score:
0–10 points

Your personality isn't dominated by an excessive need to be in control. You are likely to be comfortable with your feelings and tolerant of other people. You realize that you are imperfect, therefore you understand the failings of others. It is easy for you to let events take their own course, and surprises don't throw you off balance. You probably place a high value on spontaneity and the expression of emotions.

10–20 points

Being in control is a frequent issue with you. You have more fears and hurt feelings than you let on, but you don't work hard to resolve these feelings. Being in charge isn't necessarily that important to you, but having your way usually is. You consider yourself organized and efficient, yet it isn't a major event if things get a little out of control. You have found someone whom you can be honest and open with, but there are limits to how much you can safely say or do, even with that person.

Over 20 points

You are a controlling person. You feel that control is necessary because people hurt your feelings a lot, and your memory of this goes back into your painful childhood. To keep from being hurt more, you try to control your feelings, which basically means you are very selective about revealing yourself to others. Your overriding need to be in charge or to have things your way drives people away from you, despite the fact that you work very hard to take care of their needs. The only emotion you show easily is anger or irritability. You constantly explain your motives and give reasons for why you are the way you are, but somehow this doesn't help to get you what you want, which is other people's love and affection.

———————

The purpose of this questionnaire is not to label anyone bad for being controlling. Losing control is an extremely unpleasant state for most people, and we all exert energy to maintain control. But there is a healthy way to be in control and an unhealthy way. The healthy way is to be secure enough in yourself (meaning your worth, lovability, and achievements) that outside events do not threaten your coping skills. The unhealthy way is to manipulate people and events so that your weaknesses and insecurity are covered over. You have to be honest with yourself to follow the first way; you need to know your limits in various situations, which ones make you feel weak and which ones bring out your strengths. Self-knowledge is an anchor that makes unpredictability tolerable.

A wise person once said to me, "If my approach to a situation isn't working, I have faith that there is more to learn. Either someone else can provide me with help or the flow of events will reveal what is needed. In either case, I won't get to the solution until I first admit that my response isn't perfect." Unhealthy controlling people lack this flexibility and humility; they insist on being in charge of events and find excuses to make themselves come out on the right side of every conflict. This behavior promotes disharmony both within themselves and with their environment. Unable simply to allow, they pay the price of never truly experiencing the nourishment that comes when life is simply allowed to flow in, around, and through you.

Exercise 1: Freeing Your Interpretations

Your life can be only as free as your perception of it. Whenever we look at a situation, we see our past in it, because every event gets interpreted, and interpretations are rooted in the past. If spiders frightened you as a child, you will project that fear onto spiders today; if your father was alcoholic, your judgment about someone who drinks will be clouded by your painful past experiences. Just to realize that you are placing an interpretation on everything, no matter how trivial, is an important step toward freeing yourself from the past. Realize that you are always seeing things from one point of view. If you find yourself fighting with someone, for example, holding on to your point of view makes the other person a threat, while acknowledging that two opposing viewpoints can both be valid removes the threat.

Remember that stage 2 of the stress response—appraisal—is the only stage in which you can control your body's reaction. Once you have interpreted a situation as a threat, your body will automatically give some kind of stress reaction. So it's important to question your interpretations. Old ones usually don't remain valid beyond the original situation. The only way you can end stress is by *perceiving* it to end. There's much more to say about how to accomplish this, but in my own life, I try to approach every stressful situation with the intention of defusing its threat in myself. Five steps have been immensely helpful:

1. Realize that you have an interpretation. In a conflict situation, I try to tell myself that my viewpoint is limited; I don't have a patent on the truth.
2. Set aside the old mindset. When I feel tense, I take this as a signal that I'm holding on too tightly to my point of view.
3. Look at things from a new perspective. I focus on the feelings in my body, and as I do, inevitably my mind starts to see things slightly differently.
4. Question your interpretation to see if it is still valid.
5. Focus on process, not outcome. Stress always arises if you concentrate on how something *has* to turn out. This is the pitfall of thinking that events can be controlled or forced into predictable outcomes. To overcome this tendency to impose false control, I remind myself that I don't need to know where I'm going to enjoy the road I'm on.

When I go through these five steps, the daily annoyances that create inappropriate stress dissolve very quickly. I try to be easy on myself; sometimes a situation pushes too many buttons, and the stress response begins before I know it. When that happens, the only sensible thing to do is to ride with it; the body isn't going to return to its nonstressed state until the reaction has run its course.

The exercise is to read and think about these five steps for changing your interpretations and then apply them. At first you should apply these techniques to a troubling event from your past. Think of someone who hurt your feelings very badly and whom you cannot forgive. The five steps might carry you into this line of reasoning:

1. I feel hurt, but that doesn't mean the other person was bad or meant to hurt me. He doesn't know my entire past, and I don't know his. There's always another side to the story, despite my hurt.

2. I've been hurt like this before, and therefore maybe I was too quick to judge this incident. I need to see each thing as it is.

3. I don't need to see myself as a victim here. When was the last time I was on the other side of the same situation? Didn't I feel pretty caught up in my own motives? Did I give any more importance to the other person's hurt than mine was given this time?

4. Let me forget my feelings for a second. How did that other person feel? Perhaps he just lost control or was too wrapped up in his own world to notice my hurt.

5. This incident can help me. I don't really care about blaming this person or getting back. I want to find out the kinds of things that create threat in me. The more I think about it, the more I see this as an opportunity to take responsibility for my feelings. That makes is easier for me to forgive, since anyone who teaches me something about myself deserves my thanks.

When you begin to get into the habit of consciously and carefully examining your old interpretations in this way, you create a space for spontaneous moments of freedom. These are the moments when your old mindset clears in a flash of insight. With that flash comes a sense of revelation, because you are looking into reality itself, not a reflection of your past. All the most valuable things in life—love, compassion, beauty, forgiveness, inspiration—must come to us spontaneously. We can only prepare the way for them (a spiritual friend of mine calls this "punching a hole into the fourth dimension").

There is great freedom in insight. I know a man who for years could not go home for Thanksgiving without getting into a violent argument with his father. Then came one Thanksgiving when he was 40 and his father 75. "My father greeted me when I got off the plane, and as always, we started toward the baggage claim in a friendly mood. It takes about half an hour before my father and I take up our usual sparring roles. I tried not to tense up, but I knew that as soon as we got in the car, he would criticize my driving, and I would start to boil.

"We didn't have much to say to each other at the baggage carousel—that's usually when we run out of things to say to each other. My suitcase came down the chute, I reached for it, and he brushed me aside to carry it for me—another part of our ritual that hasn't changed in twenty years.

"This time, however, he stumbled a little picking up the heavy bag, and I noticed for the first time that he was getting old. You wouldn't think that was much of a revelation, but I realized that I have been warring with my father all this time as if I were still 7 years old and he was a hugely powerful, strong adult. I didn't take the suitcase from him, he's a proud man. But this time I didn't follow him to the car like a boy being shown up by his overweening dad. I saw that he wanted to help, and this was his way of showing he loved me. It's hard to describe how powerful that transformation felt."

This is a perfect example of how shedding old interpretations enables a different reality to shine through. In my own life, I began to notice on speaking tours that missing my jet flights, which happens to me with strange frequency, was causing more and more stress. One day I was running down the concourse, only to see the passenger ramp slowly moving away from the plane. I stopped, feeling a knot in my stomach and a sense of maddening frustration.

But then it occurred to me to ask myself, "How will my life be changed one year from now by having missed this plane?" The effect was almost magical: My heart stopped racing, my breathing calmed down, my muscles relaxed, the knot in my stomach dissolved, and my intestines stopped churning.

By questioning my interpretation, I realized that my unspoken assumptions had been my stress, not the missed flight. My body was conditioned to think, "Oh no, not this again," which is true of most stress reactions. They are anticipations. You remember the last marital fight, the last criticism of your work, the last hostile question from a lecture audience, and a full-blown stress response springs up. I felt like the rat that jumps in shock even when the shock doesn't come, for when I examined it, this missed flight had no significance. Breaking down the false interpretation released my body from its old habits.

Exercise 2: Peeling the Onion of the Past

The past is layered into us in many intricate layers. Your inner world is full of complex relationships, for it contains the past not only as it occurred but all the ways in which you would like to revise it. All the things that should have turned out differently do turn out differently in that place where you escape into fantasy, revenge, yearning, sorrow, self-reproach, and guilt. To get rid of these distractions, you need to realize that there is a deeper place *where everything is all right.*

In *Siddhartha,* Hermann Hesse writes, "Within you there is a stillness and sanctuary to which you can retreat at any time and be yourself." This sanctuary is a simple awareness of comfort, which can't be violated by the turmoil of events. This place feels no trauma and stores no hurt. It is the mental space that one seeks to find in meditation, which I believe is one of the most important pursuits anyone can follow. However, even if you do not meditate, you can approach this place of calm with the following exercise:

Write down this affirmation:

I am perfect as I am. Everything in my life is working toward my ultimate good. I am loved and I am love.

Do not pause to analyze the statement, just write it down. When you come to the end, shut your eyes and let any response surface that comes to mind, then write down the first words that came to you (write this response directly under the affirmation). Your first thought is likely to contain a lot of resistance, even anger, because no one's life is perfect and it is hard to believe that everything is working out as it should. (Typical responses: "Garbage!"; "This is nonsense"; "No!") If your reaction shows similar emotion, it is an honest one.

Now, without pausing, write the affirmation again, shut your eyes, and once more write down the first words that come to mind. Do not stop to analyze or dwell on your reaction. Continue the exercise until you have repeated the affirmation and your response twelve times. You will be surprised at how much your reactions change; for most people, the final response will be much more positive than the first. Essentially, this exercise allows you to eavesdrop on the innermost levels of your awareness.

Most people have the highest resistance at the surface of their minds, because this is where their most public and guarded reactions operate. Your social self, the one who behaves the way you're supposed to, is superficial; it was trained primarily to make a good impression and not to be too revealing. These upper layers of your awareness will not respond very profoundly to such a strong statement as "I am love." Going deeper, we hit levels of the most recent frustrations, wishes, and unreleased emotion. When you touch these layers, quite unexpected or irrational reactions can come out. The statement "I am love" may trigger an angry outburst that is related to a recent incident when you didn't feel loved at all.

Deeper still are the layers where your most entrenched feelings are stored. If you feel basically unlovable, there could be a lot of pain and resistance at this level. But beneath even the most rigid conditioning, there is a layer of awareness that agrees without equivocation to the words "I am love."

The reason you can love and be loved is that this layer of your consciousness evokes that feeling; this is where the deepest human values are known. Without such knowledge—not just of love but of beauty, compassion, trust, strength, and truth—these words would be meaningless. Love is part of essential human nature. We recognize it because it vibrates in us, however far below the conscious level. Being able to live from this level brings complete fulfillment, but that happens only when you resolve the layers of conflicts and contradictions that constitute your resistance.

When you resist the flow of life, what you are actually resisting is your own inner nature, for everything that happens to us is a reflection of who we are. This isn't a mystical statement; it is part of the apparatus of perception. To perceive is to grasp the meaning of something. A rock isn't a rock unless you are familiar with the concept of rock; otherwise a rock would be meaningless sensory input, like looking at Arabic or Russian writing if you don't understand those languages. You have to learn a foreign language, and you have to learn about all the objects "out there" in the world, but you do not have to learn how to exist. Being comes naturally; to have a human nervous system is to be. Packaged with that nervous system is human awareness, knowing that you are human as opposed to part of another species.

With this knowledge arises the primordial feelings that make us respond to love, trust, compassion, and the other essential feeling states. They are our beginning, but they are also what we seek, because each of them can grow. Living from the level of awareness that says "I am love" means living from a level where love can grow. In the early stages of personal evolution, most people wonder about these essential states. They are confused about whether they are lovable, trusting, strong, valuable, and so forth. You cannot find out about these states by trying to prove them to yourself. Earning love by acting good, being nice, learning the game of social attractiveness, etc., always ends in failure, because once you stop behaving in those trained ways, the basic attitude you are left with is doubt, which is where you began.

The end of the search for love is beyond behavior, because in time the mind decides to look inward, and when it does, the search changes into a search for the essential self, the me that knows "I am love." There is truth about yourself at every level of your awareness, but after you peel back all the layers of the onion, this is the most basic truth: You are love, you are compassion, you are beauty. You are existence and being. You are awareness and spirit. Any of these statements can be used as an affirmation, which, as the word implies, is just a way of affirming something, of saying yes. The technique is extremely powerful for reminding yourself about your nature, but more than that, it reminds you of your purpose, which is to grow to the point where "I am love" is at the surface of your consciousness, not buried in the dark depths.

Exercise 3: Living in the Present

Everything you think and feel reflects who you are. If you think and feel from a superficial level of awareness, that is who you are. To dive deeper into yourself and, hopefully, to get to that place where you are love, compassion, trust, and truth, you have to follow the path of your present responses. Someone who feels unloved can still find love in its purest form, but he will have to work through the layers of resistance that block the feeling of pure love. Your present emotions reflect the present state of your nervous system with all its past imprints. Whenever you have an experience, these imprints enter into your response, which means that most of your reactions are echoes from the past. You do not really live in the present.

However, at least you are reacting in the present, and that is where the search for your true self begins. Your emotions are the most present-centered thing you have. An emotion is a thought linked to a sensation. The thought is usually about the past or the future, but the sensation is in the present. Your mind quickly links sensations with thoughts, but when we were infants, our first experiences and emotions were much closer to physical sensations. We had no inhibitions or second thoughts about crying when we were wet, cold, lonely, frightened, etc. Our minds didn't know those powerful words *bad* and *no*. *Bad* teaches you that certain thoughts are shameful; *no* teaches you to resist your own impulses.

More complex words and interpretations came later. As adults, when we deny ourselves the immediate experience of an emotion, a screen of words is put up by the mind, and this throws us out of the present and into either the past or the future. To feel an emotion fully and completely, to experience it and then release it, is to be in the present, the only moment that never ages.

Stripped to the basics, emotions arouse only two sensations—pain and pleasure. We all want to avoid pain and pursue pleasure; therefore, all the complicated emotional states we find ourselves in are the result of not being able to obey those basic drives. Psychiatrist David Viscott has reduced emotional complexity to a single cycle that gets repeated countless times in everyone's life. This cycle begins in the present, where only pain and pleasure are felt, and ends up with complex feelings centered exclusively in the past, such as guilt and depression. The cycle of emotions is as follows:

> Pain in the present is experienced as hurt.
> Pain in the past is remembered as anger.
> Pain in the future is perceived as anxiety.
> Unexpressed anger, redirected against yourself and held within, is called guilt.
> The depletion of energy that occurs when anger is redirected inward creates depression.

What this cycle tells us is that stored hurt is responsible for a wide range of psychological distress. Buried hurt disguises itself as anger, anxiety, guilt, and depression. The only way to deal with these layers of pain is to find out what hurts as the pain occurs, deal with it, and move on. Living in the present means being honest enough to avoid the easy emotion, which is anger, and expose the hurt, which is harder to confront. When hurt is not resolved in the present, the vicious buildup of anger, anxiety, guilt, and depression can only grow worse.

The exercise is to learn the steps of how to feel in the present:

1. Realize that hurt is the most basic negative feeling. You cannot be in the present without willingness to feel hurt.
2. Be with your sensations. Resist the impulse either to deny what you feel or to turn it into anger.
3. Say what you feel to the person who caused the hurt.
4. Resolve your emotion and move on.

This may seem like an exercise in suffering, but in fact it is an exercise in freedom. Being hurt isn't pleasant, but it is real. It puts you in the present, whereas conditioned responses of anger, anxiety, guilt, and depression put you out of the present. Once you are in the present, you can follow the trail of your emotions back to their source, which is not pain but love, compassion, truth—the real you.

There is no purpose in suffering except as a guide to your truth. In and of itself, pain has no worth except as a signal that will pull you out of pain. When an infant is hurt, it cries, gets the hurt out of its system, and then relaxes. It rejoins the body's basic state, which is pleasure, ease, and comfort. If you want to feel these things, all you have to do is be yourself, but being yourself means getting past the tendency to repress or divert your emotions, which all of us learned in early childhood.

Coming to the moment by putting your attention on the pain allows you to release the pain as soon as it occurs. This release occurs naturally—it is what the body wants to do—and attention is the healing power that triggers it. Putting attention on your feelings gets you closer to the state of witnessing; you observe the pain without getting wrapped up in all the secondary blame, avoidance, and denial that usually follows. In the act of witnessing, insight becomes possible. It takes detachment to bring understanding, and if you get caught up in your hurt, you won't see the reason behind it. No one can hurt you today without triggering a hurt from your past. You have to see that in order to find yourself.

As you learn to say, "I feel hurt," and really be with that feeling, more openness will develop. The emotions that frighten us are the complex ones, because they overwhelm the natural release mechanism. You cannot simply release guilt or depression. They are secondary formations that arose once you forgot how to release hurt.

The more hurt you honestly feel, the more comfortable you will be with pain, because the ability to release it will grow. As this happens, you will feel easier about all your other emotions. (To a blocked mind, feeling "positive" emotions such as love and trust is often just as difficult as feeling "negative" emotions such as hate and distrust. Both are elauded by old unresolved hurts.) Feeling easy with your emotions means that you won't get so entangled in other people's. Instead of blaming the ones who hurt you, you will be able to forgive.

The lessons of this exercise are very profound:

- Everyone is acting from his own level of consciousness. This is all we can ask of ourselves or anyone else. However hurtful someone is, he is doing the best he can, given the limits of his consciousness.

- Forgiveness of others comes only when you can release your own hurt. The more complete your release, the more sincere the forgiveness.

- No one can really hurt you unless you give them the power to do so. This power lies in your own unresolved pain. You can take control of the old pain and reclaim power over your emotions. Until you do that, your feelings will continue to be tossed around at the whim of others.

- Outside events have no power to hurt you. The hurt comes when an interpretation occurs in your mind. You can live beyond interpretation, in a state of witnessing, the pure, untouchable awareness that is the real you.

Again, the reason this exercise defeats aging is that it puts you back into the present, and present-moment awareness never ages. It is the same when you are 5 or 85. The discovery of freedom in the present opens the door for the permanent experience of timelessness, in which past, present, and future are revealed as illusions compared to the true reality, which is always here and now.

PART FOUR

The Science of Longevity

I'VE NEVER MET Belle Odom, but I'm looking at her picture in the morning newspaper. She is a tiny old lady, smiling and waving a frilled lace handkerchief. Belle is in the paper because she has achieved the remarkable age of 109. Despite the fact that she is older than several states in the Union, her eyes look clear and alert; the accompanying article says that her mind is sharper than those of many younger residents at the nursing home where she lives.

I can imagine the fuss everyone made over Belle to get her ready for her moment in the sun. There she sits in a cheerful old-lady print dress, pink-flowered with a wide lace collar, bought for the occasion no doubt. The article rattles off some statistics about people who live to be 100 or more:

80 percent of all centenarians are women
75 percent are widowed
50 percent are in nursing homes
16 percent are black (the general population
    is only 12 percent black)

This last figure is relevant because Belle is a black woman, born and raised in rugged Texas farm country. Until she turned 100 she lived alone in a cabin without running water; now she is the star resident of a Houston nursing home. No mention is made of her health, but it is probably frail—life flickers like a guttering candle when one reaches the limits of human longevity.

At 109, Belle has moved far beyond biological probability and into a mysterious and uncertain survival. There is a riddle attached to longevity, because science still cannot predict who will live to extreme old age. Genetics does not hold the entire answer—no centenarian has ever been recorded who had a centenarian father or mother. Lifestyle is also problematic—someone like Belle, raised on a marginal diet and grinding physical labor, had a horrendous lifestyle by modern standards, yet she has outlived 99.999 percent of her generation, including those who lived in far better circumstances. Officially, the oldest survivor in American history was Delina Filkins, a country woman from Herkimer County, New York, who died in 1928 at 113. (Unofficial claims to much higher ages are frequently made, and there is little doubt that some unsung individual has survived 115 years or more.) Belle isn't challenging the record yet, but even to be a contender puts her in the longevity elite.

"Are you lonely?" a reporter asks her.

"Yes'm, sometimes I am," Belle replies. The very old are inevitably alone, having outdistanced the family and friends with whom they started out on life's journey. Belle is typical in this regard. She has buried three husbands, one brother, and six sisters. (Unlike most women of her generation, Belle had no children.) Even her nieces are far too old to take care of her now.

It's said that in a typical climbing season on Mt. Everest, an average of sixty-four climbers arrive at base camp; of this number, which is a tiny fraction of the world's skilled mountaineers, one-third attempt the final assault on the peak. Two climbers will perish in the attempt, and only four will succeed. Belle Odom is like one of those four climbers standing ten yards from the summit of human longevity, exhausted, hardly able to take another step, but there.

In the next few decades, the mountaintop is going to become much more crowded. Barring a premature heart attack or a fatal disease or accident, you and I are likely to make it at least to base camp. Ages of 85 and 90 are going to become as common in the future as they were rare in the past. Newspapers will carry notices of people reaching their hundredth birthdays as routinely as they now print announcements about the birth of twins. Only when someone reaches 110 will it be considered an event.

Can you imagine what you will be like the day you turn 100? It's a big conceptual leap, comparable to asking a 2-year-old to imagine being middle-aged. But think of yourself at 50 (perhaps you are already there) and then try to grasp this staggering fact: The day you turn 50 is going to be your second birth. In all likelihood a complete lifetime lies ahead of you, lasting at least thirty or more likely forty, fifty, or even sixty years. For every previous generation, 50 was a time for winding down. Children were grown up, off to college, possibly even married with their own children. Career was a settled matter, and a person pretty well knew whether he was a success or failure. The idealism of youth had long faded; the midlife crisis had been weathered either as a full-blown tempest or, if one was lucky, as only brooding squalls on the horizon.

But to be born at 50! Little in life has prepared us for this. Yet according to a California health department study, if medical science could wipe out just one major health risk, arteriosclerosis, the average life expectancy for women in California would rise to 100—the *average*.

Compared to your first birth, the one you will experience at 50 has both pluses and minuses. In both instances, a completely new and unknown existence opens up, but the great advantage of your second birth is that you can plan ahead. Your first birth was thrown at you, complete with total strangers who turned out to be your parents, an awkward, unformed body that had to be trained to perform the simplest tasks, and a bewildering world of chaotic sights and sounds your brain had to mold into something that made sense. By age 50, all that work has been done, and as fearful images of the "old old age" rapidly dissipate, the obvious disadvantage of the second birth—not having a new body—will not be so crippling. Disease and infirmity will be long delayed, if not conquered.

Fired by the possibilities of planning a whole new lifetime, I decided to take the opportunity seriously. I set aside all the stereotypes of old age that clutter the mind and approached my second birth (which is only four years away) with a wish list. What would I want should I live to be 100? Immediately the following desires came to mind:

I want to survive even longer, if possible.
I want to remain healthy.
I want a clear, alert mind.
I want to be active.
I want to have achieved wisdom.

As soon as I wrote down these desires, a surprising thing happened—they all seemed within my reach. Why shouldn't I have as much life as possible? As long as life is good, it's only natural to want more of it. Why shouldn't I be healthy? I know what to do to be healthy today, and I can live tomorrow the same way. My mind is clear and alert now; there is no reason why it must dim with time, assuming that I keep using it. I've always been active, so why fear that I'll sink into a chair one day, never to get up again? And if wisdom isn't mine yet, that's all the better; wisdom is a gift that arrives in its own time. My other desires would be meaningless if I didn't expect this final golden fruit to be bestowed when I am ready.

With this simple list I had turned survival from a threat into a desirable goal, because on my list were things I truly wanted. According to public-opinion polls, 80 percent of Americans say yes to the question "Are you satisfied with your life today?" A majority, however, say they don't want to live to be 100, so they must share an expectation that the road between today and 100 brings loss. This self-fulfilling prophecy can be changed only by choosing to *improve* with age. Old age is a grace if you reach it with joy, creativity, and curiosity. These qualities require living fully in the present moment, since today is the youth of your longevity.

The unquestioned assumption of the old paradigm was that as the body wore out over time, life became increasingly unfulfilling. The storehouse of possibilities ran out after a certain age, which was arbitrarily defined by each society and each individual. The new paradigm tells us that life is a process of constant transformation, not decline, and therefore is full of potential for unlimited growth. To keep unfolding new possibilities decade after decade, one has to know what these possibilities are. What should we expect physically, mentally, and emotionally in the second fifty years of life? A new science of longevity has emerged to answer these questions.

Even staunch adherents to the old paradigm now agree that automatic decline is not programmed into our bodies. Longevity comes to those who have discovered this on their own—science is merely validating the numerous improvements in bodily function that older people are already experiencing.

In this section I want to examine these new findings in the hope of discovering the most essential ones, the keys to longevity that hold true for most if not all people. Human life is incredibly resilient. It would seem unlikely that someone like Belle Odom could survive as long as she has. Many disadvantages were stacked against her: being poor and black, being deprived of adequate medical care, spending most of her life on a diet that was likely to have been high in fat and low in essential vitamins. The science of longevity must account for these anomalies, and I believe that the only way it can is to probe into issues of mind and heart that transcend physical factors. Belle is much more than her lifestyle—and so are all of us. Biologists and gerontologists have amassed fascinating information about how to survive to great old age, but new data is not enough. We need practical examples of holistic living. As an inspiring experiment in this direction, Gay Luce and her colleagues in Berkeley, California, ran Project SAGE (Senior Actualization and Growth Explorations). Founded in 1974, SAGE attempted to revitalize people between the ages of 65 and 85 with startling success. Many transformed their lives. One woman, who mournfully said her life was over when she was 74, wrote a book at age 91 and began traveling as a speaker campaigning for a decent environment for the dying. People discovered that by breath work and attention they could undo long-term symptoms—migraines, headaches, and arthritis pain. A retired woman who thought herself virtually color blind discovered through an art process that she could do interior decoration, and redid her home. There is a secret core of meaning waiting to be discovered in every life, and those who have found it are the teachers I look to for my own future survival. They have lived the years after the second birth. They are the true scientists of longevity and therefore its real geniuses.

100 YEARS YOUNG:

What the Oldest Can Teach Us

Most of us have never met anyone who is 100 years old. Historically, living to 100 was a feat so rare that it was almost freakish. Victorian-era research into the lineage of British aristocrats, who were presumably the best fed and cared for members of their society, could not unearth a single peer in the preceding ten centuries who had lived to be 100. The first was Lord Penrhyn, who died in 1967 at 101. Today in most industrialized countries, one person in 10,000 passes the century mark, and the ratio is rising faster than any other growth statistic in the population.

The oldest people alive today do not tend to be merely random survivors, but individuals who embody enviable attitudes and values. Sociologists who study centenarians are inevitably struck by their strong attachment to freedom and independence. Throughout their lives, centenarians tend to avoid being held back by constraints. Traditionally, most have worked on their own, very few in the confines of modern corporations. They prize their autonomy very highly.

As I said earlier, the word researchers apply most frequently to centenarians is *adaptable*. At some point in their lives, all have suffered losses and setbacks. But even the most intense loss, such as that of a spouse after fifty or sixty years of marriage, was mourned, and then the person moved on. Studied as a group, centenarians have other significant similarities. In his compelling book on longevity, *Prolongevity II*, Albert Rosenfeld reports from interviews conducted with twelve hundred people on Social Security who gave their ages as 100 or more. "It was clear that, though these individuals worked hard and enjoyed their work, there was a marked lack of high ambition. They had tended to live relatively quiet and independent lives, were generally happy with their jobs, their families, and their religion, and had few regrets. Nearly all expressed a strong will to live, and a high appreciation for the simple experiences and pleasures of life."

If aging were simply a matter of wearing out, we would expect all centenarians to be in poor health, trapped in bodies with many deteriorated working parts. Actually, standards of health are high among our centenarians; fewer than one in five report that they are disabled or in such poor health that they require assistance to eat, walk, bathe, and so forth. Most still get around on their own (almost always without crutches or walkers), and many continue to work, at least by keeping house and caring for themselves.

Trying to articulate a specific "longevity personality" is too constricting for centenarians—the benign, quiet, wise grandfather or grandmother is only one type among many. Living to be 100 also happens to selfish, sarcastic, and unsociable people. The common thread is a sense of self-sufficiency that runs much deeper than personality. To support this point, a 1973 study in New York of seventy-nine healthy people 87 years of age and older found that they almost never went to doctors, were never found in nursing homes, and were rarely in homes for the aged. Dr. Stephen P. Jewett, the senior psychiatrist who conducted the New York study, made clear that his subjects were more than chance survivors or lucky beneficiaries of good genes.

Granted, the seventy-nine people he studied had escaped catastrophic illness, such as heart attack and cancer, in the critical midlife period from 45 to 65 (this is when bad genes, hypertension, elevated cholesterol, smoking, alcoholism, and other negative factors tend to take their highest toll). But Jewett's subjects managed to be healthy into their late eighties and nineties, implying that some powerful positive factors were working in their favor.

Jewett's study saw longevity in broad terms, and the majority of the factors he came up with were subjective, having to do with how these people felt about themselves. In comparison, the purely objective factors linked to long life were few and very general.

PHYSICAL CHARACTERISTICS

Not seriously overweight or underweight
Little weight fluctuation over their lifetime
Good general muscle tone
Good grip
Young appearance to skin
Still drives a car and engages in physical activity

PSYCHOLOGICAL CHARACTERISTICS
(INCLUDING LIFESTYLE AND BEHAVIOR)

Superior native intelligence, keen interest in current events, good memory.

Freedom from anxiety, few illnesses, not prone to worry.

Independence of choice in their vocations. They tended to be their own bosses. They worked at farming and in the nursery business, and in the professions of law, medicine, and architecture; others headed small businesses of their own, and in a few cases large businesses. The majority did not retire early.

Most had been hard hit by the Depression, which came along in their fifties and sixties, but they recovered and built new futures.

They enjoyed life. All had a degree of optimism and a marked sense of humor. They responded to simple pleasures. Life seems to have been a great adventure. They could see beauty where others saw only ugliness.

Great adaptability. While many cherished childhood memories, all preferred living in the present with its many changes.

They were not preoccupied with death.

They continued living with satisfaction from day to day.

All may be described as religious in the broad sense, but
   none exhibited extreme orthodoxy.
They were moderate eaters but willing to experiment. No
   special diets. Diet included a high variety of foods high in
   protein, low in fat.
All were early risers. Average sleep was between six and
   seven hours, although they rested in bed for eight hours.
   (Shortened or interrupted sleep is typical in old age.)
No uniformity in drinking habits. Some drank moderately,
   some drank too much at times, some abstained.
Smoking—some abstained, a few had smoked very moderately but had long since given it up, a few were inveterate
   pipe smokers.
Medications—used less medication in their lifetimes than
   many old people use in a week.
Most drank coffee.

I have covered some of these factors previously, and I'd like to
touch on a few more first, the physical characteristics on the list,
though few, are very telling.

Longevity and Weight

Maintaining a fairly steady weight throughout life seems to be more
important than whether one is over- or underweight. As with so
many findings about longevity, this one sounds rather insignificant
but may turn out to have deep implications. A study of 11,700
Harvard graduates from the classes of 1916 to 1950 paid particular
attention to how they fared from middle age onward. Data collected
between 1962 and 1988 revealed that gaining or losing even a moderate amount of weight over a long period of time raised one's risk of
mortality.
   Compared to men who kept their weight constant, those who
lost eleven pounds or more over a ten-year period had 57 percent
higher mortality, including 75 percent higher risk of dying from a

heart attack. Those who gained eleven pounds or more over a ten-year period were only somewhat better off, with 36 percent higher mortality than the men who maintained a steady weight; their risk of dying from a heart attack jumped dramatically to 200 percent. This finding overturns the common misconception that being too fat is the main risk associated with weight; actually, as long as clinical obesity isn't present (defined as being 15 percent or more over normal body weight), carrying around some extra poundage is not correlated with shorter life span—just the reverse.

Extensive actuarial studies conducted by Dr. Reuben Andres have shown the lowest mortality among those who are 10 percent overweight and the highest mortality among the chronically under-weight. Andres's work, based on studies of millions of people in all income and social brackets, plays havoc with societal values that equate slimness with all things good and healthy; as a result, many doctors have chosen to overlook facts that do not fit in with prevailing beliefs. The Harvard study further undermines the stereotype through its emphasis on maintaining a steady weight. It also supports the long-held notion that going on crash diets is unhealthy, but calling this a purely physical finding seems misleading to me. Weight is inevitably bound up with self-image. At a young age many people, both men and women, learn to use dieting as a quick fix for a poor self-image. The thinner they are, the better they feel about themselves and the more prone they are to believe that their problems in general have been cured.

The improvement brought about by losing five or ten pounds is superficial, however, since deeper emotional issues remain untouched. Typically, the chronic dieter falls into the "yo-yo syndrome," dropping a few pounds when self-esteem is relatively high, only to gain them back quickly (and with more to spare) when self-esteem sinks again. The fact that *either* gaining or losing weight shortens one's life span makes me speculate that poor self-esteem is the real culprit. The subjects who maintained a steady weight are likely to be psychologically steady as well—this is their saving virtue, not their weight per se. Clinical obesity remains a proven risk in heart disease and type II diabetes, but being physically active may compensate for being overweight due to the fact that carrying the extra pounds provides considerable aerobic exercise to the heart.

Longevity and Exercise

The strong grip and good muscle tone of Jewett's subjects indicate that they were active people. However, there is a marked absence of pursuing organized exercise, despite the fact that exercise is known to retard aging. To understand this seeming anomaly, we have to look deeper into how much activity is actually needed to make a significant contribution to longevity.

Dr. Steven Blair and his colleagues at the Institute for Aerobics Research performed treadmill tests on more than ten thousand men and three thousand women, then followed the group for eight years to determine how much protection was provided by various levels of fitness.

It was no surprise that the least active people had the highest death rates—mortality for the most sedentary men was more than three times higher than for the fittest men, while the most inactive women had a mortality rate more than five times higher than the fittest women. What was surprising is that the most striking improvement came with fairly modest levels of activity. Someone who walked thirty minutes a day, six days a week, enjoyed a mortality rate almost as low as someone who ran thirty to forty miles per week. Blair drew the conclusion that exercising for fitness was not the same as exercising for health. As long as you perform regular, minimal activity—the equivalent of walking half an hour a day—you are gaining most of the longevity benefits conferred by exercise.

Another way to state this is that doing anything physical is much better than remaining inactive. In Blair's study, the mortality rate of sedentary people of both sexes was twice as high as for people who walked every day. Walking uses up between 290 and 430 calories per hour, depending on how fast you walk. This breaks down to an average of 180 calories for the thirty minutes that is needed to keep someone healthy. You can burn approximately the same amount of calories by:

30 minutes of dancing
20 minutes of tennis
17 minutes of uphill hiking
15 minutes of swimming

If you wanted to expend these calories in domestic chores, the times work out to:

40 minutes of housecleaning
30 minutes of weeding the garden
25 minutes of mowing the lawn
15 minutes of shoveling snow

I'm not suggesting that you count calories when you exercise; these figures are presented to indicate how easily you can maintain your health without feeling guilty that you don't jog five miles every morning or swim laps at the gym. Every time you climb the stairs instead of taking the elevator, your body uses only 4.5 calories for every flight, but this low number is deceptive. Stair climbing is excellent aerobic exercise, increasing the heart rate by ten beats for every flight climbed.

A study in Finland found that people who climbed at least twenty-five flights of stairs a day achieved a significant level of fitness. That would be too much to climb at once—the load on your heart could tax it dangerously—but anyone who lives in a two-story house can easily climb the stairs a dozen times a day; add in the opportunity to climb stairs at work or shopping (every time you see an escalator or elevator, you'll find stairs nearby), and the total of twenty-five flights a day is surprisingly easy to reach. It's just a matter of being on the lookout for opportunities.

Exercising a little every day is much better than waiting for the weekend. Start-and-stop activity is stressful on the body, which prefers short daily sessions of activity. Whether you call your activity "exercise" is up to you—some people are just not interested in sports or workouts, but you can be active by making the bed, climbing stairs, walking to lunch instead of taking a taxi, carrying a bag of groceries home on foot, etc. It takes longer, more sustained exercise to develop overall fitness, build muscles, and increase endurance; the activities listed here basically tone up the cardiovascular system by pumping the blood a little faster and giving the lungs a bit of a workout.

Performing regular aerobic exercise will make you healthier, but it will not necessarily pay rich dividends in terms of added years. In fact, detailed studies involving Harvard graduates over a period of three decades show that intensive exercise (expending two thousand calories a week, or the equivalent of running eighteen miles) lengthened life by between one and two years. Cardiologist Dean Ornish has calculated that it takes thirty minutes of running, six days a week, to burn up two thousand calories; to this time you have to add half an hour to suit up and go to the track plus another half-hour to go home, shower, and change clothes again. If a person began running at age 30, the hours spent in exercising until age 75 would add up to between one and two years. Since this is equal to the extra life you can expect to gain, the net dividend is zero. Heavy exercise gives only an illusion of adding to life span. The point is not that you shouldn't exercise strenuously, but that if you do, you should know that what you are getting is better quality of life—surely a very great advantage—not more time.

Longevity and Diet

Glaringly absent from Jewett's study is the role of diet. No mention is made of rigorous attempts to control cholesterol. There is no insistence on the use of vitamins and minerals, no recommendations on health food regimens, fiber supplements, or vegetarianism. Centenarians eat a wide variety of diets—this has been confirmed in all the studies—but the fact that they maintain a constant weight implies that they tend to eat moderately. Beyond that, it appears that many of our present dietary beliefs may need to be less rigid. This point was forcibly brought home by a recent and revealing study. In Finland, a country that has traditionally suffered the highest heart-attack rate in the world, cardiac researchers selected twelve hundred business executives who were thought to be at high risk for heart attack because they displayed one or more of the classic risk factors: obesity, high blood pressure, elevated cholesterol, and heavy smoking (each smoked more than ten cigarettes per day). Half of the men were placed on an intensive five-year program of controlled diet, regular checkups, and detailed information about their potential risks. The other group was left free to live as they liked but with regular checkups.

At the end of the five years, researchers were extremely surprised to find that death rates were much higher for the group told to cut down on cholesterol, calories, sugar, and alcohol—*including twice as many deaths from heart attacks.* This despite the fact that the heavily monitored group had been advised to eat more polyunsaturated fat (mainly margarine), replace red meat with fish, chicken, and vegetables, quit smoking, and reduce alcohol consumption. After fifteen years, the statistics were still skewed: The closely monitored group had suffered thirty-four cardiac deaths, the control group only fourteen.

By any measure, the group left to continue their smoking, drinking, and overeating should have been at much higher risk. What happened? The perverse results may or may not imply that controlling the cholesterol you eat is significant to your health. But they are certainly an indictment of the stressful nature of present-day prevention techniques.

A leading cardiologist in Britain makes the point briskly: "These results don't mean that you can stuff yourself silly with impunity. But my own feeling is that if a patient exhausted by effort and distress has his life invaded by doctors and other do-gooders wanting to constrain his eating and other behaviors, the hassle factor and loss of autonomy could prove the last straw."

The significant phrase here is *loss of autonomy.* As we have seen, a strong sense of personal freedom, coupled with personal happiness, is critical to surviving in good health to a ripe old age. Fear is not a good motivator because it creates its own stress. Yet millions of people have been indoctrinated about cholesterol, on the assumption that the price of fear is small compared to the price of high cholesterol. This is an extremely short-sighted strategy. Cholesterol has been promoted as an enemy of the body for forty years, despite the fact that every cell needs cholesterol to survive (it forms a critical part of cell membranes, among other functions), and two-thirds of the cholesterol inside us is manufactured by the liver, not absorbed through food.

The very premise that low cholesterol is beneficial has come under increasing suspicion. In a massive review of eighteen studies from around the world, covering 650,000 people in the United States, Japan, Europe, and Israel, the benefits of having low serum cholesterol were refuted. The 125,000 women studied had the same life expectancy whether they had high, low, or average cholesterol readings. Furthermore, no specific cause of death, such as heart attack or cancer, was related to cholesterol levels, either high or low (these findings are doubly important given that almost all the classic studies warning against cholesterol were based on males).

Among the 520,000 men studied, findings were somewhat more complex. Men with average to borderline cholesterol readings (200 to 240) had the same survival rates as men with low readings (160 to 200), while those with *either* very high or very low readings were worse off. Men with a cholesterol level below 160 were 17 percent more likely to die of all causes, as were men with very high readings (over 240).

This research, published in the September 1992 issue of the prestigious journal *Circulation,* represents by far the largest pool of data ever assembled. It strikes deep at our conventional notion that fat and cholesterol are "bad," but the result is still not clear. The evidence against high-fat diets remains strong, especially when one considers the additional risks posed by obesity, a common condition in countries with rich diets. Keeping fat at around 30 percent of total calories continues to be a prudent guideline.

What all this means is that a healthy diet must have two components: (1) It has to be psychologically satisfying; (2) It has to provide a balanced supply of nutrients several times a day. These are very basic requirements, but in a society that is fixated on "good" and "bad" foods, that eats half of its meals at fast-food stands and runs record-high rates of obesity, alcoholism, eating disorders, and crash dieting, it is hard to meet them. Evolutionarily, our bodies were designed to eat a wide variety of foods, but we have compromised this great range of adaptability by nutritional overload.

In *The Paleolithic Prescription,* S. Boyd Eaton and his co-authors point out that so-called primitive diets were much more concentrated in all vitamins and minerals than are modern diets while being much less concentrated in fats, proteins, salt, sugar, and calories. Stone Age man, like most tribal peoples today, ate a low-fat diet consisting largely of plant-derived foods, with only an occasional bit of meat or fish. Because all foods were fresh and had low fat content, our ancestors avoided one of the chief hazards of modern diets—high concentrations of useless calories. The human body was designed to eat all kinds of foods, but Nature provides few foods with concentrated calories.

Nuts, seeds, and meats are the most concentrated foods in the wild, and they form a comparatively minor part of the average diet of most tribal societies. Almost all native peoples must consume large amounts of fruits, grains, and vegetables—up to five or six pounds a day—in order to get the same calories that we get from one-third as much intake. (This also accounts for the faster speed of digestion on native diets and the increased bulk of elimination—up to four pounds of feces a day.)

Fruits, vegetables, and grains contain large amounts of water and indigestible fiber; therefore, one has to eat a lot of them to extract any calories to fuel the body. Besides ensuring that the intestines receive enough fiber, a native diet has the benefit of concentrated vitamins: A handful of wild greens can contain a day's requirement of vitamin C (50 to 60 mg.) with fewer than 10 calories, while a slice of toast, a doughnut, a bowl of oatmeal, coffee, and a glass of milk satisfies only 4 percent of the day's requirement of vitamin C with 500 calories. As a source of vitamin C, wild greens are 1,250 times more effective per calorie. By contrast, most processed foods contain large doses of salt and sugar, along with their extremely high ratios of fat.

Although diet was not a distinguishing feature of centenarians, improper diet is clearly linked with disease and premature aging. The most recent statistics indicate that the typical American diet contains about 40 percent fat, 130 pounds of white sugar per year, and three to five times more salt than the body actually needs. It cannot be coincidental that 86 percent of Americans over age 65 are afflicted with one or more degenerative disorders, such as heart disease, cancer, arthritis, diabetes, and osteoporosis. Although these have been long considered diseases of old age, we now view these conditions more accurately as lifestyle diseases; there are alarming signs of these same disorders in people under 50 and even in young children.

If primitive and tribal peoples survive childhood illnesses and escape accidents (the two leading causes of early death in the wild), they exhibit strong, healthy constitutions throughout life. By contrast, our modern lifestyle creates the basis for cancer and heart disease in all age groups. A hundred years ago, when Americans ate much less fat and processed food, much more fiber, and only a fraction of our intake of white sugar, the incidence of chronic disease was also proportionally lower. Returning to a more natural diet is worthwhile, given all the evidence.

Associated with diet is the question of alcohol, which has its own ambiguities. For several decades population studies in Europe have indicated that people who drink a moderate amount of wine (one or two glasses a day) enjoy lower heart-attack rates than either heavy drinkers or teetotalers. The precise mechanism is debatable, but alcohol is known to raise levels of HDLs (high-density lipoproteins, the "good" cholesterol) and dilate blood vessels, which reduces blood pressure. It also removes emotional inhibition, which may counter the tendency to bottle up emotional stress.

Weighed against this are some very negative effects, however: Alcoholism is an enormous social problem, and, as a chemical, alcohol is toxic to brain cells; it dehydrates the intestines and can reverse the assimilation of vital nutrients, particularly in the elderly. Various cancers and birth defects have been associated with even moderate drinking, not to mention the wide variety of disorders that afflict alcoholics. If we refer to Jewett's study of people who age successfully into their eighties and nineties, the fact that drinking habits varied widely suggests that alcohol alone is not a definitive factor. The only clear implication is that there are few if any 100-year-old alcoholics; they died off at a much younger age. Despite the lower incidence of heart disease that is alcohol's greatest claim to health, there is no proof that drinking significantly increases life span.

Setting Longevity as a Goal

If we summarize the physical findings from Jewett's study, we find that his subjects maintained a steady weight, ate moderately, and remained active throughout their lives. These factors are obviously not sufficient to explain longevity. Millions of people who have the same habits do not live to great old age. The psychological factors in Jewett's profile more clearly set his subjects apart. Their optimism, lack of worry, emotional resilience, capacity for enjoyment, and love of autonomy all indicate a high degree of psychological health. The fact that they are above average in intelligence also correlates well with similar studies; above-average intelligence makes it easier for a person to remain in good health, to earn a stable income, and to learn to resolve personal problems. At the other extreme, people with low intelligence often cannot take advantage of books and articles about health and nutrition; they more easily fall into low-income groups that cannot afford good housing, food, and health care. Poor, uneducated people also have the highest rates of cigarette smoking, which is a potent shortener of life.

The question arises whether longevity belongs only to those who are fortunate enough to be born with certain advantages. Psychologically healthy people tend to come from psychologically healthy families; parents with superior education and income tend to have well-educated children who go on to earn high salaries. There is no doubt that such advantages are very helpful. In a small but highly suggestive study in 1970, psychiatrist Eric Pfeiffer took thirty-four men and women, all in their late sixties, who were considered the most successful agers in the ongoing Duke University Longevity Study, one of the major projects of its kind. When he compared his successful agers with thirty-four men and women who were considered the worst agers, Pfeiffer discovered a significant difference in longevity. The men who aged best survived on average 14.8 years longer than did those who aged worst; a slightly smaller gap, 13.8 years, separated the women. This difference was not due to any single factor "but rather a constellation of biological, psychological, and social factors, amounting to what may be described as *elite status*," Pfeiffer wrote.

The marks of this elite status were as follows:

MEN

1. Financial status—70 percent of the long-lived men described their circumstances as comfortable, 80 percent of the short-lived men rated themselves as poor.
2. Self-perception of health as they aged—75 percent of the long-lived men said that their health was the same as or better than it was at 55, 80 percent of the short-lived said their health was worse.
3. Physical function (self-rated)—63 percent of the long-lived men described themselves as having no disorders or at worst mild disability, 60 percent of the short-lived fell into a range from 20 percent disability to total disability.
4. Improvement in financial status—70 percent of the long-lived men said that their income was the same as or better than when they were 55, 60 percent of the short-lived said they were worse off.
5. Marital status—95 percent of the long-lived men were married, compared to 75 percent of the short-lived.

WOMEN

1. I.Q.—the long-lived women scored about 50 percent higher on intelligence tests than did the short-lived.
2. Self-perception of health as they aged—47 percent of the

long-lived women rated their health better than when they were 55, while 53 percent of the short-lived saw their health as worse.

3. Marital status—71 percent of the long-lived women were married, 71 percent of the short-lived were not.

4. Physical functioning rating—many more of the long-lived women described themselves as healthy or only mildly disabled; many more of the short-lived described themselves as partly or completely disabled.

5. Change in financial status—many more of the long-lived women were financially better off than they were at age 55; many more of the short-lived had grown poorer.

The notion of an aging elite supports the idea that biology can be influenced by outside factors. Coming from a disadvantaged background doesn't automatically disqualify someone from bettering him- or herself, and insofar as a person achieves a stable income, good health, and a satisfying marriage, he is adding to his chances of longer life. But can longevity, in and of itself, be set as a conscious goal? Although most of us try to attain the best life we can, we do not always equate that goal with long life. Longevity has been a conscious primary goal for only a small number of people throughout history. However, the insights of those few are important to consider.

In the nineteenth century, when only one in ten people lived to be 65, anyone who survived to 90 or 100 qualified as a source of wisdom about longevity. At the turn of the century, an Englishman, Dr. G. M. Humphrey, professor of surgery at Cambridge, examined nine hundred patients who were over 90. He sorted out fifty-two who were thought to be centenarians and made a list of their habits. The majority, he found, were moderate or light eaters, consumed little meat and some alcohol, rose early, and liked to do outdoor work. A large majority, over 80 percent, reported that they were excellent sleepers—most averaged over eight hours a night for most of their lives. (As usual, the women centenarians vastly outnumbered the men, thirty-six to sixteen. Almost all had been married; most had raised large families.)

These characteristics fall into the same patterns as those we see in modern studies; they also gave rise to what we could call the longevity movement, as consciously trying to live a long life became more feasible. The late Victorians were riding a crest of increasing life expectancy. The work of Pasteur and Koch had raised huge optimism about wiping out epidemic disease; social reform was improving housing, sanitation, and working conditions. Instead of assuming that long life was a gift of providence, people began to take responsibility for their existence; they began to believe that their own efforts made a difference. Thus the first seeds of conscious life extension were planted.

Several long-lived doctors in their nineties in the Victorian era wrote books on longevity. All were fierce advocates of a simple diet and abundant exercise. Alexandre Gueniot, a Parisian physician who lived to be 103, disclosed that every morning when he arose to work on his book at age 99, he reached his study by climbing three flights of stairs. His English counterpart, Sir Hermann Weber, a doctor who lived to be 95, was adamant about the role of constant exercise: In his nineties he recommended one to three hours of walking every day and taking vacations that included mountain climbing and hiking.

Other long-lived authorities of the day believed in the virtues of country living, of keeping active in old age, and of maintaining close social ties with family and community. It is also interesting that many of the nonagenarian doctors advised vegetarian diets with small amounts of dairy products; most believed that calorie consumption should be low, around 2,500 a day, which is frugal for an adult who exercises several hours daily. Certain incidental advice crops up that cannot be proven scientifically but still seems valid: Weber and Gueniot both thought highly of massages and deep breathing exercises (we would call them aerobics) to "stimulate the vital organs."

None of this advice has ever been contradicted, and much of it has been reinforced by modern prevention techniques. In the 1930s, writer Maurice Ernest in his book *The Longer Life* examined the biographies of centenarians across many European cultures and back to ancient times. Ernest concluded that understanding just a few physical processes would extend our lives to 100 or 120 years; he gave the following prescriptions:

- Eat frugally
- Exercise and get plenty of fresh air
- Choose a congenial occupation
- Develop a placid or easygoing personality
- Maintain a high level of personal hygiene
- Drink wholesome liquids
- Abstain from stimulants and sedatives
- Get plenty of rest
- Have a bowel movement once a day
- Live in a temperate climate
- Enjoy a reasonable sex life
- Get proper medical attention in case of illness

Of all these factors, frugal eating is the one that has caught the imagination of almost every person who consciously tried to live a long life. For centuries the literature of longevity has been filled with testimony about the virtue of strict dietary abstinence. A fifteenth-century Venetian nobleman named Luigi Cornaro is famed in gerontology because he resolved, after a roaringly dissolute youth, that he would mend his ways, pursue a healthy course of life, and try to survive to at least 100. He succeeded spectacularly. In an age where the average person was fortunate to live to 35, Cornaro lived to 103 and remained active and clear-headed to the end. His method for achieving this feat was to abstain from drinking and to eat very sparingly: In essence, he fasted from age 37 onward, following ancient Greek and Roman notions of frugal diet as the secret of longevity.

Cornaro's prescription gained scientific credence centuries later, at least in animal experiments. In the 1930s Dr. Clive McKay of Cornell University took newly weaned rats and fed them only 60 percent of the calorie intake of a rat with food available all the time. This restricted diet was supplemented with adequate vitamins and minerals. The diet-restricted rats grew very slowly compared to normal rats, but they appeared extremely healthy throughout their

long lives; they could be held in a growth-retarded cycle for a
thousand days, by which time all the rats on unrestricted diets had
died. When the restricted rats were allowed to return to a full diet,
they started growing normally, and they showed interest in sexual
activity, which had been missing before.

To date, McKay's method of "undernutrition"—supplying
complete nutrients on a very-low-calorie diet—is the only proven
way to extend the maximum life span of animals. Follow-up research indicated that the average maximum life span of approximately a thousand days for fully fed rats could be extended to
sixteen hundred days for undernourished rats, an increase of 60
percent. Would the technique work for humans? Perhaps. But the
test cannot be done on newly weaned babies, given the risk of
stunting their growth and the obvious ethical objections. A human
diet restricted to 60 percent of normal calories—roughly fourteen
hundred calories per day for an average adult—is on the borderline
of fasting. It would be intolerable to impose this on children, and
since young adults can't see signs of the aging process yet, they don't
have much incentive to prevent it. Cornaro took up his fast in
middle age, which may be early enough.

Dr. Roy Walford, a noted gerontologist at UCLA and an outspoken advocate of undernutrition, is one of the few scientists actually to take up the method himself. Walford believes that cutting
back on calories is safe and effective long after infancy. To support
this view, he started mice on a restricted diet at the equivalent age
of 30 to 33 in humans and found that they lived 20 percent longer.
Unlike the animals who followed a restricted diet from birth, these
did not outstrip the maximum age of mice. On the other hand, a 20
percent increase in life span represents about fifteen years for humans. The animals displayed excellent health all their lives and aged
with a fraction of the heart disease and tumors of fully fed mice.

Walford did not subject the animals to total fasting every day.
Earlier research had shown that eating a restricted diet only every
other day was highly effective in increasing life span. In addition, the
mice were tapered into their new diet gradually, allowing their
bodies to shift their metabolic set point to accommodate dietary
restrictions without abrupt changes.

Your metabolic set point is a brain mechanism that regulates how fast your body burns fuel. It also indicates when you feel hungry or satisfied. If you try to impose a diet on yourself that disagrees with your metabolic set point, the brain will create cravings for food until more is supplied. By changing the metabolic set point gradually, Walford coaxed it into line with the meager calories called for in undernutrition. He advises the same tapering process for people who adopt his method, taking several months or years to adjust to a 40 percent reduction in caloric intake.

This graduated plan forms the basis of Walford's diet, which he believes will allow anyone to surpass Cornaro and live to age 120 or older. "The idea is to lose weight gradually over the next four to six years," he says, "until you're 10 to 25 percent below your set point. That's the weight you'll drift toward if you neither overeat nor undereat. Usually it's what you weighed between ages 25 and 30." The gradual restriction of calories has to include careful food selection to make sure that all vitamins and minerals are included—undernutrition is not the same as malnutrition. From a physician's viewpoint, Walford's diet would lead to almost certain improvements in health, particularly in the areas of cancer and cardiovascular disease.

Instead of eating anything like the 37 percent fat that the average American consumes daily, or even the 30 percent advised by prevention experts, Walford's regime cuts fat to a marginal 11 percent—approximately the fat in one tablespoon of vegetable oil, plus traces in grains, vegetables, and fruits. Although this intake is so minimal that only the most intensely motivated person could realistically expect to live on it, 11 percent fat is normally not dangerous over the short term. The widely publicized program for reversing heart disease devised by cardiologist Dean Ornish contains only this much fat, as does the Pritikin Plan and the Duke University "rice diet" that preceded it.

Another advantage of dietary restriction is its elimination of useless calories and processed foods. On a regimen of twelve hundred to fifteen hundred calories a day, there is no room for cakes, cookies, ice cream, hamburgers, and french fries. Sugar and fat have to be excised to make room for an abundance of whole foods. This is desirable even if longevity doesn't result from Walford's plan. Some gerontologists point out that the animals who are of real interest are not the diet-restricted ones but those that were allowed to eat all they wanted. Dr. Leonard Hayflick, one of the country's leading research gerontologists, says that the argument should be reversed: "The restricted mice are merely being allowed to reach the limit of their life span. It's overfeeding that kills the control group."

This contention makes a good deal of sense when applied to humans; the rampant degenerative disease that afflicts our society in old age indicates that we are being held back from the long, healthy life spans that a few achieve—approximately 15 percent of people over 65 have no major degenerative disorder such as heart disease, cancer, diabetes, arthritis, or osteoporosis.

No one has yet discovered why calorie restriction extends life span in animals. Walford speculates that it postpones a breakdown in the immune system. Presently a huge government facility in Arkansas has been turned over to undernourishing thirty thousand rats, with similar extensive trials being run on monkeys. In the near future, announcements of the results, which have been favorable so far, will no doubt be widely aired.

It seems unlikely that many people will ever undertake severe calorie restriction as a longevity program, given its rigors, but my cultural background predisposes me to favor the principle of occasional fasting. In India there is a tradition, centuries old, that longevity can result from taking little or no food one day a week (in the form of fruit juice, warm water with honey, or low-fat milk). The principle at work is simple: The digestive system is allowed to take a rest, to recover its balance and flush out accumulated impurities. Modern physiology has not accepted these principles, yet every spiritual tradition boasts long-lived people who adhered to them. The success of frugal eating, I believe, is that it must be blended with a lifestyle in which fasting is neither a punishment nor a discipline but a respite from daily activity. The time one would ordinarily devote to eating would be spent quietly, alone. Fasting would then allow the body to participate in a feeling of peaceful non-doing.

It seems to me that centenarians tend to be far ahead of gerontologists in what they know about living. There's something woefully lacking in any fragmentary approach to life, however intriguing any single fragment happens to be. Dietary restriction doesn't address the rich psychology of humans, and what we know about longevity so far indicates that this factor is extremely important. I recently read an interview with an inspiring 100-year-old woman named Edna Olson. She is very devout; all her life she has sung and prayed and written poetry expressing her faith. When asked about her life, she said, "I was only about 2 years old when God spoke to me. He told me he was God and He wanted me to believe in Him, and He said, 'I will take care of you.'

"And He has. He said, 'Don't tell your mother yet. She'll just say you're a silly child and you don't know what you're talking about. I will send you dreams.' And God did send me dreams in the morning—before I woke up—and they would always be true dreams. They would tell me what I should do. That's how I've lived my whole life."

A woman nourished by visions, or thirty thousand rats on short rations—I know the juxtaposition seems strange, but I cannot conceive of survival without vision. Even if I don't wake up to dreams from God, every new day has to mean something to me, and if it does, I believe the battle is won. However, this emphasis on personal qualities of heart and mind is at odds with current gerontology. The cutting edge of the field lies in biotechnology, and the most exciting breakthroughs, reported with extravagant hopefulness by the media, have to do with youth hormones and genetic engineering. Are these the true hope? There is an appealing simplicity to the idea that youth is only a matter of injecting the right chemical or manipulating a wayward gene. In many people's minds (including those of many gerontologists) the science of longevity ultimately boils down to finding a magic bullet, a substance that will chemically alter our cells' propensity to age. We therefore need to evaluate this perspective and ask why the kind of longevity that seems to be achievable in test tubes is so far removed from the kind achieved by real-life centenarians.

LONGEVITY UNLIMITED?

The Future of an Unlikely Survivor

It makes sense that the strongest creatures should live the longest, but if that were the case, the naked ape would be a poor candidate for longevity. As infants, we emerge from the womb in a state of utter helplessness, unlike Arctic caribou, for example, whose off-spring drop onto the tundra straight from the womb, immediately gain their wobbly bearings, and within a few hours are contentedly walking along with the herd. As we know, human newborns cannot even sit up or roll over.

The things we can do straight from the womb—suck, swallow, salivate, hiccup, blink, yawn, sneeze, cough, stretch, cry, and sleep—aren't very useful for survival, except for the first two, sucking and swallowing, which enable us to eat. (A baby also exhibits certain reflexes that must have helped our remote ancestors to survive: A newborn human has a grip so strong that it can support its own weight if lifted, perhaps an echo of infant monkeys clinging to their mother's fur; this ghost from the genetic past fades away after about two months, however.)

Most creatures have evolved some way to protect their DNA from the elements, either with a shell, feathers, fur, or scales. But human skin is bare and so thin that it is easily punctured. Our DNA is vulnerable to wind, rain, cold, and heat; even remaining in the sun for a few hours makes us susceptible to cancer. After years of maturing—far longer than any other mammal requires—humans still cannot run fast enough to escape lions and tigers, and if we choose to stand and fight, our teeth, fingernails, and fists provide hopelessly inadequate defenses.

So it makes little sense that man lives longer than any other warm-blooded creature, upward of 115 to 120 years. At least one man in current times, a Japanese offshore islander named Shige-chiyo Isumi, reached the limit of this range. Born two months after Lincoln was assassinated in 1865, Isumi died 120 years, 237 days later, in 1986. Isumi-san was reported by his doctor to be healthy and alert until just a few months before his death. In his eleventh decade he still took a daily walk and drank the local rice beer. In *The Guinness Book of World Records* there is a beguiling picture of Isumi, looking like an Oriental sprite with his long, snowy beard, surrounded by a dozen children born in his village since his 110th birthday.

Other people without reliable birth certificates may have lived as long as or longer than Isumi. Arthur Reed, an American, was thought to be 124 when he died in 1984, which means that he was born the year Lincoln was first elected. Presently the oldest person alive is said to be a Frenchwoman, Jeanne Louise Calment, age 117. Since governments and health authorities are haphazard at best about keeping up with long-lived individuals, the most notable are generally reported for publicity value to *The Guinness Book of World Records,* which recently listed three women, a 112-year-old from Wales and two 115-year-olds from the United States, as the oldest in the world. (The fact that all these potential record holders are women is in keeping with an advantage women hold over men throughout life; among centenarians, women outnumber men two to one.)

Most longevity charts list the giant tortoise, which is cold-blooded, as the longest-lived creature, with a life span of at least 150 years. A specimen that old was recorded living in an old fort on the island of Mauritius in the Indian Ocean. This particular tortoise was an adult when captured, and it did not die of old age but by accident when it fell through a rotted cannon emplacement. Technically speaking, a coral colony can be considered a single, extremely long-lived organism; even though individual polyps do not survive for long, the entire colony goes on for thousands and perhaps tens of thousands of years.

Among mammals, our closest competitors for longevity are the great whales, who may live to be 100 or more—one blue whale was observed to return to its seasonal feeding grounds off Australia for nearly a century. Elephants can survive under the best conditions to about 70, but among small mammals, life spans shrink drastically, so that mice, shrews, and rats reach only 1 to 3 years of age under optimum conditions. Domestic dogs and cats can survive to 20 and 30 years respectively.

Biologists use two measures for how long any animal can live. There is *maximum* life span (the outer limit of longevity for a species) and *average* life expectancy (how long the members of a species normally live in the wild). There is often a huge divergence between these two numbers. Nature is extravagant with birth and equally extravagant with death, allowing many more creatures to be born than ever survive to breeding age. At least half of the small animal and bird population, regardless of species, dies every year. Creatures as diverse as the praying mantis and the brilliant tropical fish in the Great Barrier Reef will spawn hundreds or thousands of young for every one that survives. A humpback whale may theoretically have a maximum life span of over seventy years, but in today's polluted seas, newborn humpbacks seem to have an average life expectancy of only two or three years. This shocking shortening of life is tragic, because if not enough baby whales mature to breeding age, the species will dwindle into extinction.

Even without man's destructive interference, living to old age is one of Nature's great improbabilities. The only feasible way to measure an animal's maximum life span (and this is only approximate) is to observe it in a zoo, which serves as a sort of longevity museum. Animals in zoos are kept well fed and free from predation until they die of old age. Thus we have learned how peculiar longevity can be. Generally, the smaller an animal is, the shorter it lives, which is why elephants live thirty-five times longer than do shrews. Having stated this fact, we immediately run into complications. Some small animals, particularly if they are cold-blooded, survive a very long time: Fresh-water mussels and sea anemones can live a century.

Despite their high heart rate and fast metabolism, birds do not wear themselves out quickly: Eagles, condors, owls, and parrots can live past age fifty and up to seventy. Something about the flying life gives them durability, for even bats live three to four times longer than do mice of their size. Man himself is much smaller than an elephant but lives longer. All these anomalies indicate that there are few fixed rules about how Nature determines life span.

Humans have the capacity to think about being immortal, but the closest DNA has come is in primitive organisms—algae, plankton, amoebas, and microbes, to name but a few—whose existence is too simple to allow for aging. Any amoeba floating in a roadside ditch today sprang from the first amoeba that ever appeared; rather than aging and dying, the ancestral amoeba prolonged its existence indefinitely by dividing into carbon copies of itself, time after time. Immortality was the first survival strategy DNA learned, hundreds of millions of years before complex plants and animals appeared—bringing the complex syndromes of aging with them. A coral reef never gets cancer; streptococci are immune to Alzheimer's.

Fifty years ago, it still seemed possible that human cells were potentially immortal, that they could divide indefinitely if given a chance. The most convincing support came from a famous experiment begun at the Rockefeller Institute in 1912. Dr. Alexis Carrel, an eminent French surgeon and Nobel laureate, took a sample of fibroblasts (cells found in connective tissue such as cartilage) from chicken embryo hearts and began to raise them in a nutrient solution. The cells thrived, divided, and then divided again. The fibroblasts divided so enthusiastically that they eventually filled the flasks to overflowing, at which point Carrel poured off the excess and topped the nutrient solution with fresh broth. Under this regimen, the cells multiplied unchecked for thirty-four years, finally coming to a halt only when the project was abandoned two years after Carrel's death. Carrel had a flair for theatricality, and as the fame of these chicken cells spread, he invested them with supernatural qualities. "The tending of the cells was very like a religious rite," Albert Rosenfeld recounts. "In fact, everything that went on in Carrel's lab took on a ceremonial air as his celebrity grew. He even made his technicians carry out their solemn high duties in flowing black robes with hoods."

Carrel died believing that he had solved a crucial part of the aging puzzle: Cells could live forever provided they were given the right environment. Unfortunately, Carrel was discovered to have made a serious mistake in technique. When he added new batches of nutrient medium, which was also derived from chickens, he was accidentally introducing new embryo cells at the same time. It was these cells that kept on dividing after the previous generation of fibroblasts died.

The final hope that human cells were immortal was dashed by acccident in the late 1950s when Leonard Hayflick, a young Philadelphia researcher, could not get a batch of human embryonic cells to multiply past a certain limit. No matter how carefully he cultured them, the cells died after about fifty divisions. However, Hayflick's failed experiment turned into a breakthrough, as he realized that he had discovered the outer limit of cell longevity. What came to be known as "the Hayflick limit" was born. Besides overturning Carrel's results, Hayflick also observed that as they approach their fiftieth division, cells divide more slowly and begin to look older, accumulating yellowish waste products.

Other experiments revealed that the Hayflick limit was apparently part of DNA's programmed memory, for cells raised in vitro (i.e., in test tubes under laboratory conditions) seem to remember how close to their limit they are. If cell cultures are frozen after making twenty divisions, for example, they will reproduce thirty more times after being thawed out, and then they will die. This implies that a fixed timetable is being followed. The Hayflick limit therefore strongly endorses the idea that aging is controlled by a biological clock. Now a senior spokesman for aging-clock theories, Hayflick believes that humans have a fixed maximum life span, using the simple logic that if our cells have a fixed limit on their life, we cannot exceed it.

In support of this theory, when cells extracted from old people are raised in the laboratory, they die after many fewer divisions than do younger cells, implying that they were already close to the Hayflick limit; giving them a new environment with perfectly controlled nutrients does not extend their life. Likewise, skin from old mice, when grafted onto younger mice, continues to age and die according to the donor's life cycle.

The Hayflick limit is apparently not the same for all cells, however. Roy Walford of UCLA conducted later experiments showing that white blood cells may reach a limit of only fifteen to twenty divisions, and lower limits have been seen in cells from short-lived animals such as mice and rats. In order to overcome the Hayflick limit, researchers have had to resort to artificial conditions unknown in Nature. Bone marrow can be taken from old mice and implanted inside young ones, then as they age, the marrow can be extracted and transplanted again. In this way, marrow cells have survived four or five generations of host mice, far beyond the Hayflick limit. Challengers have pointed out that raising cells under glass is still not a perfected art; they surmise that when better conditions are developed for tissue culture, cells might divide more than fifty times.

DNA and Destiny

How does the Hayflick limit affect our chances for living past a certain age? Even though the Hayflick limit is often considered the most significant experimental finding in research on aging, its relevance to real life is unknown. In the laboratory, every generation of cells is the offspring of a limited number of mother cells. On the other hand, babies are not born with a full complement of cells; new ones are produced throughout life. Your bone marrow, for example, generates immature blood cells that grow up to become mature ones. At various stages of early development, and sometimes throughout life, every organ contains a mixture of primitive, partly mature, and mature cells. Mature ones are those that have differentiated, choosing to become a heart cell as opposed to a stomach cell, a brain cell as opposed to a kidney cell.

The same DNA exists inside every cell, but through differentiation, it expresses certain characteristics and represses others. Some theorists would get past the Hayflick limit by proposing that a cell doesn't begin its career of fifty divisions until it has become differentiated. At various stages of our lives, some primitive cells divide and become mature while others remain primitive. Thus the body is equipped with backup resources. Even if every cell has to obey the Hayflick limit, they don't have to obey it together. Whether this escape clause will ever be accepted depends on understanding how cells choose to differentiate in the first place, and geneticists are still far from knowing that.

One whole class of cells—cancer cells—is devoid of growth limit. Freed from genetic restraint, cancer cells divide wildly until the host body dies; if raised in vitro, even this limit is removed. Most malignant cells cultured in laboratories around the world are descendants of tissue taken from a few individuals, now long deceased.

One undisputed victory for Hayflick is that he took aging to the cellular level. His method of "aging under glass," as he once dubbed it, is accepted as the norm by biologists. Hayflick declared that "the primary cause of age changes can no longer be thought of as resulting from events occurring at the supercellular level, i.e., at cell hierarchies from the tissue level and greater. The cell is where the gerontological action lies." According to this logic, looking at how organisms live is much less important than looking at how their cells live.

This logic dominates today's biology of aging, but it strikes me as pure reductionism. The logic I have followed throughout this book is that the whole is far more important than the parts; a person's life determines the activity of his cells, not vice versa. And yet these aren't irreconcilable approaches, for no one can outlive his cells—that much is certain. Biologists such as Hayflick tend to regard DNA as all-powerful and far removed from daily life—a kind of biochemical Jove whose dictates cannot be overruled. "It is as if DNA *used* us to keep *itself* going," Albert Rosenfeld mourned. Yet this is only one point of view. If you look at life through the eyes of a geneticist, it means nothing that a very old person has a strong will to live or enjoys the simple pleasures of life. And indeed such facts may be insignificant in terms of DNA's original programming, but as the outcome of a life well spent, it is enormously significant—indeed, it is the *most* significant thing.

Outside the biologist's test tubes and flasks, DNA gets influenced by your every thought, feeling, and action. The stress hormones that play such a critical part in aging are regulated by

RNA, which is a copy of DNA; even though the DNA itself may sit quietly in its vault, its active twin is constantly changing its instructions. When you make a lifestyle change that reduces stress, the RNA in your cells responds by churning out fewer stress hormones.

The Hayflick limit renders the whole aging process meaningless; it becomes a mechanism to be tinkered with in a laboratory dish, devoid of breath, motion, warmth, experience, memory, love, hope, courage, sacrifice, will, curiosity, and everything else that makes life worth living. Unfortunately, manipulating cells is still the dominant activity in gerontology and attracts the most excitement. In 1990 the media announced that researchers from the University of Wisconsin had injected synthetic human growth hormone into a small group of elderly men between the ages of 61 and 81. The result was sudden rejuvenation that reversed biological aging by as much as twenty years. Over the course of the six-month trial, muscle mass and strength steadily returned; fat melted away without dieting; memory and other brain functions improved; vigor and stamina were renewed.

This artificially regained youth was greeted with tremendous public excitement. Popular accounts breathlessly compared it to the fantasy rejuvenation in the hit movie *Cocoon*. The subjects themselves were deeply affected. "I started feeling the changes after three months. I felt much stronger—I mean, I never felt stronger in my life," recalled one retired Waukegan factory worker. The experiment involved only men whose natural levels of growth hormone were extremely depleted. Most old people have adequate, if reduced, levels of growth hormone; those who do not have sufficient growth hormone age faster and more severely than normal. When these subjects began the experiment they were exhibiting excessive biological aging; therefore, restoring their hormone levels made a dramatic difference. For the first time in years, many of them could travel, take long walks, or work in their gardens.

But the improvement was not permanent. After the extremely expensive treatments (around $14,000 a year) were withdrawn, the ravages of age gradually returned. Muscles shriveled again, fat reappeared, strength waned, and the men were left with no lasting benefits except perhaps a trace of improved memory. "It was wonderful while it lasted. Maybe someday I can try it again," one man said wistfully. Told that the next experiment would be expanded to include women, he said approvingly, "I think they should have a chance to feel like we did."

These words, quoted from a glowing newspaper account, trouble me. One cannot assume that injecting growth hormone does not have long-term side effects. This may not prove true for older people with abnormally low levels of naturally occurring growth hormone, but for normal people, extra growth hormone is useless for rejuvenation purposes.

Interfering at a gross level with the body's function does not really affect the source of the problem. Giving a drug, even one the body produces itself, can effectively push the physiology one way or another, but the body remembers what it wants to do, and until that memory is changed, there will always be imbalance. Anyone who has dealt with diabetes knows the many metabolic imbalances that insulin-dependent diabetics suffer from, and the careful juggling of dosages necessary to avert insulin shock and coma. The replacement hormone is the right molecule, but what is missing is the innate intelligence to use that molecule. Diabetes, hypothyroidism, and aging itself are due to lost intelligence, not depleted molecules.

Inevitably, any "miracle" of rejuvenation achieved with chemicals will disrupt the body's intelligence. When human growth hormone was given to stunted children, the experimenters ran into serious side effects and several fatalities. The argument that aging is caused by abnormal hormone production is convincing to me, but hormones function to carry messages, and messages ultimately are controlled in awareness. By increasing your inner intelligence, by enhancing your happiness and fulfillment, you can defeat aging in a lasting, meaningful way, without chemicals and their potential side effects. The responsibility for changing this awareness lies with each individual.

The "Aging Gene"

In addition to hormone treatments, much hope for defeating aging is being pinned on genetic engineering. Forty years ago, after Watson and Crick decoded the chemical structure of DNA, the hunt for an aging gene became inevitable. By finding this gene, scientists could possess the control switch for immortal cells, even if Nature had failed at the task. In several American universities, researchers have been announcing breakthroughs in locating genes that control aging in yeast, fruit flies, and finally humans.

Michael West, a molecular biologist at the University of Texas in Dallas, working with tissue-cultured human cells, isolated two "mortality genes" whose effect is to speed the aging process in these cells. Labeled M-1 and M-2, the two genes can be chemically switched on or off, driving the aging process backward or forward at will. In normal aging both M-1 and M-2 appear to be switched on. By turning off the M-1 gene, West is able to restore a cell's youth and double its overall life span, measured by how many times it divides. Apparently West has discovered how to override the Hayflick limit at will.

The results are even more dramatic when the second mortality gene, M-2, is switched off. The cells continue to divide indefinitely and remain youthful forever. Turning M-1 back on again, West found, caused the cells to resume normal aging. This may be the one and only aging gene, although other contenders are offered by competing researchers. By general consensus, aging seems to be polygenic, involving the cooperation of several or perhaps many genes at once. Also, finding these switches doesn't mean that one has found out what operates them. There may be unknown brain mechanisms that control the genetic switches, and these mechanisms would almost certainly vary according to each individual's life and experience.

The fact that the body can record the passage of time is beyond dispute. Proponents of a biological aging clock have tracked the body's internal biorhythms to a tiny cluster of neurons in the hypothalamus known as the superchiasmatic nucleus. No larger than the end of a pencil, this clump of tissue regulates the body's sense of time. But finding the body's biological clock didn't solve the mystery of aging, because the hypothalamus is connected to the rest of the brain, the endocrine system, and the immune system. Any or all of these could be involved, for they all possess formidable intelligence of their own.

Our bodies are intelligent everywhere. Brain chemicals aren't secreted just from our heads; our skin, stomachs, intestines, and hearts produce them. White blood cells floating through the immune system are outfitted with the same receptors for neurotransmitters—they form a kind of "floating brain." The skin secretes more endocrine hormones than does the endocrine system itself. M-1 and M-2 are fascinating fragments in this vast intelligence network. Michael West has formed a company to see if a drug can be found to manipulate these genes. But just as using interferon to fight cancer was found to cause horrendous side effects, massive expense, and poor results, West's efforts have far to go before achieving any benefit for cells outside glass dishes. Genetic engineering to date involves highly risky procedures such as bone marrow transplants, which are drastic operations. Presently, the most advanced organisms to have their life extended by genetic manipulation are fruit flies, yeasts, and roundworms. I think the application of this technology to humans is unlikely.

Yet optimism pervades this branch of gerontology and trickles down into the popular press. "If we develop ways to repair aging tissues with embryonic cells, we could add thirty years of healthy human life in the next decade," said a professor of medicine in Virginia, echoed by a colleague in Texas: "Possibly in thirty years we will have in hand the major genes that determine longevity, and will be in a position to double, triple, even quadruple our maximum life span. . . . It's possible that some people alive now will still be alive four hundred years from now."

A more restrained researcher in Louisiana said, "We may find it possible to extend life span considerably more, perhaps by 100 percent—which would give us an extra 100 to 120 years." Other gerontologists shy away from specific numbers but lack nothing in enthusiasm. "I think we may well be able to lengthen human life far beyond anything we ever dreamed possible," said a researcher in Colorado whose work has been successful with a nematode, a transparent roundworm the size of a comma.

Something disturbing lies beneath the surface of the wild predictions made by geneticists with regard to aging. Americans like to imagine that technical ingenuity will solve any problem. Like IBM engineers tweaking computers to make them faster and more efficient, gerontologists aim to improve the human machine. The theory is that given a little biochemical retooling, our bodies can be made more efficient, less prone to breakdowns, and slower to wear out. If any field was dedicated to the proposition that the body is mindless and inherently defective, genetics is it.

Like other reductionist models, the genetic view of aging ignores life as a whole. Unlike the Pacific salmon, humans are not the pawns of biological destiny. Populations exist right now that have largely overcome high blood pressure, artery disease, and childhood infections, with low rates of major cancers, and so on. The problem is that no single culture combines all of these favorable traits. As we try to reach a longevity that satisfies the desires of the whole person, we will find that DNA can change to suit our higher expectations. Adapting to new conditions is what the body's intelligence is all about. If you were a research biologist in the Stone Age, and you had a perfect map of human DNA, could you have used it to predict the rise of civilization? Would you have foreseen Mozart, Einstein, the Parthenon, the New Testament? Could you have known that by the year 2000, improved living conditions would add six decades to early man's life expectancy?

The wonder of DNA is not that it runs my life but that it can unfold previously unknown possibilities as they arise in my heart and mind. In other words, DNA serves my purposes, not the other way around. There are societies where longevity is highly valued, and it is there, in real-life settings, that we have found our best laboratory. Instead of relying on isolated individuals who achieve extreme longevity, we can examine a whole population who were instilled with that ambition from childhood on. The results have been remarkable, despite the absence of scientific involvement.

Secrets of the "Long-Living"

Abkhasia, a remote mountain region of southern Russia, is a land of almost mythical old age. It is the only place I have ever heard of where there is a separate word for great-great-great-grandparents, which is applied only to the living. The legendary longevity of the region excited world attention in the late 1960s when Western visitors were invited to meet the "supercentenarians" of Russia. These were rural villagers, almost all of them illiterate field workers, who were reputed to have reached incredible ages of 120, 130, and upward of 170.

Outside the Soviet Union, such claims hardly seemed credible. It was widely accepted by gerontologists that the upper limit of human life span was between 115 and 120. Even that was a theoretical limit, since at that time no one with a reliable birth certificate had ever lived beyond 113. But in Russia the oldest of the supercentenarians, a man named Shirali Mislimov, was reputed to have been born in 1805, seven years before Napoleon marched on Moscow. Mislimov lived in a remote village in the state of Azerbaijan west of the Caspian Sea, where he died in 1973 at the incredible age of 168. Toward the end, he had been secluded from visitors due to ill health. If they could not visit the oldest man who had ever lived, Westerners could interview the oldest woman of all time.

She was Khfaf Lazuria, a native of Abkhasia who claimed to be approximately 140. With a mixture of fascination and skepticism, foreign visitors, including doctors and news correspondents, began to trickle in. From the first moment, Abkhasia was an enchanting place to anyone who came there from the crowded, polluted cities of the United States and Europe. The countryside was green and idyllic. Most Abkhasians lived at altitudes between seven hundred and a thousand feet above sea level, in neat two-story homes, often built out of walnut, with wide verandas and airy rooms.

The climate in the hills just inland from the Black Sea was temperate year-round, somewhat on the brisk side at a mean temperature of 50 to 55 degrees. But the rugged Abkhasians relished this slightly chilled air, claiming that it contributed to their long life. Except for the kitchen stove, their houses generally had no heat.

Although the region had suffered from malaria and typhus epidemics until the lowland swamps were drained by Soviet engineers in the 1930s, Abkhasia boasted five times more centenarians than any other part of the world, and 80 percent of the "long-living"— the word *old* was never applied to them—were active and vigorous. It was common for both men and women to work in the local tea fields for decades past the official Soviet retirement age of 60— champion tea pickers were given certificates when they reached 100.

When one party of curious American journalists showed up at his gate, Vanacha Temur, age 110, stepped smartly out of his garden to greet them. Vanacha—he was always called by his first name— spotted a baby among the visitors and, smiling with delight, insisted that a cow be milked to provide refreshment. He offered the adults baskets of apples from his best trees and passed around tumblers of the local applejack. Before he consented to talk about himself, he spoke with simple conviction about the need for world peace and harmony between America and the (former) Soviet Union. Needless to say, his visitors were completely charmed.

Rare among the long-living Abkhasians, Vanacha possessed a certificate of his baptism, a rarity in that region where record keeping is minimal at best. According to the date on his document, Vanacha was 106, but he explained that his parents had waited four years to baptize him because they were too poor to pay the priest. "Vanacha's vigor, even at 106, was incredible," one of the visitors wrote. "A man of about five feet with twinkling blue eyes and an elegant white mustache, he was the personification of a kindly and playful grandfather. He credited his slim, wiry body to light eating, horseback riding, farming, and walking in the mountains."

Although Vanacha Temur was considered one of the healthiest

of the long-living (an American doctor measured his blood pressure at a youthful 120/84), he was not atypical. In a careful survey of all Abkhasians over age 90, 85 percent were judged to be mentally healthy and outgoing, only 10 percent had poor hearing, and 4 percent had poor eyesight. Both men and women in the culture shared a passion for racing horses, and it was a point of pride for centenarians to appear on horseback in village parades.

In America the concept of remaining extremely active into old age was just beginning to gain medical credence, but for centuries in Abkhasia sedentary retirement was unknown except in cases of disability. Typically, older workers shortened their hours in the fields as they approached 80 and 90; instead of laboring for ten to fifteen hours, they might quit after three to five hours. Yet, this toil was not forced on them. Love of hard work was deeply ingrained among the Abkhasians, and records showed that a woman of 109 was paid for forty-nine full workdays in the tea fields one summer.

The entire Caucasus mountain range had been famed for centuries as a "longevity belt." Bordered by the Black Sea on the west and the Caspian Sea on the east, three separate Russian states laid claim to supercentenarians: Georgia (which contains the state of Abkhasia), Azerbaijan, and Armenia. A mixture of races lives throughout this whole area, which is only sparsely industrialized; the religion shifts from Moslem to Christian depending on where you go, and the climate varies widely from high alpine (the Caucasus is the tallest range in Europe, cresting at eighteen thousand feet) to subtropical. These details were important to gerontologists, because with such a wide diversity of culture, race, and climate, there was no isolated gene pool to account for the longevity of the region, nor was there one favored geographical locale—a Shangri-la in Russia—responsible.

In the late 1960s and early 1970s, the heart-attack epidemic following World War II reached its peak, and cancer rates had not significantly changed since the 1930s (the same holds true today, after another three decades of lavishly funded research). The long-living had avoided both scourges to a remarkable degree, and much of the credit for this, besides frequent exercise, went to diet. Favored with rich land and a climate suitable for corn, tomatoes, and all manner of truck produce, the population subsisted on home-grown vegetables and dairy products, with small amounts of nuts, grains, and meat to round out the fare. (Yogurt, a staple in their diet, has long had a reputation as a longevity food; to capitalize on this, one American yogurt company ran a series of delightful ads showing an 89-year-old Abkhasian sampling their product while his cheek is being pinched by his 117-year-old mother.)

Despite the fact that most of the long-living consumed cheese, milk, and yogurt every day, total intake of fat and calories was unusually low by Western standards, between fifteen hundred and two thousand calories a day. In order to eat that frugally, many Americans would have to *cut* fifteen hundred to two thousand calories from their diets! Daily fat intake for Abkhasians was sixty grams, exactly half of the U.S. average. Although they liked to drink the local applejack, only a few supercentenarians smoked, and this rarely included women, who traditionally shunned this practice as a prerogative of male life. Almost all were married and had been since their twenties. Since the region had few paved roads, it was customary for people to walk distances up to twenty miles a day.

One of the first Americans to penetrate this amazingly healthy culture was Dr. Alexander Leaf, an enlightened Harvard Medical School professor who was an early champion of prevention. To bolster his belief that exercise and diet were the cornerstones of lifelong good health, Leaf made a pilgrimage to all the places in the world where legendary longevity was to be found. Abkhasia excited him enormously; there Leaf witnessed firsthand people surviving in good health to unheard-of old age.

On his visit to Abkhasia in 1972, Leaf struggled to keep up with Gabriel Chapnian, a short, sprightly elder who easily climbed a steep hill to reach his garden at the age of 117. At 104, Markhti Tarkhil still rose at dawn and plunged into an icy stream for his morning bath. Leaf wrote, "Markhti attributes his long life to God, to the mountains, and to a good diet—and he warns against eating without pepper! His 'best' age was 18, but he agrees with Vanacha that he regarded himself as a young man until the age of 60. 'I still feel young, I sleep well, ride my horse, eat well, and swim every day, so I still feel like a youngster, even though not so strong as I once was.' "

As we in the West age, our bodies lose muscle mass and replace it with fat—at 65, almost half the body weight of both men and women is fat, double what it was in their twenties. By comparison, nearly all the long-living Abkhasians had lean physiques, with erect spines and firm muscles. Long after retirement, the oldest people thrived on outdoor life—they tramped up to the high grazing areas in summer and dug potatoes in their gardens. Even in cases where coronary arteries were blocked or other damage had occurred to the heart muscle, the walking and climbing in which everyone engaged seemed to offset physical limitation.

When Leaf brought back photographs of the long-living for *National Geographic* in 1972, millions of readers saw a face of old age that had never been seen before in this country and scarcely imagined. Twenty years later, we are facing a huge increase in all age groups over 65, and the long-living Abkhasians are more and more fascinating to us. In their culture the "new" old age has existed for generations. They traditionally led lives in which all the right ingredients came together for conscious, purposeful longevity—not just a longevity of survivors but of "youth in old age," the title Leaf chose for his book.

Abkhasians managed to redefine youth so that it was not opposed to long survival. Someone could be chronologically old and yet young by their standards. Jotting down his impression of one 98-year-old named Tikhed Gunba, Leaf wrote, "Tikhed's blood pressure was 104/72 and his pulse was regular at 84 [beats per minute]. He seemed a very placid individual with much 'mileage' left. In the presence of two centenarians, Tikhed was still regarded as a youngster."

The Supercentenarian "Hoax"

Why, given this idyllic situation, haven't we all heard of Abkhasia? The reason is that confusion and mistrust quickly clouded the initial reports brought back by Westerners. What made Abkhasia so interesting in the mid-1970s was not lifestyle but the phenomenon of supercentenarianism. The then-Soviet government wanted to reap a harvest of propaganda by claiming that their oldest people survived beyond anything known in the noncommunist world. Tremendous focus was placed on individuals such as Khfaf Lazuria, the most celebrated of the long-living.

Khfaf Lazuria was reported to be the oldest woman who had ever lived. She died in 1975, claiming to be 140, which meant that she had been born in 1835 during the reign of Czar Nicholas I, at the same time as Andrew Jackson was president of the United States. While alive, Khfaf Lazuria was a tiny wisp of a woman at four feet two inches. Although frail, she moved nimbly, was always eager to meet visitors, could thread a needle without glasses, and was a lively storyteller.

Rare for a woman in Abkhasia, she liked to smoke cigarettes, a habit she had picked up, she said, at age 100. (Since she was too old to be taken for a woman, she liked to joke, she might as well act like the men.) Among her colorful stories, Khfaf recounted her early memories of "the big war in the North," which Leaf guessed must refer to the Crimean War of 1853–56. That was also the period when she was abducted by Turks and not returned home until ten years later, around the year Lincoln was assassinated. Perhaps even more remarkable than Khfaf Lazuria's claim to superlongevity was that her immediate family boasted grandparents, parents, brothers, sisters, and cousins who had lived to be 100. This made them far and away the centenarian family of all time.

Spellbound, Leaf accepted these tales completely, therefore it came as a blow when large inconsistencies began to surface. As it turned out, Khfaf Lazuria had told every visitor a somewhat different story about herself, freely changing her age, the number of husbands she'd had, how long her parents had lived—in fact, few details remained constant. Leaf can be forgiven for not knowing, as no casual visitor could, that one of the cherished customs in Abkhasia was lying to strangers! Western visitors who lingered long enough to acquaint themselves with the area learned that the Abkhasian love of exaggeration was legendary, particularly if tall tales were being spun to an outsider.

When consulted about how old they thought the long-living actually were, local gerontologists who had been sent into the region by the then-Soviet government estimated that some of the long-living were certainly quite old, upward of 115, but no one in the region who claimed to be 120, much less 140 or 168, could supply reliable documents. In fact, since 90 percent of the local churches had been destroyed by the Soviets under Stalin, almost no old records of births, communions, or marriages existed in Abkhasia.

The final blow came when Zhores Medvedev, one of the most respected Soviet geneticists, defected to the West in the early 1970s. Medvedev had traveled throughout the Caucasus and was intimately acquainted with the methods of the gerontologists who worked there. In London he revealed weaknesses in all the claims of superlongevity: Up to 98 percent of Abkhasia old people were illiterate and many did not even know their birthdays. For them, keeping track of time was haphazard, particularly considering that there was an overlap of the Christian and Moslem calendars in that region (the Moslem calendar is based on a ten-month year). Soviet records before 1930 were nonexistent, and suspicions of a deliberate hoax were raised when Medvedev pointed out that Stalin had been born in Georgia. Zealous attempts to convince him that he would live a long life—something that most absolute despots are extremely eager to believe—had added political fuel to the Abkhasians' folkloric pride in reaching extreme old age.

The bubble quickly burst. In the cold light of day, there was really no convincing evidence that families in the Caucasus had produced several generations of centenarians. When the American yogurt company originally conceived their campaign of the mother pinching her son's cheek, they wanted to find a mother and son who were both over 100 (this seemed plausible in a society where women married around 20), but this proved impossible. Nobody could find a family in which parents and offspring were both centenarians. Most investigators concluded that the Georgian supercentenarians were products of a traditional culture in which being as old as possible had always been a cause for great social respect.

Why We Need Abkhasia

Despite the inconsistencies in his findings, Dr. Leaf stood by the principles of age prevention he saw at work in the Caucasus. His work made a significant difference in turning Americans toward more exercise and better diet, particularly in terms of heart-attack prevention, but mounting skepticism forced him to retract his support of superlongevity. Abkhasia shouldn't be dismissed, however; in a world where the vast majority of societies condition their people to expect short lives and condemn the elderly to a marginal existence, this one society fostered a conscious ideal of old age as the most rewarding phase of life—and the reward was open to all who wished to achieve it.

To me, Abkhasia was the place where the traditional concept of "old" never took root. The word was banished, and in its place the long-living pursued an ageless lifestyle—they galloped their horses, worked under the sun, and sang in choirs in which the youngest member was 70 and oldest was 110 (contrary to Soviet propaganda, which boasted that the minimum age was 90). Abkhasia proved that growing older can be a time of *improvement*. Abkhasians toasted one another with the words, "May you live as long as Moses," and they venerated the long-living as people who were achieving an ideal.

By far the greatest advantage the long-living enjoyed was this: They trusted in their way of life. Abkhasians struck Western visitors as remarkably attuned to the rhythms of life, precisely what we have lost in this country. It's worth quoting at length from Dan Georgakis, an American writer who traveled to Abkhasia after the bubble burst and still found much to admire. In his book *The Methuselah Factors* Georgakis wrote, "Abkhasians dislike being rushed, loathe deadlines, and never work to exhaustion. In the same vein, they consider it extremely impolite to eat quickly or to eat too much. . . . Their routines have a tempo more linked to biological rhythms than the helter-skelter patterns that predominate in most developed countries."

One gets the sense of a people who have reached a natural balance. Rather than struggling to break unhealthy habits, their culture had woven good health into their overall view of life. Seventy percent of their food consisted of vegetables and dairy products, and a further unique aspect of the traditional diet was the insistence on freshness.

"Vegetables were picked just before cooking or serving, and if meat was to be part of the menu, guests were shown the animal before it was slaughtered. Whatever the food served, all leftovers were discarded, because they were considered harmful to health. Such concern for freshness guaranteed that a minimal loss of nutrients took place between garden and table. Most food was consumed raw or boiled, with nothing fried."

Light eating and heavy exercise made it easy for Abkhasians to preserve the lean body outlines considered most pleasing in their culture (as in ours), but there was a deeper significance to this than vanity. "The Abkhasians have been among the few people in the world so appreciative of the ill effects of fat that even their children and infants remain slim." The traditional love of horses added another tempo to this integrated way of life that already embraced work and diet. "From the earliest possible ages, even at 2 and 3, children were taught to ride. Horses provided the main sport, and the ability to do equestrian tricks was a mark of individual worth. The horses were never used as work animals, only for recreation and sports."

In every society, expectation rules outcome. In a culture where wealth is the highest goal, the entire society will focus on making money, prestige will accrue to those who make the most, and the poor will be regarded as failures. In Abkhasia, a great value was placed on longevity; therefore the entire society felt motivated to live up to that ideal. In America, the reverse is true; old age is not valued, much less exalted.

This helps account for the flagrant manner in which we waste the last years of life in our society. An extremely pessimistic study from the government's Centers for Disease Control underscores this point. To assess the health of people at the end of their lives, researchers evaluated seventy-five hundred individuals who had died in 1986. Their families were asked if the deceased person could still perform five minimal daily activities in the year before he or she passed away: dressing, walking, eating, going to the toilet, and bathing. On average, only 12 percent of people who died after age 65 could be classified as "fully functional" according to these minimal standards.

At the opposite extreme, 10 percent of the subjects needed assistance to perform three or more of these daily activities in the last six months of life; these people were classified as "severely restricted." The bulk of elderly Americans falls between these two extremes, in a shadow land between self-sufficiency and dependence. It is disturbing enough to realize that only one person in seven can take care of life's simplest needs but the figures get worse the closer you inspect them.

In the youngest age category, from 65 to 74, only one-fifth of the people could be classed as fully functional. About 15 percent showed confusion when asked where they were; 13 percent had trouble remembering what year it was; 10 percent could not reliably recognize family and friends. A higher percentage of people who died from heart attacks remained fully functional than did those who died from cancer. Fully 49 percent of heart-attack victims could perform all five activities the year before they died, compared to only 4 percent of cancer sufferers. Women, besides suffering more years of disability, were hit harder than men: They were 40 percent less likely to be able to take care of themselves in the last year of life than were men and 70 percent more likely to fall into the severely restricted category. Another factor that increased the likelihood of disability was not being married.

Researchers consider this study highly significant because few others have looked as closely at the health status of old people in the critical last year of life. We have to be careful not to extend the findings too far—since the vast majority of the elderly are not in their last year, they are much less likely to be severely restricted. But the CDC figures give us a sobering look at how far the "new" old age still has to go.

Huge differences divide the American and Abkhasian cultures. One would have to go back to 1920 to find a time when the majority of Americans lived in rural areas. A lifetime of light eating and considerable physical activity is something we have to consciously learn again, but to fixate on those ingredients would cause one to miss the spirit of Abkhasia, which to me is far more inspiring as a motivation to survive to 100. I recently received a letter from a concerned woman named Mary Ann Soule, inviting me to a conference on "conscious aging." She ended it with the following eloquent statement:

> If we continue to succumb to modern America's stereo-
> typic vision of aging, fearing the changes in our bodies,
> resisting the natural transitions of life, and avoiding the
> unknown territory of death, we will deny ourselves and the
> whole of civilization the gifts of age: mature perspective,
> seasoned creativity, and spiritual vision.

The truth of this comes through every day when I talk to older patients. One of them, a retired office manager, once ruefully remarked to me, "I always wanted to live a long time, but I never wanted to grow old." He said this ironically; it went without saying that he couldn't have one without the other. But why not? He was quite healthy and active, yet unfortunately he *saw* himself as old, which in America means entering a no-man's-land of lost dignity and uncertain self-worth. After his 1972 visits with the long-living, Alexander Leaf came away "feeling that to live to be 100 was a most natural and simple thing. It took only a brief time back in Boston before the feeling was just another exotic memory."

This country has recently experienced an unparalleled boom in centenarianism. The number of Americans who are 100 or over is currently estimated at 35,800—double what it was ten years ago and expected to double again before the year 2000. This figure comes from the Census Bureau, which accepts people's reported ages without verification. (A detailed investigation of Social Security recipients who reported their age as 100 revealed that 95 percent were exaggerating; this is easy to do, since being 97 or 98 carries much less mystique than being 100.)

Even assuming that a certain number of respondents have inflated their ages to cross the magical century mark, statisticians agree that at least 1 in 10,000 Americans is 100 or older. This is a historic number, and yet it is only an average. Some regions of the country already boast incredibly high ratios of longevity. In Iowa, where life expectancy is the highest in the nation, 1 person out of 3,961 is over 100, followed by South Dakota, with 1 out of 4,168. By contrast, some areas are far below the national average in centenarians: The last two states on the Census Bureau list are Utah, which reports only 1 centenarian per 19,358 people, and Alaska, with 1 in 36,670. By historical standards, however, even these low figures are astonishing. What they imply is that we have won the struggle for longevity and now face the challenge of becoming a land where the long-living are still young.

Senility: The Darkest Fear

Most of us would find it easier to bear the physical afflictions of old age than the mental ones. In India, where I grew up, age is still equated with wisdom. Rural villages are run by the *panchayat*, a council of five elders who have gained respect and authority because of their venerable age. In the West, the longer one lives, the more one is suspected of mental incompetence. Alzheimer's has probably surpassed cancer for the dubious honor of being the most feared disease in America. I know 60-year-olds who obsessively pore over articles about Alzheimer's and panic whenever they forget a friend's telephone number, so convinced are they that contracting Alzheimer's is only a matter of time.

"Put at its crudest," Anthony Smith wrote in *The Body,* "the advances of medicine are enabling more and more of us to achieve senility." That is too dark a view. Only 10 percent of people over 65 exhibit any symptoms of Alzheimer's, but there is no doubt that this figure escalates with increasing age, and after 75, up to 50 percent of the elderly may show some evidence of the disease. One dark legacy from the "old" old age was the belief that senility is a normal, inevitable aspect of aging. Paradoxically, the most important factor in bursting this myth was Alzheimer's itself. The disorder was discovered as early as 1906 by Alois Alzheimer, a prominent investigator and physician in Munich. He dissected the body of a 55-year-old woman who had been mentally deteriorating for three years before her death. In her brain Dr. Alzheimer found visible damage that could not be explained as normal aging: twisted, tangled nerves and hardened deposits of chemical plaque.

No one had ever before linked senility with a specific disease, and by discovering the one named after him, Dr. Alzheimer struck a decisive blow to the theory of "normal" senility. However, social attitudes often last long beyond their time, and it took seventy years for the importance of Alzheimer's discovery to be fully grasped. In recent decades, recognition of Alzheimer's disease has increased dramatically, as it has been realized that the illness afflicts over 1 million Americans, or around 50 to 60 percent of all people who exhibit senile dementia. Dementia is the medical term for a host of symptoms associated with the general term senility: forgetfulness, confusion, disorientation, short attention span, irritability, and decreased intelligence.

Lewis Thomas dubbed Alzheimer's "the disease of the century" and spoke eloquently of it as "the worst of all diseases, not just for what it does to the victim, but for its devastating effects on families and friends. It begins with the loss of learned skills, arithmetic and typing, for instance; it progresses inexorably to a total shutting down of the mind. It is, unmercifully, not lethal. Patients go on and on living, essentially brainless but otherwise healthy, into advanced age, unless lucky enough to be saved by pneumonia."

Alzheimer's patients go in and out of lucidity in the early stages of their ordeal. In his book *The Myth of Senility,* Dr. Siegfried Kra of Yale quotes a colleague's wife, herself a successful physician and children's writer, who was forced to retire due to Alzheimer's in her midfifties. At the outset she still had lucid periods, particularly in the early hours between three and five in the morning; during that time she gave utterance to the dark transformation that was taking place inside her. All she could manage were halting phrases that are all the more poignant given how much she had loved words and how well she had used them:

> I have a neurological problem. Who needs it? No one.
> Nobody likes me. I don't like myself either.
> I used to be a physician, I used to drive a car. What do I
>   want? I don't want to be here.
> I am afraid of everything.
> All I am is garbage. I belong in the garbage can.
> You need a new wife. This one is no good anymore.
> No one knows my name anymore—because I am nothing.
> I've lost everything—the health service, typing, and writing.
>   I don't have any skills. All I do is eat. I have to go away.
>   I can't read my own writing.
> I've lost a kingdom.
> I don't sing anymore. I probably won't sing again.

What is the source of this terrible disease? Much speculation has been offered: a rare "slow virus" that takes decades to mature; a defect in the immune system that causes the victim's own antibodies to attack the brain; increased accumulation of aluminum in the neurons. None of these causes has been proved. Although high levels of aluminum have been found in the brains of Alzheimer's patients, elevated levels of the metal are not found in the patients' bloodstreams.

Some popular books have sounded the alert against using aluminum foil, aluminum cookware, and deodorants based on aluminum salts, but millions of people use these products without acquiring Alzheimer's. Some physiological abnormality is more likely to be at fault; perhaps the blood-brain barrier that normally excludes aluminum from entering the brain has broken down, allowing these deposits to develop. Another reason to suspect that the brain itself has gone awry is that at least one critical neurotransmitter, acetylcholine, is deficient in Alzheimer's patients, impairing the ability of brain cells to communicate with one another.

Alzheimer's is presently incurable. There is no viable prevention, although investigators believe they have found indications of genetic markers for the disease in some families. After the onset of the disease, medical care is limited to tranquilizing or sedating the patient. These efforts do not affect the outcome but help reduce the psychological distress that patients and family so acutely feel. The real hope lies with cases of dementia that are not the result of Alzheimer's, for once the myth of "normal" senility was overcome, it became apparent that more than one hundred different treatable disorders could mimic the symptoms of senile dementia, including thyroid deficiency, strokes, and syphilis.

How the Brain Resists Aging

Aging of the brain is not enough to cause Alzheimer's or any of these other disorders. Over time the structure of the brain is known to change. It grows lighter, for example, and shrinks slightly. One of the clichés of neurology is that the human brain loses roughly a million neurons per year as it ages; this created a convenient rationale for seeing the onset of senility as the result of a decaying brain.

However, the flaw in this explanation is that people who *don't* become senile presumably have lost the same number of neurons (this has to be left to conjecture, since reliable neuron counts can't be made in living people). At present it isn't known why one old brain stays lively and creative—one thinks of Michelangelo designing St. Peter's when he was nearly 90 or of Picasso painting at the same age and Arthur Rubinstein playing the piano in Carnegie Hall—while another starts to deteriorate. One theory, based on animal research, is that our brains grow new connections as we age. As more neurons die, these new connections may compensate for the loss in some individuals.

No two brain cells ever actually touch physically. They reach toward each other across a gap, or synapse, using hundreds or thousands of hairlike filaments called dendrites. The effect is like that of two twiggy trees almost intertwining in the wind (the word *dendrite* is derived from the Greek word for "tree"). Just at the point where two filaments almost meet, a chemical signal can be sent from one neuron to another. The basic chemicals involved are well known. One of them is acetylcholine, which is deficient in Alzheimer's patients; another is dopamine, the lack of which leads to Parkinson's disease. No one knows precisely why some neurons grow fifty dendrites for sending messages while others grow ten thousand. One encouraging finding, however, is that by remaining mentally active, older people may actually be growing new dendrites all the time.

This much-publicized news was founded on brain research by Marian Diamond at Berkeley, who showed that the brains of rats grew or shrank according to the kind of experiences they were exposed to. Rats confined to small cages and deprived of social interaction with other rats began to develop shrinking cortexes and a loss of dendrites. On the other hand, if an old rat was put back into rat society and given lots of stimulation, its brain expanded and grew new dendrites. This helped to give a physiological explanation for something we have all observed: Lonely, isolated old people are much more likely to be confused, disoriented, dull, and vacant than are their peers who remain actively involved with family and friends.

Because of our materialistic bias, growing new dendrites sounds very scientific and reassuring. In actuality, the situation turns out to be more complex. To have more dendrites is not the same as having a more developed brain. Babies are born with many more dendrites than adults have; the process of maturation consists of pruning the excess, whittling the cortex down to its most useful connections. However, it is still encouraging to find that old brains may be capable of replacing lost dendrites as they are needed.

It was long thought that we are born with a set number of brain cells that never divide to form new ones, yet recently it has been found that the DNA in neurons is active, which may lead to new conclusions. Some neurologists also doubt that the brain is actually losing a million neurons a year. Robert Terry, a neuroscientist at the University of California at San Diego, determined that there is no significant decline in neuron density in three important areas of the brain. The number of large neurons does decrease, but is offset by an increase in smaller neurons. Also, large neurons appear not to be dying but shrinking.

Two other neuroscientists, Samuel Weiss and Brent Reynolds at the University of Calgary in Alberta, found that they could stimulate dormant brain cells to active life. They cultured mouse neurons in the laboratory and gave them a chemical called epidermal growth factor, causing some immature, inactive brain cells to divide and form mature ones. The human brain is almost certainly storing such dormant cells perhaps as a replacement reserve.

It is also encouraging that the brain has its own natural mechanisms for activating itself in old age. New dendrites grow longer and sprout new branches past age 80. As neurons shrink, they create new synapses, which in turn stimulate more electrochemical activity in the brain. Natural substances stimulate this growth and repair— in particular nerve growth factor (NGF), one of a class of proteins known as trophic factors. NGF seems to have important functions. At Johns Hopkins, NGF prevented the degeneration of old neurons in rats and monkeys; when injected into the brains of old rats, it significantly improved their spatial memory. One hope is that Alzheimer's patients can regain function using chemicals that induce neuron activity (nerve growth factors have already been tried in Sweden with some success).

All this good news about the aging brain lifts our expectations that to keep one's faculties intact is completely normal. "Older people may not be as quick in timed tests," neuroscientist Robert Terry remarked, "but they don't lose judgment, orientation, or vocabulary. There is no way that people like Picasso, the cellist Pablo Casals, or Martha Graham could have continued to be so successful on half a brain."

Preserving intelligence in old age.   To document whether decline in intelligence is a natural part of aging, researcher Lissy Jarvik at

Columbia conducted studies on twins beginning in 1947. The subjects showed no significant drop in I.Q. from ages 65 to 75. Often there is a sharp drop in intelligence in the year preceding one's death, but there are many inconsistencies from individual to individual, and also from one intelligence test to another. Old people cannot simply be lumped together; it is the individual, not old age alone, that makes the difference.

As corroborating evidence, we can turn to a long-term study at Duke University that found no general decline in intelligence among older subjects (ages 65 to 75) unless they were suffering from high blood pressure. It is well known that small, often barely detectable strokes are associated with hypertension, which may be at work here. Whatever the specific cause, sickness, not the aging process itself, seems to create the decline in mental functioning so long associated with senescence. Although the neurological picture is not yet clear, it is completely realistic to expect to survive with your memory and intelligence intact.

The topic of aging and I.Q. provides a perfect example of how linear thinking misinterprets the complex changes that time brings. It isn't enough just to say that growing older is better or worse than being young. The human mind develops with experience along various lines. Brain studies help to indicate that organic changes keep up with the mind in its journey of expansion, but it is also important to trust the process itself, to realize that the mind *wants* to expand.

Psychologists are beginning to verify that human development extends into old age through higher states of awareness such as wisdom. One prominent German researcher, Paul Baltes, is committed to the idea that any decline in the brain's physical structure with age is offset by new mental accomplishments. As a person ages, certain types of memory tasks take more time to perform: For example, when Baltes asked people to pair words and places (such as car and Eiffel Tower, table and Berlin Wall, keys and Golden Gate Bridge), he found that older people could not duplicate the speed of recall displayed by younger ones.

"The situation is entirely different, however, when we look at the kind of knowledge that is transmitted from generation to generation through culture," Baltes wrote. In one test, Baltes presented his subjects with a hypothetical situation such as the following: What would you do if a friend called on the phone and announced that he was going to commit suicide? Or if a 15-year-old girl told you that she was thinking of getting married right away?

Baltes says, "The response we get to these and other dilemmas varies widely, and over the years, we have developed a 'wisdom scale' on which we place the answers. Take the problem of the 15-year-old girl. A participant might respond: 'A 15-year-old girl wants to get married? No, no way, marrying at that age would be utterly wrong.' Even after further cuing about possible extenuating circumstances, this person continues to insist that the problem is a simple one with one answer: 'Marriage is not possible.'

"Another answer might reflect a deeper knowledge of the human condition: 'Well, on the surface this seems like an easy problem. On average, marriage for 15-year-old girls is not a good thing. Thinking about getting married, on the other hand, is not the same as actually doing it. I guess many girls might think about it without getting married in the end. And then there are situations where the average case doesn't fit. Perhaps in this instance the girl has a terminal illness or is all alone in the world. Or as I think more about it, this girl may not be from this country in the first place; perhaps she lives in another culture or historical period where girls marry early.' "

On the "wisdom scale" Baltes found that older people did very well—more than half of the wisest responses came from subjects over age 60. Not all older people are wise, but they generally outperform younger people, reversing the results of the memory tests. Baltes feels that wisdom is a "software" achievement that culture uses to outwit biological limits. In his nineties the great pianist Arthur Rubinstein was still playing concerts, and when asked how he kept up such demanding activity, he cited three wise strategies: perform fewer pieces, practice each piece more frequently, and—to compensate for loss of speed and manual dexterity—slow down for a few seconds just before the music enters a particularly fast passage (your playing will then sound faster than it really is!).

These findings by Baltes point to mysteries that cannot be tested, for wisdom is more than experience. Socrates held that wisdom could not be taught but only known directly. Although we can sense it in the atmosphere around a wise person, their sagacity cannot be weighed, measured, or readily defined. Jonas Salk said of wisdom, "It's something that you know when you see it. You can recognize it, you can experience it. I have defined wisdom as the capacity to make judgments that when looked back upon will seem to have been wise."

But what confers wisdom? Being unteachable, it is only conferred by growing into it. An Indian adage holds, "This is not the kind of knowledge you acquire but the kind you must become." Having spent hours with Maharishi, who seems to me a profound sage, I don't feel that I have absorbed his wisdom, but I do know that to be genuine, wisdom must be as intimate to a person as breathing. Wisdom is in what you are, not in what you do.

As the new old age obliterates the prejudice against old people, I believe we will witness a flowering of the visionary qualities that age can bring at its best. Vision is the hidden bond that unites youth and old age. In middle age we compromise our ideals in order to achieve success and security; wisdom isn't something we have much time for. The young are still impetuously idealistic, but the old can balance and enhance that through wisdom, perhaps the greatest gift of the human life cycle in its mature years.

The Limits of Medicine

Medical findings on the aging brain allow us to close the gap between our low expectations of growing old and the rich possibilities that actually exist. They are also misleading, however. Most people assume that medicine has been chiefly responsible for improving the health of old people and extending their life span; therefore, they look to doctors for cures for cancer, heart disease, Alzheimer's, and other degenerative disorders common to the elderly. This ignores the fact that successful aging is far more than the avoidance of disease, although that is important. It involves a lifelong commitment to oneself every day; a doctor can assist in making this commitment, but medicine is not a surrogate for it.

Modern medicine's role in helping us live longer is growing weaker by the decade. In the great era of the microbe hunters that began in the 1870s and lasted almost a century, medicine made undeniable advances, wiping out infectious diseases of all sorts. This past success is one of the reasons why Americans are willing to bear the crushing cost of health care in this country, which has already passed $700 billion and is heading toward $1 trillion in the coming decade. We take it on faith that this enormous outlay will buy extra life, just as investment in penicillin research and the Salk vaccine did, but the overall contribution of medicine—past, present, and future—may be greatly exaggerated.

Since 1900, the average American life span has increased by 50 percent, yet much of that increase does not affect anyone who has already survived infancy and early childhood. If you examine the chart on page 251, it reveals how little extra life recent generations have gained in adulthood. Two graphs have been overlaid here. The lower one indicates life expectancy as measured from birth; this is relevant when we speak of the tremendous increase of twenty-six years in life expectancy between 1900 and 1990. The upper graph, however, indicates life expectancy measured from age 50, and although it also rises steadily, the increase between 1900 and 1990 is modest. A 50-year-old man today can expect to live only eight years longer than did his counterpart in 1900.

The fact is that medicine in this century has made remarkable strides in eliminating infant and childhood mortality, chiefly by reducing childbirth deaths and communicable disease such as polio, smallpox, measles, pneumonia, and influenza. By contrast, the impact on adult mortality has been much less dramatic, and there are persuasive facts to show that medical research is still not returning the benefits society once hoped to achieve:

• *Cancer.* The age-adjusted death rate from cancer has not changed in fifty years. Earlier detection gives us the illusion that cancer patients are living longer than they did in the past, but modern treatments apparently do not prolong life overall. If they did, people would be dying of cancer at older ages than in the past;

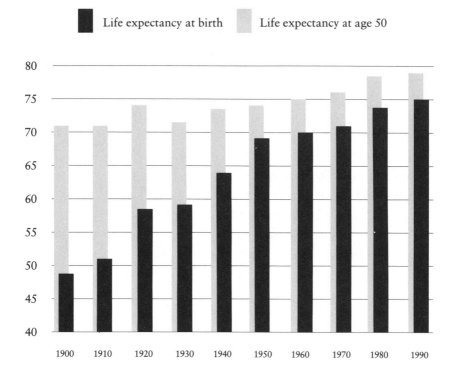

but this is not the case. Cancer deaths occur at about the same age as they did in our grandparents' day, and the overall mortality rate—about 20 percent of deaths are due to cancer—has remained constant since at least the late 1940s. In fact, the recent rise of lung cancer among blacks and women, which is linked to more cigarette smoking in these groups, has slightly increased the cancer death rate.

•   *Heart disease.* I have already discussed the ambiguous state of affairs regarding heart attacks. Mortality rates are falling—at the slow pace of 1 or 2 percent a year—but the underlying cause, coronary artery disease, is far from being eradicated. Despite massive prevention campaigns, damaged arteries are showing up in children as early as age 10, with widespread artery disease being common in half the population by age 20. The two leading surgeries for heart patients, the bypass graft and balloon angioplasty, are often effective in alleviating the pain of angina. However, repeated studies have failed to prove that either of these expensive, traumatic operations actually increases the patient's life expectancy.

• *Degenerative disorders.* We still lack effective treatments for many chronic diseases such as arthritis, diabetes, multiple sclerosis, and osteoporosis. Modern medicine can sometimes assist through the use of drugs to ease the pain or slow the progression of these diseases, but we cannot cure the patients or even explain why they got sick in the first place.

• *Medications.* Dependency on drugs, particularly sleeping pills and tranquilizers, continues to rise. It has been estimated that the average American over 70 who is *healthy* takes 3.5 kinds of drugs, both over-the-counter and prescription. Someone who is sick may take 10 drugs or more. A 1988 study in California concluded that overmedication is the leading health hazard among the elderly. Some of these drugs exist for no better reason than to relieve the side effects of earlier drugs.

There is also a huge problem with compliance, since many patients either don't take the proper medication or misuse it. At least half of older patients fail to comply with instructions for medication for glaucoma, the leading cause of blindness in this country; millions more fail to use antihypertensive drugs correctly. They recklessly mix them with tranquilizers, alcohol, cigarettes, and sleeping pills, and untold cases of needless illness and death are the result.

• *Addictions.* After focusing public attention on addictions for twenty years, America is becoming more addicted every year rather than less. No effective treatment has been found for alcoholism ("effective" means curing at least 50 percent of patients). Drug taking has reached down to the grade-school level; smoking is on the rise among blue-collar workers, young women, and minorities. Twenty-five years after the Surgeon General's report on the dangers of tobacco, 58 million adults—almost a third of us—still smoke; 75 percent of them say they are trying to quit but can't.

• *Medical costs.* The cost of health care continues to reach all-time highs, making a long stay in the hospital catastrophically expensive for most people. Hospital beds range from $500 to over $2,000 a day, depending on whether intensive care is needed, and bills in excess of $100,000 for treating a single life-threatening illness are common. About one-fourth of all health care costs occur in the last year of life, when expensive efforts to stave off life-threatening illness are common. (Inevitably, the last illness—the one the doctor can't cure—is the most expensive.) Unless there is an unforeseen turnabout, the spiraling cost of health insurance may wipe out the profits of many Fortune 500 companies before the year 2000.

• *Social awareness.* Medical research has raced ahead of the average person's comprehension. Most Americans cannot accurately describe the role of cholesterol in the body, the function of genes, or the nature of the immune system. Few people can list the major carcinogens in order of danger (many think that *any* chemical can cause cancer).

Given these dismal trends, it is highly unlikely that we are entering a golden age of longevity spurred by medicine. It has been estimated that curing heart disease and cancer would net an increase in life expectancy of fewer than ten years (the logic here is that since both disorders strike primarily after age 65, people who die from heart attacks and cancer are already near the end of their life expectancy; they are being deprived of relatively few years of life).

However, there is a positive side to medicine's current crisis: It throws into high relief the need for personal initiative. Longevity is still an individual achievement; it comes primarily to those whose expectations are high enough to reach for it. America could become a land where no one ever grows feeble and crippled by age, but for that to happen, we need to see the entire human life cycle as a rising curve. Today, fortunately, few "normal" signs of aging have gone unchallenged, and major studies have proved that we have expected far too little of the aging body, which holds great potential for improvement at very advanced ages.

Not Older, Better

In 1958, a unique project began in Baltimore, where eight hundred men and women between the ages of 20 and 103 volunteered to be examined as they aged. Each returned every year or two to go through an extensive battery of tests. The Baltimore Longitudinal Study of Aging, as it is officially known, grew to be the most famous of its kind. Its basic purpose was to determine how different bodily organs change over time. Hundreds of separate findings have emerged, and in general they fully support the optimism of the new old age.

Some key findings:

• As people age, their physical status varies widely from individual to individual, and by the time they reach 80 and 90, the differences have grown to be tremendous.

• While physical performance always declines over time as measured in a group, this does not always hold true for each person. Some people manage to retain lung capacity while everyone around them is losing it; others actually improve in kidney function or the amount of blood their hearts pump with each stroke. In most of these cases, the person kept up the use of the organ in question; "use it or lose it" was the key.

• Mental function is also maintained with use. For instance, someone who earns his living solving problems tends to retain that ability as he ages, even though that function declines for the group as a whole.

• The most complex organs, such as muscles, are the first to diminish. Losing muscle tissue is the main reason why people are unable to perform as much work as they age.

• Being moderately overweight in middle age apparently doesn't shorten one's life span (this depends, however, on avoiding the harmful side effects of being overweight, such as diabetes, hypertension, and congestive heart failure).

• Remaining sexually active throughout one's early and middle years gives one the best chance of remaining active into old age. Again there was tremendous variance from person to person. Married men between ages 60 and 80 might have sex as little as three times a year or as much as once a week or more. Most subjects believed that regular sexual activity, however, was good for their health.

• When asked to perform light to moderate exercise, men in their sixties were as efficient as men in their twenties, but the older men had to use more of their total physical capacity. (The Tufts researchers found that older bodies benefit just as much from exercise as do younger ones; the gain in muscle mass from twelve weeks of weight-lifting was the same for 60-year-olds as for much younger subjects.)

• Old people metabolize alcohol as well as when they were young, but its effects get stronger. After taking a drink, an older person will show poorer reaction time, memory, and decision-making than a younger person.

• High levels of cholesterol do not keep rising with age but peak at about 55 (somewhat earlier for men and later for women).

• Although sugar tolerance declines with age, this leads to type II diabetes only in some people; others do not acquire the disease despite the change in their body's ability to use glucose in the bloodstream.

This represents only a fraction of what the Baltimore researchers discovered, but it is enough to confirm one of the main points I started out with: Everyone grows more unique with age, and that uniqueness includes the possibility for improvement on any front. Of 650 men, only 12 actually managed to improve their kidney function, while the vast majority suffered decline in function or remained the same, but that small handful is enough to give us a glimpse of untapped possibilities.

The new paradigm tells us that we are constantly making and unmaking our bodies at the quantum level, which means that we are constantly unfolding hidden potential. Some of this potential is negative, some positive. The field takes a neutral attitude; what we wish and expect for ourselves governs the response we get. If we consider how to improve physical and mental function every day for the rest of our lives, three values emerge that must be part of everyone's intention:

1. longevity itself, since life is a primary good
2. creative experience, which keeps life interesting and makes us want more of it
3. wisdom, which is the collective reward of long life

It's impossible to set limits on what can be achieved in each area. Creativity and wisdom inspired Picasso, Shaw, Michelangelo, Tolstoy, and other long-lived geniuses to the day they died. Verdi wrote one of his greatest operas, *Falstaff,* at the age of 80, and the German naturalist Alexander von Humboldt completed his greatest work, *Cosmos,* at 89. There is immense beauty and dignity in these autumnal achievements; the dome of St. Peter's seems even more masterful for the fact that Michelangelo designed it in his ninth decade.

Psychologists who study creativity say that artists and writers often can produce more new ideas in their sixties or seventies than in their twenties. One interesting variable is that the later you take up any creative pursuit, the more likely you are to pursue it into old age. Eliot Porter, one of America's premier landscape photographers, did not publish his first picture until he was past 50; Julia Child came to television when she was past midlife. In both cases, success steadily increased through the next three decades.

Creative experience may enhance the structure of the brain itself. Chinese studies of old people in Shanghai indicate that less educated people have higher rates of dementia and Alzheimer's disease; the implication is that educated people, having been trained to use their minds, stimulate healthy brain activity. PET scans show increased blood flow to the brain during periods of creative thought; a distinctive EEG of coherent rhythms across all bands of brainwave activity is associated with the "Aha!" or "Eureka!" experience that characterizes art and creativity in general. Also, it's a myth to think that it harms the brain to get too wrapped up in mental work. As long as it is enjoyable, concentrated mental activity gives rise to alpha-wave patterns typical of "restful alertness," the relaxed but aware state also found in meditation.

Certain desirable neurotransmitters such as serotonin also increase during pleasurable creative activities (again, the same change is associated with the restful alertness found in meditation). The neurological picture is still debatable, but the real-life results—more years of fulfilling existence—are not. It would appear, then, that to want as much life, creativity, and wisdom as possible is very desirable. If your expectations in these areas are low, you are not likely to exceed them, while setting very high standards makes every decade worth looking forward to. (I am fond of Lord Byron's line, drilled into my head as a child in India: "A man's reach should exceed his grasp, or what's a heaven for?") A sense of "active mastery . . . is the ego state most clearly associated with longevity," wrote David Gutmann, aging researcher at the University of Michigan. This conclusion came after studying long-lived people from many diverse cultures and periods of history. Active mastery means having autonomy over one's life and circumstances, not power over others. Beyond any body of evidence about aging and how to prevent it, the single most important factor is that you make something creative from your existence.

The renowned religious writer Huston Smith once declared, "In order to live, man must believe in that for which he lives." People languish and die when their core of belief is gone. The most meaningful thing you can live for is to reach your full potential. At any given age the body and mind you experience are but a tiny fraction of the possibilities still open to you—there are always infinite new skills, insights, and depths of realization ahead of you.

These latent potentials are closed off to the vast majority of people, who barely have skills to fill sixty-five years of existence. Therefore, it is extremely important to begin to develop your skills consciously, breaking free of social expectation and setting yourself the goal of becoming a master. The underlying reason why old people feel marginal in our society, cut off from the mainstream of activity and social value, is that they themselves do not have a positive ideal of the very stage of life they find themselves in. To help you carve out your own ideal life, I have listed ten *keys to active mastery*. They summarize much of what we have learned so far about aging and awareness. They are also meant to be practical ideals, ones you can aspire to in action every day (we will detail the kind of action in the "In Practice" section that follows).

TEN KEYS TO ACTIVE MASTERY

1. Listen to your body's wisdom, which expresses itself through signals of comfort and discomfort. When choosing a certain behavior, ask your body, "How do you feel about this?" If your body sends a signal of physical or emotional distress, watch out. If your body sends a signal of comfort and eagerness, proceed.

2. Live in the present, for it is the only moment you have. Keep your attention on what is here and now; look for the fullness in every moment. Accept what comes to you totally and completely so that you can appreciate it, learn from it, and then let it go. The present is as it should be. It reflects infinite laws of Nature that have brought you this exact thought, this exact physical response. This moment is as it is because the universe is as it is. Don't struggle against the infinite scheme of things; instead, be at one with it.

3. Take time to be silent, to meditate, to quiet the internal dialogue. In moments of silence, realize that you are recontacting your source of pure awareness. Pay attention to your inner life so that you can be guided by intuition rather than externally imposed interpretations of what is or isn't good for you.

4. Relinquish your need for external approval. You alone are the judge of your worth, and your goal is to discover infinite worth in yourself, no matter what anyone else thinks. There is great freedom in this realization.

5. When you find yourself reacting with anger or opposition to any person or circumstance, realize that you are only struggling with yourself. Putting up resistance is the re-

sponse of defenses created by old hurts. When you relinquish this anger, you will be healing yourself and cooperating with the flow of the universe.

6. Know that the world "out there" reflects your reality "in here." The people you react to most strongly, whether with love or hate, are projections of your inner world. What you most hate is what you most deny in yourself. What you most love is what you most wish for in yourself. Use the mirror of relationships to guide your evolution. The goal is total self-knowledge. When you achieve that, what you most want will automatically be there, and what you most dislike will disappear.

7. Shed the burden of judgment—you will feel much lighter. Judgment imposes right and wrong on situations that just are. Everything can be understood and forgiven, but when you judge, you cut off understanding and shut down the process of learning to love. In judging others, you reflect your lack of self-acceptance. Remember that every person you forgive adds to your self-love.

8. Don't contaminate your body with toxins, either through food, drink, or toxic emotions. Your body is more than a life-support system. It is the vehicle that will carry you on the journey of your evolution. The health of every cell directly contributes to your state of well-being, because every cell is a point of awareness within the field of awareness that is you.

9. Replace fear-motivated behavior with love-motivated behavior. Fear is the product of memory, which dwells in the past. Remembering what hurt us before, we direct our energies toward making certain that an old hurt will not repeat itself. But trying to impose the past on the present will never wipe out the threat of being hurt. That happens only when you find the security of your own being, which is love. Motivated by the truth inside you, you can face any threat because your inner strength is invulnerable to fear.

10. Understand that the physical world is just a mirror of a deeper intelligence. Intelligence is the invisible organizer of

all matter and energy, and since a portion of this intelligence resides in you, you share in the organizing power of the cosmos. Because you are inseparably linked to everything, you cannot afford to foul the planet's air and water. But at a deeper level, you cannot afford to live with a toxic mind, because every thought makes an impression on the whole field of intelligence. Living in balance and purity is the highest good for you and the Earth.

———————

Life is a creative enterprise. There are many levels of creation and therefore many levels of possible mastery. To be completely loving, nonjudgmental, and self-accepting is an exalted goal, but the important thing is to work from a concept of wholeness. Because society lacks a vision of the road's end, the eminent psychiatrist Erik Erikson laments, "Our civilization does not really harbor a concept of the whole of life." The new paradigm provides us with such a concept, knitting body, mind, and spirit into a unity. The later years should be a time when life becomes whole. The circle closes and life's purpose is fulfilled. In that regard, active mastery is not just a way to survive to extreme old age—it is the road to freedom.

IN PRACTICE:

Breath of Life

In its most complete sense, active mastery means handling the whole of life. It is a process of integration, for ordinarily many aspects of the mind are quite separate from and out of tune with the body, and both are separate from spirit. Sitting quietly and being aware of yourself, you will notice that your perception is taken up with mental "noise" (random thoughts, emotions, memories) and occasional physical sensations that may or may not have anything to do with what is going on in your mind. Usually the perception of spirit is completely lost or ignored; even in moments of silent witnessing, those welcome pauses when one is detached from the common turmoil of mental events, most of us do not recognize that we are contacting our essential selves.

Bringing all these ingredients back into unity isn't possible on either the mental level or the physical level alone. Paying attention to one automatically tends to exclude the other. Unity can be accomplished at very deep levels of awareness through meditation, when the duality of mind and body is transcended, but meditation is restricted to the special time set aside for it. How do we integrate the remaining hours of our active daily lives?

Thousands of years ago the ancient Indian sages gave an answer in the form of *Prana,* the subtlest form of biological energy. Prana is present in every mental and physical event; it flows directly from spirit, or pure awareness, to bring intelligence and consciousness to every aspect of life. You sometimes see Prana defined as "life force" or "life energy," but what is more important than a definition is to get experiential knowledge of it. If you can experience Prana, you can begin to nurture and preserve it. The critical importance of life energy has been recognized in many cultural traditions; the Chinese know it as *Chi* and control its flow through acupuncture, meditation, and specialized exercises such as tai chi. Other names for the breath of life appear in Sufism, mystic Christianity, and the teachings of ancient Egypt. What is universally agreed on is that the more Prana you have, the more vital your mental and bodily processes. Balanced Prana gives rise to the following qualities:

RESULTS OF BALANCED PRANA

Mental alertness	Proper formation of tissues
Responsive nervous system; good motor coordination	Sound sleep
Balanced bodily rhythms (hunger, thirst, sleep, digestion, elimination, etc.)	Strong disease immunity
Enthusiasm	Physical vitality
Spiritual realization	Sense of exhilaration

These are the natural qualities of human life when it is balanced and whole. Depleted Prana is directly linked to aging and death. Nothing can remain alive when Prana is absent, because Prana is intelligence and consciousness, the two vital ingredients that animate physical matter. The experience of Prana can be had in many ways: When you are flushed with sudden energy, feel the inrush of sudden alertness and clarity, or simply perceive that you are "in the flow," your attention has been drawn to Prana. Some people sense it as a streaming or buzzing energy in their bodies. These sensations tend to get passed off as something else (ringing in the ear, tingling nerves, increased circulation of blood), but that is only a reflection of how we were taught to perceive our bodies.

In India the body is perceived first as a product of consciousness and only secondarily as a material object. Conserving Prana is considered extremely important, and the ancient teachings give the following basic rules to ensure balanced and vital Prana in the body at all ages:

Diet. Eat fresh produce, preferably home grown. The highest Prana is in food eaten straight from the garden. Stale food rapidly loses its Prana; in fact, anything stale, musty, or moldly indicates the absence of life energy and should be avoided. Processed food is also very low in Prana. Drinking water should be pure; the best is spring water or mountain water from melted snow. Polluted water is deficient in Prana.

Exercise. Physical activity increases Prana by bringing energy into the body, unless carried to the point of exhaustion. Exhaustion and fatigue are critical signs that Prana has been depleted. (In Western medicine we recognize this change as well; when exercise is carried beyond the body's oxygen reserves, it has to gain energy by metabolizing its own tissues. See the discussion of catabolic and anabolic metabolism, pp. 151–152.)

Breathing. The body's main source of Prana is through the breath, which on a gross level brings in oxygen and on a subtle level brings in life energy. Prana is thus literally identified with the breath of life. The ancient sages considered the quality of a person's life to be reflected in the quality of his breathing. When breathing is refined, slow, and regular, the circulation of Prana is reaching all levels of body and mind, promoting a state of complete balance.

Behavior. Actions can damage or nourish the body's Prana. Harsh, tense, conflicted behavior (what we today call stressed behavior) disturbs the flow of Prana. Refined behavior that comes from a sense of ease and self-acceptance promotes balanced Prana. The attitude of nonviolence (*Ahimsa*), sometimes called reverence for life, is at the root of life-nourishing behavior.

Emotions. Four negative emotions—fear, anger, greed, and envy—throw Prana out of balance and are to be avoided. Positive emotions, particularly love, increase Prana. Love is considered the most basic emotion that human awareness can feel; therefore, it is the closest to the source of life. The burst of well-being you feel when you fall in love is due to the fact that you unconsciously open the channels of awareness that allow more Prana to flow. Emotions that are repressed through shame and guilt cause these channels to constrict. When Prana is kept from flowing in this way, pockets of inertia and stagnation develop, eventually promoting disease. Depression is a state of almost complete nonflow and is associated with chronic illness, premature aging, and early death.

Thus, a healthy life, as measured by the conservation of Prana, demands the following:

- Fresh food
- Pure water and air
- Sunlight
- Moderate exercise
- Balanced, refined breath
- Nonviolent behavior and a reverence for life
- Loving, positive emotions; free expression of emotion

Think of the difference between a salad fresh-picked from your garden and one made from the same vegetables bought in the supermarket. Contrast a picnic in the mountains with lunch at a hamburger stand, or the taste of cool well water with water from a city tap. Freshness indicates the presence of Prana; staleness indicates its absence.

The factor least understood in our culture is balanced breath, which in India is considered the most important. The word *breath* implies more than the physical act of drawing air in and out of the lungs. Breath is the junction point between mind, body, and spirit. Every change of mental state is reflected in the breath and then in the body. Gross indications such as posture as well as distinct bodily sensations are directly related to one's style of breathing.

Changes of feeling are registered immediately in the pattern of breathing. Anger produces shallow inhalation and strong, panting exhalation. Fear creates rapid, shallow, ragged breathing. Sorrow creates spasmodic, broken breathing—the kind that arises when you are sobbing. On the other hand, positive emotions such as joy induce more regular breathing as the chest cavity relaxes. In moments when the mind stops, struck with beauty or revelation, so does the breath—that's what people are referring to when they say that looking into the Grand Canyon for the first time is breathtaking. At a subtler level, entering into the silence of deep meditation slows the breath, and what spiritual masters call "the rapture of God"—contemplating Spirit directly—is reflected in little or no breathing.

This phenomenon also works in reverse—changing the breathing pattern also causes altered emotions. As a young intern on duty in the emergency room, I was taught to calm down agitated patients just by sitting next to them and asking them to breathe slowly, deeply, and regularly along with me. As we fell into a relaxed breathing rhythm, our bodies spontaneously followed suit, and their agitated emotions were stilled. In the chart on page 266 are some examples from common experience of how the link between breath, body, and emotion works.

As you can see, when joy, love, and compassion are at work, breathing is at its most spontaneous and relaxed. The various systems of Yoga in India teach many kinds of highly controlled breathing exercises, known as *Pranayama*, to balance the breath, but their actual goal is not to produce controlled or disciplined breathing under ordinary circumstances. Rather, paying attention to the breath is a vehicle for releasing stress and allowing the body to find its own balance. Once in balance, yogic breathing is spontaneous and refined, so that the refined emotions of love and devotion can be carried throughout the body at all levels. When your cells experience the fullness of Prana, they are receiving the physical equivalent of these emotions.

The following two exercises are for balancing your breathing. They are not full-blown Pranayamas, which should be done in

EMOTION	BODILY SENSATION	BREATHING PATTERN	POSTURE
BEREAVEMENT, LOSS, SORROW	Hollow, empty feeling, especially in the pit of the stomach. Body feels sluggish, listless, and weak	Spasmodic, sighing, and superficial breath, as in sobbing	Posture conveys the impression of
FEAR AND ANXIETY	Tight muscles; racing heart; dry mouth; increased sweating; pounding head	Rapid, shallow, ragged, and irregular	un-ease. Closed, contracted,
ANGER	Tense body; feeling of pressure, especially in area of chest; hands may tighten into fists; widening of nostrils	Shallow inhalation; strong panting exhalation	hunched in one aspect or another. Stiff
GUILT	Feeling of being burdened by weight; feeling pushed down	Confined breathing; feeling of suffocation; unable to fully take in the breath of life	neck and back
JOY, LOVE, COMPASSION	Openness of posture; muscles relaxed; warm feeling in the body, especially in the heart; palms open; feeling of energy in the body	Deep, regular, spontaneous, comfortable, smooth, easy	Posture conveys impression of ease; open; relaxed; shoulders wide, back erect and comfortable; neck floating easily on spine

(The breathing patterns described above are present when the emotion is overwhelming and completely overshadows a person's stability. However, these breathing patterns are present in a subtle form whenever the emotion is being experienced.)

conjunction with meditation and Yoga postures,* but when properly done, these exercises will give you the experience of Prana as a light, sparkling, flowing sensation in your body. Usually, your muscles will become noticeably warm and relaxed. Mentally, balanced breathing is reflected in a sense of calm, lack of tension, and quietness, as the static of restless thinking gives way to silence.

Exercise 1: Body Breathing

Sit still in a chair listening to soft music, or outside listening to the wind in the treetops. As you listen, gently let your attention flow out of your ears as you easily exhale. Repeat for a minute, then do the same thing through your eyes, letting your attention go outward on the breath, slowly and gently. Repeat this through the nostrils, the mouth, then sit quietly just listening to the music with your whole body.

Now allow your attention to sink into your chest. Feel where your heart center is (at the point where the breastbone and ribs join) and breathe out through it, letting your attention go with the breath. Continue gently for another minute, then sit quietly, aware of your body. This exercise takes about two minutes but can be extended by doing another cycle or two.

This exercise consciously links respiration and the nervous system, helping to promote their smooth integration. It is a delightful exercise to conduct outdoors, sitting next to running water or under a tree when the wind is gently stirring its leaves. Feeling your awareness as it flows out on your breath gives you a powerful sense of being at harmony with Nature.

---

*Pranayama forms an important part of the traditional Ayurvedic procedures I employ in medical practice. The interested reader may refer to my earlier book, *Perfect Health* (New York: Harmony Books, 1990), which details the complete program of Maharishi Ayurveda, a revival of the most powerful knowledge from India's ancient "science of life."

Exercise 2: The Expanding Light

Stand in your stocking feet with your eyes closed, arms down at your sides, and vividly relive the sensation of your last exhilarating experience. Recapture the feeling of being happy, vibrant, and carefree. (You can use a visual image, a loving memory, a moment of triumph from the past—anything that brings the sensation of exhilaration back to you; do not worry if it is only faint, just have the intention of being with it.)

As you do this, inhale slowly through your nose and begin to spread your arms out slowly. Imagine that as you inhale, your breath is expanding from the center of your chest. It is an expanding light that makes your arms float effortlessly open, and as the light expands, your happy, exhilarated feeling expands with it. You can visualize this as a glowing blue-white ball of light if you want, or just as a sensation. Let the light grow as slowly or quickly as it wants, spreading from the center of your heart, reaching out to the tips of your fingers, up to your head, and down to your toes. You'll also be smiling, so let that grow, too.

At the point of maximum extension, start slowly exhaling through your nose and bring your arms back down to your sides. Do this slowly, taking longer to exhale than to inhale. Take the expanded feeling/light back down into your chest, until it is small and localized in your heart again. As your arms come back down to your sides, let your head drop forward.

Now repeat the exercise on the next breath, expanding the feeling again—don't pay attention to your physical movements, but stay with the feeling. You want to open and close it like a flower with each breath.

As you continue, you can begin to open up even more, throwing your head back, expanding your chest, and rising on tiptoe on the outward stroke. As you exhale, slump like a rag doll, bending at the knees and waist. Don't speed up the movements, however, just proceed slowly and rhythmically. You'll notice that this is an extremely pleasant exercise, because as you open, your body fills with breath, awareness, and enjoyment all at once—the sensation is light, warm, tingling. As you close, the body relaxes and slumps under its own weight, becoming more grounded and still. You are exploring a complete range of feeling, which allows the subtle breath to penetrate into every channel.

The Vata Connection

As we get older, there is a natural tendency for Prana to diminish; this must be countered to preserve youthfulness. In India, longevity was traditionally assigned to a branch of learning called *Ayurveda,* derived from two Sanskrit roots, *Ayus,* or "life," and *Veda,* meaning "science" or "knowledge." This ancient "science of life" is usually referred to as India's traditional medicine, but there is a deeper spiritual basis for Ayurveda. The most famous verse from the ancient Ayurvedic texts says, *Ayurveda amritanam* ("Ayurveda is for immortality"). The meaning is twofold: Ayurveda is for promoting longevity without limit, and it does this from a belief that life essentially is immortal.

According to Ayurveda, the life energy, or Prana, is channeled throughout our bodies by a "wind" known as *Vata.* Vata is one of the three metabolic principles (*doshas*) that give form to every living thing, be it a mosquito, an elephant, a human being, a planet, a star, or the entire cosmos. Vata is responsible for movement of every kind. In the human body it is divided into five parts:

Prana Vata regulates the nervous system.
Udana Vata regulates cognitive skills, speech, and memory.
Samana Vata regulates digestion.
Vyana Vata regulates circulation.
Apana Vata regulates excretion.

All five aspects of Vata are controlled by the first and most important, Prana Vata, for as the name implies, this dosha brings in Prana, the life force, which is then distributed to the rest of the body. When

Prana Vata is out of balance, there is general disruption throughout the system. Ayurveda holds that old age is a particularly sensitive time for such imbalances. Vata is naturally higher in old age, and if a person has not been careful to keep Prana Vata in balance, the following symptoms will result:

SYMPTOMS OF VATA IMBALANCE

Physical symptoms	*Mental/behavioral symptoms*
Dry or rough skin; wrinkles	Insomnia
Chronic underweight; muscle wasting	Worry, anxiety
	Constipation
Weak kidneys; loss of bladder control	Depression
	Fatigue
Weak or irregular heartbeat	Confusion, restless thoughts
Constipation	
Common arthritis	Intolerance to stress
Nonspecific aches and pains	Intolerance to cold
Weakened immunity (susceptibility to colds, pneumonia, and other infections)	

You'll immediately notice the close match between these disorders of imbalanced Vata and aging. As the "wind" of the body, Vata is cold, drying, and piercing. When Vata is aggravated, it is as if a withering wind begins to stir inside. Usually the first place to which aggravated Vata will travel is the joints, initiating a range of joint problems beginning with minor aches and pains (these cause trouble especially during winter, the season that is worst for Vata disturbance) and ending with degenerative arthritis if the aggravation persists.

Since every cell contains Vata dosha, the effects of aggravating it are not confined to the joints. The whole body begins to shrivel and dry up; the bowels become dry, tight, and constipated; racked with insomnia and worry, the person languishes, prey to ever-increasing aches and pains. Millions of prescriptions for painkillers, tranquilizers, and sleeping pills are written by baffled doctors who cannot explain why elderly patients start exhibiting such symptoms, since usually there is nothing organically wrong. In medical terminology, *organic* means that a physical organ shows signs of disease or malfunction. Physicians tend to dismiss symptoms without organic cause as psychosomatic or idiopathic (unexplainable).

Old people rarely suffer from just one of the symptoms of Vata imbalance and many suffer them on a broad scale. If multiple drugs are prescribed for each symptom, new imbalances begin to pile up, for the body cannot help but react with imbalance to painkillers, diuretics, tranquilizers, sleeping pills, beta blockers, and all the other medications commonly prescribed for the elderly. Whether we like it or not, a symptom is something the body wants to express—it is a message—and drugs suppress that expression.

How fast you age is intimately linked to the speed and intensity of Vata aggravation. Some people are extremely prone to Vata imbalance, while others are not. Some people may get aggravated Vata in their fingers, leading to arthritis, while others get it in their intestines, leading to chronic constipation.

What can cause Vata imbalance? Ayurveda follows the principle of complementarity—"like speaks to like." What this means is that any quality Vata dosha possesses will be stimulated by the same quality outside your body. These qualities are as follows.

QUALITIES OF VATA DOSHA

Dry
Cold
Changeable
Rough
Moving

Light
Subtle
Quick
Leads other doshas

Anything in your environment that contains the above traits will increase Vata. For example:

Dry weather; dry foods (crackers, cereals, potato chips, etc.)
Cold weather; cold food and drink
Changeable: sudden life changes; death in family; loss of job; mood swings; sudden change of season; etc.
Rough-textured materials next to the skin; rough words or behavior
Moving: travel; falling down; physical exercise or labor; exposure to drafts or wind
Light foods that have a high air content, particularly raw fruits and vegetables
Subtle changes of mood, a subtle draft
Quick: any activity, physical or mental, requiring speed; being made to rush

Let me illustrate how these qualities (called *gunas* in Sanskrit) interact. If my kidneys detect a fluid shortage in my bloodstream, they secrete a specific chemical messenger—angiotensin 2—which gets carried to the hypothalamus in the brain and is converted into a mental event: I feel thirsty. This feeling then prompts me to act by getting a glass of water.

In Ayurvedic terms, what has happened is a steady flow of one impulse of intelligence—Vata—as it registers the needs of 50 trillion cells simultaneously. Vata has the quality of being dry, and it increases under any kind of dry condition. Dry crackers, dry desert heat, dry cold from air-conditioning, and even dry wit all serve to increase Vata. Dryness make us thirsty because our bodies detect this increased Vata, and the signal will persist until something wet, such as a drink of water, brings the opposite quality into play and Vata falls back into line.

Vata is the easiest dosha to push out of balance, but also the easiest to bring back. Since Prana Vata, the most important aspect of this dosha, regulates the nervous system, it shifts with the slightest thought or sensation. By doing the things that are needed to keep Prana Vata in balance, we have a complete system for conserving Prana and defeating the aging process at an extremely subtle level. This means we must pay some attention to Vata every day, which is in fact quite a natural and easy thing to do. Vata can be "pacified"—i.e., kept in balance—through various lifestyle measures.

PACIFYING VATA

To keep Vata dosha in balance, you need to keep the following qualities in mind:

Regular:	regular habits; mealtimes; bedtime; work schedule
Warm:	warm, well-cooked food; sunshine; avoidance of cold food and drink
Nourishing:	rich, nourishing, even heavy foods in cold weather; nurturing emotions
Relaxing:	taking time for adequate rest; avoidance of stressful situations, overexcitement, and overexertion
Stable:	stable relationships and work; stable home life
Calming:	quiet, orderly work environment; gentle massage (particularly good is warm oil massage using sesame oil)
Steady:	steady supply of food and water to body; not skipping meals or going on an empty stomach

A dosha is pacified by qualities it lacks. Because Vata tends to make people erratic, irregular, and inconsistent, it is helpful to counter with the oposite—steadiness and regularity. Small matters such as not skipping meals and going to bed on time pay large dividends in pacifying Vata. Prolonged exposure to stress creates serious Vata imbalance, so special attention has to be paid to giving yourself a quiet, orderly work environment. Cheerful conditions at work greatly relieve the Vata tendency to uncertainty and insecurity.

When you are under the influence of Vata, you will naturally seek warmth; keeping warm in winter and sunbathing at other times of the year soothes this dosha. Your diet should emphasize well-cooked, nourishing foods; Ayurveda considers even heavy, oily food to be good for Vata (which is why long-cooked stews and soups seem so appealing in winter). Avoiding cold salads, iced drinks, alcohol, and dry or uncooked food in cold weather will also correct the body's tendency to develop aggravated Vata at those times. In general, stimulants of any kind, including coffee, tobacco, and alcohol, create Vata imbalance.

When out of balance, Vata leads to light, interrupted sleep; this is best countered by going to bed early and avoiding late-night reading and television. The body also wants some periods of calmness, relaxation, and peace during each day. Transcendental Meditation is ideal, since exposing the nervous system to deep silence allows it to harmonize all the synchronized bodily rhythms that Vata regulates. Peaceful, loving family life is an ideal many people feel has slipped away in recent decades, but from the viewpoint of Vata dosha, it is vital.

Vata has a special affinity with warm oils; daily massage with warm sesame oil on the feet, head, and lower abdomen is one of the best measures for relieving deep stresses in the nervous system. The oil should be applied gently and slowly before the morning bath and again before bedtime. Special attention to balancing Vata should be paid whenever you are recuperating from illness or under emotional stress; suffering from jet leg; displaying depression, chronic fatigue, and exhaustion; or have been physically wounded—all of these conditions cause severe Vata disturbance.

If you detect chronic symptoms of Vata imbalance, the following specific measures should help:

- Include sweet, sour, and salty tastes in your meals; these are balancing for Vata. This dosha calls for more sour and salty foods than does any other.
- Avoid bitter, astringent, and pungent (spicy) tastes. Astringent is counted as a taste in Ayurveda; it is found in dry-tasting foods that pucker the mouth (beans, lentils, pomegranates, tea).
- If you feel uncomfortable living in a dry, cold, windy climate, consider moving to a warm one, which is more conducive to Vata balance. Everyone who lives in a cold climate would do well, according to Ayurveda, to make sure that their home and workplace has warm, humidified air. Avoid drafts and prolonged outdoor exercise in winter. Warm, hearty food eaten at regular intervals is a good anti-Vata measure in cold climates.
- If possible, eat all meals sitting down in a peaceful, quiet, friendly setting. Food eaten on the run disturbs Vata. Avoid any kind of dieting, fasting, or spending any length of time with an empty stomach.
- If you have an irregular appetite—a common problem when Vata is imbalanced—try eating several small meals throughout the day (the last one should be at sundown, or at least a couple of hours before bedtime).
- Avoid prolonged travel without rest in between flights or long drives. In cases of jet lag, take adequate time to rest and/or sleep as soon as you have reached your destination. Drink plenty of fluids en route; herb tea or plain hot water is helpful on jets; liquor and cold drinks tend to aggravate the jarring effect on Vata dosha.
- Aroma therapy or warm baths with a few drops of fragrant oil help soothe Vata. Choose scents that are warm, grounding, and soothing, such as wintergreen, sandalwood, camphor, cinnamon, basil, orange, rose geranium, and clove.

•   In cooking, herbs and spices should be sweet and/or heating in quality: ginger, black pepper, turmeric, cinnamon, mustard, mint, cayenne, horseradish, cumin, nutmeg, cardamom, green coriander, fennel, basil, oregano, rosemary, sage, and thyme.

PART FIVE

Breaking the Spell of Mortality

*By your art, Spirit, you defeat
the withering of death.*

RIG VEDA

T HE ULTIMATE BOUNDARY to human life is death, and for thousands of years we have tried to travel beyond that boundary. Despite the obvious mortality of our bodies, moments arise when the clear perception of immortality shines through. The poet Tennyson wrote of experiences he had in his youth when his individual self "seemed to dissolve and melt away into boundless being." This radical shift out of ordinary experience "was not a confused state," he recalled, "but the clearest of the clear, the surest of the sure, utterly beyond words—when death was an almost laughable impossibility."

Because they are totally subjective, such immortal feelings do not fit in to the worldview of science, and therefore we tend to label them religious. But thousands of people have been privileged to catch glimpses of the reality that encloses space and time like a vast multidimensional bubble. Some people seem to have contacted this timeless realm through near-death experiences, but it is also accessible in everyday life. Peeking through the mask of matter "we have a certain feeling, a certain longing that we can't quite put into words. It's a striving . . . a wish for something greater or higher in ourselves." With these words the philosopher Jacob Needleman pointed to what he called "our second world," which anyone can access under special conditions.

Our first world, Needleman wrote, is "the world we live in every day, this world of action and activity and doing," ruled by everyday thoughts and emotions. But like flashes of spiritual lightning, there are moments when the second world makes itself known, full of peace and joy and a clear, unforgettable sense of who we really are—"vivid moments of being present in oneself," Needleman called them. If the second world is inside us, so is the first, because ultimately there is nothing verifiably "out there." Everything to be seen, felt, and touched in the world is knowable only as firings of neuronal signals inside our brains. It all happens in here.

Who you are depends on what world you see yourself living in. Because it is ruled by change, the first world contains sickness, aging, and death as inevitable parts of the scenery; in the second world, where there is only pure being, these are totally absent. Therefore, finding this world within ourselves and experiencing it, even for a moment, could have a profound effect on the process of sickness and aging, if not death itself.

This possibility has always been accepted as fact in the East. In India and China, some spiritual masters are believed to have lived hundreds of years as a result of achieving a state of timeless aware-ness. This is considered one of the options open to a spirit who has attained *Moksha*, or liberation, although not every master takes the option of extending his life span. In the West, such powers are viewed with extreme skepticism. But the new paradigm assures us that there is a level of Nature where time dissolves, or, to turn it around, where time is created.

This level is extremely enigmatic, even by quantum standards, since it existed before the creation of space and time. The rational mind can't conceive of such a state, because to say that something existed before time began is a contradiction in logic. Yet the ancient sages believed that direct knowledge of timeless reality is possible. Every generation has affirmed that assertion. Einstein himself expe-rienced episodes of complete liberation from space-time boundaries: "At such moments one imagines that one stands on some spot of a small planet gazing in amazement at the cold and yet profoundly moving beauty of the eternal, the unfathomable. Life and death flow into one, and there is neither evolution nor eternity, only Being."

It has taken three generations for the new paradigm to show us that Being is a very real state, existing beyond change and death, a place where the laws of Nature that govern change are overturned. Death is ultimately just another transformation, from one configu-ration of matter and energy to another. But unless you can stand outside the arena of change, death represents an end point, an extinction. To escape death ultimately means escaping the world-view that gives death its terrible sense of closure and finality.

"I'm very afraid of death," an Indian disciple once confessed to his guru. "It's haunted me since I was a child. Why was I born? What will happen to me when I die?"

The guru considered the matter thoughtfully and said, "Why do you think you were born?"

"I don't understand your question," the disciple stammered.

"Why do you think you were born?" the guru repeated. "Isn't it just something your parents told you that you took for granted? Did you actually have the experience of being born, of coming into existence from a state of nonexistence, or didn't it happen that one day in childhood you asked where you came from, and your parents told you that you were born? Because you accepted their answer, the idea of death frightens you. But rest assured, you cannot have birth without death. They are two poles of the same concept. Perhaps you have always been alive and always will be. But in accepting your parents' system of belief, you entered into an agreement to fear death, because you think of it as an ending. Perhaps there is no ending—that is the possibility most worth exploring."

Naturally the disciple was shocked, because, like the rest of us, he didn't see death as a belief he had agreed to. What the guru was pointing out is that birth and death are space-time events but existence isn't. If we look inside us, we find a faint but certain memory that we have always been around. To put it another way, no one remembers *not* existing. The fact that such metaphysical issues arise shows how unique humans are. For us, death isn't just a brute fact but a mystery, and it must be unraveled before the mystery of aging—the process that leads to death—can be solved. The very deepest questions about who we are and what life means are wrapped up in the nature of existence.

When the spell of mortality is broken, you can release the fear that gives death its power. Fear of death reaches much further into our lives than our conscious minds are willing to concede. As David Viscott wrote, "When you say you fear death you are really saying that you fear you have not lived your true life. This fear cloaks the world in silent suffering." Yet by seeing through the fear you can turn it into a positive force. "Let your fear of death motivate you to examine your true worth and to have a dream for your own life," Viscott encouraged. "Let it help you value the moment, act on it, and live in it."

I want to go even further and suggest that when you see yourself in terms of timeless, deathless Being, every cell awakens to a new existence. True immortality can be experienced here and now, in this living body. It comes about when you draw the infusion of Being into everything you think and do. This is the experience of timeless mind and ageless body that the new paradigm has been preparing us for.

THE METABOLISM OF TIME

One of Einstein's brilliant contributions to modern physics was his intuition that linear time, along with everything happening in it, is superficial. Time seems to flow and move; clocks tick off their seconds, minutes, and hours; aeons of history unfold and disappear. But ultimately, Einstein held, this vast activity is all relative, meaning that it has no absolute value. John Wheeler, an eminent physicist, wrote, "The very idea of space-time is a wrong idea, and with that idea failing, the idea of 'before' and 'after' also fails. That can be said so simply, and yet it is so hard for the lesson to grab hold in the world."

One proof that it hasn't yet grabbed hold is that people continue to age, following a straight-line process as faithfully as if it really existed. Yet if Einstein was right, aging is an illusion. It depends on "before" and "after," two concepts that have been bankrupt for almost a century. The mystic Sufi poet Rumi understood this truth centuries ago when he wrote, "You are the unconditioned spirit trapped in conditions, the sun in eclipse." Time and space are conditions, and when we see ourselves bound in them, we have lost touch with reality and bought into a fiction.

Einstein displaced linear time with something much more fluid—time that can contract and expand, slow down or speed up. He often compared this to subjective time, for he noted that spending a minute sitting on a hot stove seems like an hour, while spending an hour with a beautiful girl seems like a minute. What he meant by this is that time depends on the situation of the observer. For physicists, the notion of expanding and contracting time allowed for better calculations of various phenomena occurring near the speed of light, which was Einstein's absolute, the universal yardstick that could not be changed or exceeded. Time had to expand and contract in order to keep the speed of light constant.

We all have a sense that time expands and contracts, seeming to drag one moment and race the next, but what is our constant, our absolute? I believe it is "me," our core sense of self. To borrow from Einstein's example, if two men are sitting with the same beautiful girl, the time might drag for one, because the girl is his sister, while it flies for the other if he is in love with her. This means that each of us has personal control over our sense of time. Consider all the subjective qualities we attach to time. We say things like:

> I don't have time for that.
> Time's up.
> Your time's running out.
> How the time flies.
> Time hangs heavy.
> I love you so much, time stands still.

These statements do not say anything about time measured by the clock. The clock doesn't lie about how much linear time has elapsed "out there." But subjective time, the kind that exists only "in here," is a different matter. All the above statements reflect a state of self. If you're bored, time hangs heavy; if you're desperate, time's running out; if you're exhilarated, time flies; when you're in love, time stands still. In other words, whenever you take an attitude toward time, you are really saying something about yourself. Time, in the subjective sense, is a mirror.

In medicine we realize that people who don't have enough time are probably going to develop health problems. The discovery of Type A behavior, for example, revealed that heart attacks were linked to a sense that there's never enough time; for a Type A, the next deadline is always a threat, and his *struggle with time* contributes to his ingrained frustration and hostility. Hostility then sends a message to the heart that constricts blood vessels, drives up blood pressure, elevates cholesterol levels, and generates various kinds of arrhythmias, or irregular heartbeat.

This happens to more people than just Type A's. As April 15 approaches, tax accountants have been observed to develop temporary elevations in blood pressure and cholesterol that disappear once the tax deadline is past. Their subjective sense of time is enough to put their bodies at risk. This points to a deeper lesson. Ask someone to make an omelet. A skillful cook can accomplish the task in about two minutes. Now alter the situation slightly by saying, "Make an omelet, but you only have two minutes to do it." This will often make even the accomplished cook feel tense and harried. Time pressure causes stress hormones to be released into the body, which in turn elevates heartbeat. If the person struggles against this reaction, his situation only gets worse. Now his heart has to put up with time pressure and frustration. When heart patients are given demanding tasks under a deadline, a significant number grow so agitated that their heart muscles actually suffer ischemic or "silent" heart attacks ("silent" in this case means that damage is occurring but without any sensation of pain).

The element of time pressure also alters behavior, attitudes, and physiological responses. So subjective time can be an incredibly powerful force. It's no accident that the word *deadline* contains the word *dead*. A deadline implies a threat: "If you don't meet this limit, you're finished." The threat may be subtle or blatant, but it is almost always present. If it were not, we would not feel anxious under time pressure. Sometimes we expose the threat more clearly in phrases such as "I'm under the gun" or "His time is up" (which may sound like a neutral phrase until you remember that we apply it to people who are about to die).

Some people are much more sensitive to time pressure than others. A nervous cook can get so rattled by the two-minute deadline that he drops the eggs, burns himself, and can't accomplish a task at which he excels when time is not a consideration. Another cook will blossom under the challenge and finish the omelet even quicker than before. One feels time pressure as a threat, the other as a challenge. One feels thrown out of control, the other feels impelled to test his sense of control and improve upon it.

All of us, however, feel the pressure of a serious, threatening deadline over which we have no control—death itself. If you believe that you have been allotted a certain span of time for your existence, the deadline of death will exert the same kind of stress as that felt by the nervous cook rushing to finish his omelet and botching the job. How much better not to feel any time pressure, to blossom fully despite the fact that death exists. The attitude that life is a blossoming, not a race, can be achieved. But to do that, you can't believe that time is running out. Sending that message to your body's cells is the same, ultimately, as programming them to age and die. Yet the fact is that linear time *is* moving inexorably forward, and to overcome that, we must find a place where a different kind of time, or no time, can be experienced and internalized.

The Quantum Mechanical Body

To a skeptic, this proposition must sound purely subjective, but quantum events that defy linear time take place within our cells continually. DNA's intelligence operates simultaneously in the past, present, and future. From the past it takes the blueprint of life, applying to the present only the tiniest fraction of the information needed for cellular function (perhaps a billionth of its total data base), and reserving for the future the information that will be relevant years from now. The double helix is the quantum storehouse of your future; here time is compressed and locked away until needed. At the instant you were conceived, your genes gained control of an entire lifetime of events that would unfold in precise sequence. Your hands, for example, emerged in the womb first as amorphous blobs of cells, then as stubby knobs that turned into fishlike fins, amphibian feet, animal paws, and finally human hands. Those blobs, knobs, fins, feet, and paws are still present today as stored data in your genes, as are the hands of your infancy, childhood, adulthood, and old age. At the quantum level, you live all these ages at once.

Because we are both physical and quantum, human beings live multidimensional lives. At this moment you are in two places at once. One is the visible, sensual world, where your body is subject to all the forces of nature "out there." The wind chaps your skin and the sun burns it; you will freeze to death in winter without shelter; and the assault of germs and viruses makes your cells sick. But you also occupy the quantum world, where all these things change. If you get into the bathtub, your consciousness doesn't get wet. The limitations of physical life count for much less in the quantum world, and often for nothing. The cold of winter doesn't freeze your memories; the heat of a July night doesn't make you sweat in your dreams.

Put together all the quantum events in your cells and the sum total is your quantum mechanical body, which operates according to its own unseen physiology. Your quantum mechanical body is awareness in motion and is part of the eternal field of awareness that exists at the source of creation. The intelligence inside us radiates like light, crossing the border between the quantum world and the physical world, unifying the two in a constant subatomic dialogue. Your physical body and your quantum mechanical body can both be called home—they are like parallel universes that you travel between without even thinking about it.

PHYSICAL BODY:
A FROZEN ANATOMICAL SCULPTURE

"I" sees itself as:

—made of cells, tissues, and organs
—confined in time and space
—driven by biochemical processes (eating, breathing,
     digestion, etc.)

QUANTUM MECHANICAL BODY:
A RIVER OF INTELLIGENCE CONSTANTLY RENEWING ITSELF

"I" sees itself as:

—made of invisible impulses of intelligence
—unbounded in time and space
—driven by thoughts, feelings, wishes, memories, etc.

To all appearances, the physical body occupies a few cubic feet of space; it serves as a fragile life-support system for seven or eight decades before it must be discarded. The quantum mechanical body, on the other hand, occupies no well-defined space and never wears out. How big a container would you need for the dream you had last night, or for your desire to be loved? Even though a person's total genetic material could easily fit into a teaspoon, what is most important about genes—their intelligence—occupies no physical space.

At the level of the quantum mechanical body every aspect of an experience is wrapped into one point that is beyond the three-dimensional world. A photograph of a new bride gives us a literal record of how she looked, and a tape recording can capture her voice, but these are the crudest fragments of experience; unless she saves them as mementos, the texture of her bridal gown and the taste of her wedding cake appear to be lost forever.

But in quantum space everything is there at once, and through the simple act of remembering, the bride can recapture a complete world. By some further miracle, every other experience the bride ever has will be tinged with this new addition to her memory. Being a married woman becomes a part of her brain's view of her whole life from that moment on.

The images imprinted on your quantum mechanical body are as complex as you are. In short, these images *are* you. You live out your stored images, manufacturing your own version of time, and in the process you program the kind of body required by your version of time. Let me give a concrete example of how this works.

In his fascinating book of psychiatric case studies, *Love's Executioner,* Irvin Yalom recounts the story of Betty, a 27-year-old unmarried woman who came to him for therapy. Betty was a very difficult case from the start. Hard in manner, aloof and complaining, she kept up a litany of grievances about the fact that no one liked or accepted her. She worked in public relations for a large department store, and every slight she suffered from customers, co-workers, and bosses was dragged into her diatribe.

As Yalom listened, he was struck by the odd fact that throughout Betty's tireless description of her miseries, she never mentioned something very obvious—her weight. Although barely five feet two inches tall, Betty weighed 250 pounds. She and everyone else knew that her appearance was disturbing, yet she had turned her entire existence into an elaborate game to disguise this fact. Not mentioning her weight was a shield of silence, covering up the deeper pain she could not confront.

Yalom realized that it would be too difficult for Betty to tackle her obesity without first coming to terms with her psychological distress. He spent months trying to penetrate her defenses, and eventually they started to dissolve. One day Betty announced dramatically to Yalom that she was going to lose weight. She outlined a plan of attack that was remarkably disciplined and well organized. With great seriousness she launched into a diet, joining a support group and religiously avoiding any temptation to binge. She signed up for weekly square-dancing and set up a stationary bicycle in front of her TV. As the pounds quickly began to come off, Yalom noticed a remarkable thing.

As Betty lost weight, she began to have vivid dreams and flashbacks of painful incidents in her past. The underlying traumas that Yalom could hardly budge in therapy were now melting away with the fat. Betty began having wild mood swings, which at first seemed random. Then Yalom noticed that they followed a coherent pattern: She was reliving various traumas that had occurred when she was at certain weights. It turned out that Betty had grown steadily fatter since she was 15.

The last time Betty had weighed 210 pounds, for example, was when she decided, at age 21, to move to New York. She had grown up on a small, poor ranch in Texas, an only child trapped with a depressed, widowed mother. On the day that her diet took her back down to 210 pounds, Betty had a vivid flashback of how difficult leaving home had been. Quite literally, time was locked up inside her, blended into her cells.

"Thus her descent from 250 pounds set her spinning backward in time through the emotionally charged events of her life: leaving Texas for New York (210 pounds), her college graduation (190 pounds), her decision to drop the pre-med curriculum (and to give up the dream of discovering the cure for the cancer that had killed her father) (180 pounds), her loneliness at her high school graduation—her envy of the other daughters and fathers, her inability to get a date to the senior prom (170 pounds), her junior high graduation and how much she had missed her father at that graduation (155 pounds)."

Yalom was quite excited to see how tangible and alive a past memory could be: "What a wonderful proof of the unconscious realm! Betty's body had remembered what her mind had long forgotten." I would go even further and say that her body was a kind of mind in itself, a storehouse of memories that had taken physical form in fat cells. Betty's experience had become Betty; instead of just metabolizing hamburgers, pizzas, and milk shakes, she had metabolized every emotion—sad longings, frustrated hopes, bitter disappointments—associated with each bite of food.

Shedding weight was her deliverance from the past, and as the old body went, a new Betty was created. She rapidly gained insight into herself; she rediscovered deeply buried desires and shed tears over hurts she had concealed from herself for many years. Her body contours began to emerge: first a waist, then breasts, then a chin and cheekbones. With her new shape, Betty found the courage to venture into a social life. Her weight had made her an outcast since her early teens; now she went on her first date, and men in her office were attracted to her, no longer put off by her armor of defensiveness.

In the end, the metamorphosis did not fully succeed. The most traumatic event in Betty's life had occurred just before her adolescence, when her father suffered a long, protracted death from cancer; she had weighed 150 pounds then and had never managed to get that thin again. Now, as she got down to 155 pounds, her diet became a grim struggle—her body refused to let go of even one more ounce, no matter what, and her flashbacks became harder to face.

"Soon we spent entire sessions talking about her father. The time had come to unearth everything. I plunged her into reminiscence and encouraged her to express everything she could remember about his illness, his dying, his appearance in the hospital the last time she saw him, the details of his funeral, the clothes she wore, the minister's speech, the people who attended. . . . She felt her loss as never before and, over a two-week period, wept almost continuously." This time was very difficult for both doctor and patient. Racked by nightmares of her father's death, Betty said that she died three times a night; Yalom felt intensely guilty for dragging her back to a time when she had lost not just her father but her dream of happiness.

Betty balked at uncovering any more buried feelings. It became clear that her mind could not cross this last, too-threatening threshold. Neither could her body. Too many griefs and unrealized hopes had turned into Betty. At about that time she quit both her diet and her therapy. The 150-pound barrier held, embodying the loss of a father who would never return to her. Yalom regretted that she was only a partial cure, yet he also had to admit his relief—the ordeal had deeply shaken both of them.

Like Betty, everyone becomes their past, but we also have the power to reverse that process, to free up frozen time and release pent-up memories that no longer serve us and prevent our happiness. You are constantly making and unmaking your body at the quantum level. The word *unmaking* is necessary because life is not all creation; old, outworn experiences need revision as new ones come along. Sometimes a person feels compelled to try to shatter the entire body of experience he or she has created over the years; people who suddenly change jobs or plunge into divorce without provocation are often motivated by an inability to revise their inner world.

They may project the blame outward, onto an unsuitable job or unloved wife. What has actually become intolerable, however, is their internalized experience. Toxic memories have accumulated inside the person to the point where perfectly neutral situations—meeting the boss at the water cooler, watching the wife brush her teeth in the morning—arouse deep-seated negative emotions. Running away is an attempt to relieve these emotions, but the tactic rarely works because what we want to run away from has become part of ourselves.

Time-bound versus Timeless Awareness

Throughout this book I've argued that how you age depends on how you metabolize your experience. And in the final analysis, how you metabolize time is the most important aspect of this process, because time is the most fundamental experience. A key lesson in the spiritual teachings of J. Krishnamurti was this: "Time is the psychological enemy of man," meaning that we are psychologically undermined and deprived of our real selves by the feeling that time is an absolute over which we have no control. We somehow forget that we can choose whether to make time our enemy in the first place.

It's possible to have actual experiences of timelessness, and when that happens, there is a shift from time-bound awareness to timeless awareness.

Time-bound awareness is defined by:

- External goals (approval from others; material possessions; salary; climbing the ladder of professional success)
- Deadlines and time pressure

- Self-image built up from past experiences
- Lessons learned from past hurts and failures
- Fear of change, fear of death
- Distraction by past and future (worries, regrets, anticipations, fantasies)
- Longing for security (never permanently achieved)
- Selfishness, limited point of view (typical motivation: "What's in it for me?")

Timeless awareness is defined by:

- Internal goals (happiness; self-acceptance; creativity; satisfaction that one is doing one's best at all times)
- Freedom from time pressure; sense that time is abundant and open-ended
- Little thought of self-image; action focused on the present moment
- Reliance on intuition and leaps of imagination
- Detachment from change and turmoil; no fear of death
- Positive experiences of Being
- Selflessness; altruism; sense of shared humanity (typical motivation: "Can I help?")
- Sense of personal immortality

Although I have described them as opposites, there is in fact a whole range of experience running from completely time-bound to completely timeless awareness. A person who dreads his mortality, who is consumed by success and deadlines and depends solely on external motivations, would be almost pathologically time-bound, yet we can all see some of these traits in ourselves. On the other hand, the saint who lives only for God, whose experience of Being is constant and certain, represents the extreme freedom of timelessness. Most people do not manifest either extreme; and yet in many ways our deepest traits and attitudes are based on how we relate to time and metabolize it. To discover where you are on the scale of time-bound versus timeless awareness, answer the following questionnaire.

QUESTIONNAIRE: HOW DO YOU METABOLIZE TIME?

Read the following sentences and check off each one that applies to you fairly often or that you generally agree with. Some of the statements in Part 1 may seem to contradict others in Part 2, but that doesn't matter. Even if you have seemingly opposed traits and opinions, answer each statement on its own.

Part 1

1. There's barely enough time in the day to do all the things I have to.
2. I'm sometimes too exhausted at night to get to sleep.
3. I've had to abandon several important goals I set for myself when I was younger.
4. I'm less idealistic than I used to be.
5. It bothers me to let unpaid bills sit around.
6. I'm more cautious now about making new friends and entering serious relationships.
7. I've learned a lot from the school of hard knocks.
8. I spend more time and attention on my career than on my friends and family.
9. I could be a lot wiser about how I spend my money.
10. Life is a balance of losses and gains; I just try to have more gains than losses.
11. In a loving relationship, the other person should be counted on to meet my needs.
12. It sometimes hurts to remember the people I have let down.

13. Being loved is one of the most important things I can think of.
14. I don't like authority figures.
15. For me, one of the most frightening prospects about old age is loneliness.

Part 1 score _____

Part 2

1. I do what I love, I love what I do.
2. It's important to have a greater purpose in life than just family and career.
3. I feel unique.
4. Near-death experiences are very real.
5. I often forget what day it is.
6. I would describe myself as a carefree person.
7. It's a good thing to bring sexual issues out in the open, even when they are disturbing.
8. I work for myself.
9. It doesn't bother me to miss reading the newspaper or watching the evening news.
10. I love myself.
11. I've spent time in therapy and/or other self-development practices.
12. I don't buy into everything about the New Age, but it intrigues me.
13. I believe it is possible to know God.
14. I am more leisurely about things than most people.
15. I consider myself a spiritual person; this is an area of my life I work on.

Part 2 score _____

• • •

Evaluating your score. Although everyone usually checks at least a few answers in both sections, you will probably find that you scored higher in one section than the other.

If you scored higher on Part 1, you tend to be time-bound. For you, time is linear; it often runs short and will eventually run out. Relying on outside approval, motivation, and love, you have not grappled with your inner world as much as with the external one. You are likely to value excitement and positive emotions more highly than inner peace and nonattachment. You may cherish being loved by others too much and lose the opportunity to find self-acceptance.

If you scored higher on Part 2, you tend to be timeless in your awareness. Your sense of loving and being loved is based on a secure relationship with yourself. You value detachment over possessiveness; your motivations tend to be internal rather than external. At some time in your life you have had a sense of being larger than your limited physical self; your life may have been shaped by decisive experiences of God or your higher Self. Where others fear loneliness, you are grateful for your aloneness—solitude has developed your ability to know who you are.

————————

Most people have very little notion of how much effort they expend to keep themselves trapped in time-bound awareness. In their natural state, both body and mind attempt to discharge negative energies as soon as they are felt. A baby cries when it is hungry, thrashes when it chafes, and falls asleep when it becomes exhausted. Once you reach adulthood, however, spontaneous expression has largely been squelched in favor of behavior that is safe, socially acceptable, calculated to get what you want, or simply habitual. This loss of spontaneity is a result of not living in the present, which

I discussed earlier. But there is another result I haven't discussed: the loss of timelessness.

When the human organism is discharging its negative experiences efficiently, the mind is empty of past or future concerns; there is no worry, anticipation, or regret. This means that the mind is left open to Being, the simplest state of awareness. To support the mind in this open state, the body must be relaxed and flexible. Without stored stress, the aging process cannot gain a foothold. Thus, the most natural and easy experience anyone can have is that of timeless mind and ageless body. Unfortunately, normal life is far from this state. We are all time-bound, and only on the rarest occasions— generally when we least expect it—do we manage to break in to a conscious experience of our true nature. And in a world hungry for spiritual contact and so desperately lacking it, one taste of the timeless creates an earthquake in a person's awareness.

I'd like to offer an example of someone whose life was completely changed by such an experience, the spiritual teacher and writer Alan Watts. As a young man, Watts was inspired to try to find the right attitude toward meditation. He knew that meditation was practiced in the great spiritual traditions so that a person could escape the bonds of everyday existence, but his meditations were uncomfortable, boring, and did little more than remind him of how limited he was.

Watts had noted that many of the methods of the East are contradictory and mutually exclusive. Some masters say the mind should watch itself, some say that it is absolutely forbidden for the mind to watch itself. Some say that the mind should be controlled like a wild elephant tied to a stake, others say it should be allowed to run free. In sheer disgust he decided to reject them all. One day he took no special attitude and found, amazingly, that this letting go of expectations was enough to free him.

"In the force of throwing them away," Watts wrote, "it seemed that I threw myself away as well. For quite suddenly the weight of my own body disappeared. I felt that I owned nothing, not even a self, and that nothing owned me. The whole world became as transparent and unobstructed as my own mind. The 'problem of

life' simply ceased to exist, and for about eighteen hours I and
everything around me felt like the wind blowing leaves across a field
on an autumn day.''

This is a wonderfully evocative depiction of what it is to go
beyond time and space. The sense of freedom, of throwing away the
old baggage, arises automatically once a person stops relating only
to his limited self. What is this thing you call "me"? A reference
point built up from memories. Just as a bride has a specific reference
point that she can call on to relive her wedding day, the content of
your mind is built up of similar reference points—holographic packages of old experience—that you use to define who you are. "I" am
the one who was born in 1946, went to Catholic school, was afraid
to tell my mother I wet the bed, got a stuffed elephant for Christmas
when I was 8, married too young, dropped out of college, and so on,
endlessly. The buildup of memory accumulates until a rigid structure has been amassed. This is your self-image.

In moments of deepest awareness we completely transcend self-
image. Paradoxically, this is when the spiritual masters say the Self
is truly experienced, for the total absence of self-image leaves pure
selfhood exposed. Compared to the rigidity of your ordinary sense
of "I," the Self is a living, flowing sense of identity that is never
exhausted. It is a state beyond change, no matter whether you
experience it as a baby, a child, a young adult, or an old man.

Alan Watts had an unobscured experience of the Self, which is
available to everyone. You don't have to do anything to find the
Self—you have to stop doing anything. You have to stop identifying
with your self-image and its context of memories and linear time. "I
use memory," an Indian master once remarked, "I don't let memory
use me." This is a crucial point. Memory is just frozen time. It is
impossible for the time-based mind to see the timeless, for what we
call time is actually quantified bits of immortality. Reality is an
ocean, but we take it away in teacups.

When Watts fell into Reality, the ocean of timelessness, his
perception changed. Instead of feeling bound up and suffocated
(which is how all of us feel, although we might not be able to
articulate it), he had an "oceanic feeling," a phrase coined by Freud
to indicate the sense of merging with the whole. Time-based exis-

tence isn't whole and never can be, because it is by definition made of fragments.

Toppling Linear Time

When Einstein popped the bubble of the space-time illusion, he didn't do it just in his mind; something very real happened. One of Nature's absolutes was suddenly gone. By taking down linear time, Einstein took down three-dimensional space with it, for our perception of space from the air, showing us that the runway lights are ten feet apart, totally changes when the observer changes his position. From the vantage point of a higher altitude, the runway lights get closer and closer together, until finally one rises to outer space, and the lights disappear.

At the core of reality, Einstein said, linear time evaporates completely, pooling out like a stream overflowing its banks. In the physics before Einstein, a particle whizzing past an observer was thought to follow a straight-line trajectory, the kind that arrows, cannonballs, and bullets follow after they are fired.

$$A \longrightarrow B$$

Here are two points separated in time, and the arrow represents the most basic event in the universe, the passage of time from point A to point B. The reason why you can move through time is that particles and energy waves do, forming the basis of past, present, and future. Some particle was once at A, is now traveling toward B, and eventually will get there. But with great mathematical precision, Einstein (aided by a pioneering generation of other great physicists) proved that reality looks more like a pool of expanding rings (see page 300). Time turns into probability waves, and space is filled with ambiguous, foggy regions where a bit of matter might once have passed through or could be expected to show up.

Our two points A and B are known to be somewhere inside

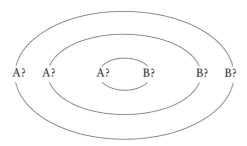

A?   A?   A?   B?   B?   B?

these expanding rings, but there is no definite past, present, or future, only possibilities of position. Maybe a particle is here, maybe there. When the position is determined, then the time scale emerges with it. A and B could be close together at the center or apart somewhere farther out. Linear time fools us into thinking that one minute follows another with equal spacing, but change your reference to subjective time: Two seconds sitting on a hot stove are much further apart than two seconds with a pretty girl. Einstein proved that the spacing between any two events is totally arbitrary; in reality there is only the *possibility* of intervals.

Toppling linear time didn't make Einstein very happy—he personally preferred to believe that three-dimensional things and events were real. Nonetheless, a supreme act of liberation was achieved for science. Younger physicists were jubilant, and in Einstein's wake we now have "superspace," a realm exploding with new dimensions, new geometries, and any kind of time one can imagine. In superspace, stars are no longer separated by black emptiness; infinite energy pulsates through the void, spinning itself out along invisible strings and loops. Time can get sucked into black holes and spewed out of "singularities," compressed seeds of space-time that enfold infinite duration in zero space.

In superspace time does not have any fixed direction; it can just as easily go backward as forward. A particle departing from A can show up at B before it left, defying our linear expectations. This may seem impossible to comprehend, but imagine a jet taking off at night. As a passenger sitting inside the plane, you see the runway lights rushing past you in a row, following a sequence in time. Once you are airborne, however, you can look down and see that the lights weren't moving at all. They exist in a pattern that you experienced as moving time. Linear time always appears to be moving, but when you break out of the three-dimensional viewpoint, it is possible to look down, survey the larger picture, and realize that time itself does not move.

The standard picture of Nature endorsed by most physicists has two layers that we can understand either through the senses or through scientific theory:

PHYSICAL CREATION

....

QUANTUM FIELD

The physical world arose from the quantum field, which is the source of all matter and energy. But that raises the obvious question: Where did the quantum field come from? Quantum reality is already at the very edge of time and space; beyond it there is no where or when. Therefore, the source of the quantum field must be nowhere and everywhere, and the date of its birth was no time and anytime. In other words, the question has no answer that makes sense within our ordinary framework of space-time.

Here again, Einstein offered a solution. When he had completed his work on the General Theory of Relativity, which some physicists consider the most profound act of thought achieved by any single human being, Einstein went on to postulate a unified field theory that would draw together all the laws of Nature and give them a common foundation. His famous theorem $E = mc^2$ had proved that matter can be converted into energy—in the terminology of physics, Einstein had unified the two—and now he set out to unify space and time as well. In essence he would replace the two-layer model of the cosmos with a three-layer one (see page 302).

Since he had already proved that space-time is an illusion, this new layer of the unified field had to be the Reality behind the illusion, the wholeness beyond all dimensions. Unfortunately, Einstein died before he was able to find mathematical expression for his unified field theory. Thirty years after his death, younger colleagues such as John Wheeler and David Bohm took up the task, despite the

PHYSICAL CREATION

....

QUANTUM FIELD

....

UNIFIED FIELD

fact that most physicists were extremely skeptical. It seemed impossible to come up with a true unified field theory, because it would have to be nothing less than "the theory of everything." Today, skepticism has turned to hope, and a theory of everything is considered a viable goal by such notable thinkers as Stephen Hawking and Roger Penrose.

However, we do not have to wait for the theory of everything to be proved in order to grasp that the unified field is identical to the It of Alan Watts's timeless experience, the totality that is perfectly ordered and that includes all space-time events in a seamless web. When the spiritual masters declare, "I am That," they are affirming the most complete sense of belonging. They realize that the unified field exists in, around, and through them. However, for us to share this experience we have to overcome a very imposing obstacle—the fear of death. For the vast majority of people, death represents the cutoff point where life ends and the unknown begins. But the post-Einstein universe has no beginning and end, no edges in time and space. To join this larger reality, each of us must redefine where our own life begins and ends—or whether it begins and ends at all.

THE SPELL OF
MORTALITY:

Overcoming the Illusion of Death

The unified field is inside ourselves, anchoring us to the timeless world with every breath, every thought, every action. Some people are much more aware of this connection than others, and for them death becomes much less threatening. Once, as a young man when he was at the depths of ill health and depression, Einstein wrote to a close friend, "I feel myself so much a part of all life that I am not in the least concerned with the beginning or the end of the concrete existence of any particular person in this unending stream."

This sense of being one with things brings safety and the absence of threat. If harboring threat inside us is what gives rise to aging, then we cannot afford to live with our present fear of death. In actuality, death is not the all-powerful force our fear tells us it is. In Nature, death is part of the larger cycle of birth and renewal. This year's seeds sprout, grow, blossom, and set next year's seeds. The cycles of endless renewal are not beyond death—they incorporate death, using it for a larger purpose. The same is true inside our bodies. Many cells undergo aging and death as a choice, not because they have been forced into extinction by the grim reaper.

Even to assume that death exists is a half-truth, for there are many levels of yourself that know nothing of extinction. Your atoms are billions of years old and have billions of years more life left in them. In the remote future, when they are broken down into smaller particles, atoms will not die but just get transformed into another configuration of energy. Atoms are nothing but transformed energy to begin with, yet we do not say that the primordial "energy soup" died when it got locked up into the orderly patterns of hydrogen, helium, and the other elements. Gravity and its kindred subatomic forces holding your body together will never die, although in some unknowable future they may withdraw into the larger force fields that gave birth to them in the Big Bang. As long as we are composed of these deathless ingredients, why not see ourselves in the same light?

In the Grip of Illusion

To break free of the grip of death, you need to see that it is based on a very selective view of reality that was conditioned into you before you had a conscious choice. Go back in your mind to the time in early childhood when you first realized that there was death. These first encounters are generally very shocking. A 4-year-old is stunned when she wakes up one morning to find that a pet canary, cat, or dog has simply stopped being alive. What's happened? Where did my pet go?

Parents rarely can supply a good answer to those questions. They say something like, "Your pet has gone to heaven to be with God." This usually doesn't settle the matter. Saying that a pet went to heaven conveys what the parents *hope* is true, but underneath they fear death as much as children do and understand it just as little. Young children have good antennae for parental doubts and evasions. The tears stop and the pain eases, but at a deeper level a faint suspicion is born: Maybe this could happen to me.

Then when a child is somewhere between ages 4 and 6, the parents confirm that the fearful intimation is true. "Grandmother has died and gone to heaven, and one day you will die, and so will Mommy and Daddy." You may not remember this moment—many children prefer to deny it and vow to be Peter Pan, forever young— but whether you remember it is irrelevant. The moment you confronted death, some psychologists argue, you bought into a notion that has gripped humanity for centuries. Your belief in death as an extinction doomed your body to decay, age, and die, just as did so many before you in exactly the same way.

It isn't death that hurts us but the dread of its inevitability. We all felt an ache, a hole in our hearts that was left when the first cherished thing in our lives died. A gap was left for fear to fill, and since nothing else has filled it since, we haven't yet been able to confront death. Loss is the most potent cause of anxiety and also the most difficult to face.

In adulthood, aging reminds us of loss; therefore it forces us to look into this gap that was opened in childhood. To free oneself from death is the goal of all religions: "O Death, where is thy sting? O grave, where is thy victory?" Saint Paul asks in his letter to the tiny Christian band in Corinth. He then supplies the answer: "The sting of death is sin," meaning error or the fall from grace. In other words, death is the result of man's separation from the Divine, which is without death. By implication, immortality is our true life.

But what about the pet canary, cat, or dog who died in our childhood? It perished without having any such theological beliefs. However, to say that an animal died is to put things in human terms. Look out the window at a tree. Is it alive or dead? It is both at the same time: Its old leaves are dead, as is the seed the tree sprouted from. The wood inside the trunk is dead, except for the thin ring of cambium, less than one-sixteenth of an inch thick, that feeds the leaves, which themselves are largely composed of nonliving fibers of cellulose. When leaves turn in autumn, their dead skeletons fall to the ground, but until then they are part of the living tree.

Moreover, the food, air, and water circulating through the tree are no more alive than when they were locked up in rocks and raindrops; the soil that sustains the tree is only ground-down stone and decayed compounds from prior trees. What we call a living tree is a composite of life and death, and any division between one and the other is mostly in our heads. Any plant or animal is just one stage in the constant cycling and recycling of elements that goes on eternally. That whole cycle is life, and the cycling is the living. The fact that we try to freeze the cycle into stop-motion and say, "Now this tree is alive, now this tree is dead," represents how our minds work. Fearing decay and disintegration, we label them death when in fact they are only change.

Like the tree, the canary is just a stage of life. At an earlier time the canary was an egg, before that a fertilized cell, and before that,

birdseed being eaten by its mother, who turned the food into the egg
that was to be laid. After the canary dies, it will decompose, its
elements will nourish plants, and the plants will set seed to feed
other birds. How much of this endless round, if any, is death, and
how much is just our view of things—including ourselves? You may
think that death is an awful event awaiting you in the future, when
in actuality parts of your body are dying every second. Your stomach lining dies partially every time you digest food, only to be
replaced by new tissue. The same is true of your skin, hair, toenails,
blood cells, and every other tissue.

You may assume that death is your enemy, but all these cells are
dying in order to keep you alive. If your stomach lining didn't die
and get replaced over and over, gastric juices would sear a hole in
your stomach wall after a few hours, and then all of you would die.
The line between what is living and what is dead gets very blurry the
closer you look. Parts of your body are much more alive than others.
Muscles have a faster metabolism than fat; brain, heart, and liver
cells rarely if ever duplicate after birth, while stomach, skin, and
blood cells replace themselves in a matter of days, weeks, and
months.

A strange fact of human anatomy is that if we could somehow
remove all the cells in our bodies, the remaining form would still
look very much like a person. Our structural parts resemble a
free-standing coral reef composed of mineralized bone, plus liga-
ments, tendons, connective tissue, and water, with all our cells
tucked away inside, the way coral polyps are tucked in the calcified
reef they have secreted.

Like the reef, which carries the ocean around within it, we are
about two-thirds salty brine. But these dead parts of ourselves exchange their atoms freely with the environment: If hurt they heal; if
pressure is put on them, they slowly change form to relieve the
stress. So how much of the body is alive and how much dead?

Even to say "my body" implies a division that doesn't necessarily exist. Is the air in my lungs part of my body? If so, what about
the air I'm about to inhale or the air I just exhaled? The world "out
there" is composed of trillions of atoms that either once were or
soon will be me, and the whole packet of matter and energy we call

Earth is necessary to keep me alive. I could as easily say that I am just a cell in this larger body, and since I need the whole planet to sustain myself, everything on Earth is part of my body. If that is true, then nothing should be considered dead—rotting carrion, the worms and fungi that feed off them, even the bones of my ancestors are caught in the same tidal wave of life that carries me on its crest.

Some people recoil from all this talk about death, denying any interest in it. They don't fear death, they say, or if they do, it doesn't haunt them or hold the kind of power over them I have been describing. Why dwell on such a morbid subject? Isn't it healthier simply to accept the inevitable and live for today? The answer to this objection is that unconscious forces are at work in us. We may all concede that we are going to die, but except in moments when we have to be present with the dead or dying, our dread is kept under wraps. This is almost a biological necessity—I can't imagine how I could keep going if the thought of my own death came to the surface of thought more than once or twice a year. (Being a doctor, I am forced to see death much more often than that, but closing the eyes of a deceased cancer patient doesn't automatically bring my own mortality to mind. I may feel sad, but I do not see my own eyes closing.)

The fact that we all protect ourselves from dread doesn't mean that we have control over it. From within its dark pit, fear is still exerting control over us. For one thing, the very fact that we can't stand to imagine our own death invests it with tremendous power, as if death had an electrified fence around it with 10 million volts running through it and a huge sign reading DO NOT TOUCH! We don't. And because death is fenced off in the mind, we don't really know much about it. Fear of death should be renamed ignorance of death.

I feel quite sure that nothing makes people age faster than fear. Grief runs a close second; every doctor has witnessed the appalling deterioration that can befall widowed men and women. But nothing beats fear at this particular game: A patient who has received the diagnosis of terminal cancer can wither away very quickly, almost before your eyes. Not that this always happens. There are inner qualities that fight off fear, such as courage or faith in God, and some people can summon these qualities in times of dreadful crisis. But if fear gets through, it will do its work sure enough. The point is not that death is a fiction, but that our belief in death creates limitations where none need exist.

The Uses of Dying

One assumption we all tend to make is that death is somehow unnatural and, by implication, evil. I cannot agree. Nature is very tolerant and flexible about how death is used, or not used; and in the larger picture, questions of good and evil tend to look rather arbitrary. If you consider how life operates from the genetic level, DNA long ago discovered the secret of creating ageless cells, in the form of amoebas, algae, bacteria, etc., whose generations extend back without interruption. The appearance and disappearance of any single amoeba is insignificant, for life keeps cranking out amoebas from the same genes. Nature also went on to assemble more complex ageless creatures. The hydra, for example, is a primitive water animal that can grow new cells as fast as old ones are shed. Composed of a foot, a thin stalk, and a flowerlike cluster of tiny tentacles, the hydra is always growing at one end and dying at the other, renewing its entire body every two weeks. Its cells exist in perfect flow, with new ones moving along the assembly line to fill in the places where old ones are dying. This is creation and destruction in perfect balance, leaving no room for death. Time therefore cannot catch up with the hydra; it only dies by accident, lack of food, drought, or some other external cause.

The secret of eternal youth, then, is a balanced metabolism, a constant chemical flow that processes food, air, and water in perfect equilibrium, without losing a stitch to entropy. DNA learned to manage this balancing act hundreds of millions of years ago. In that sense, death is a late development on the evolutionary chain, but even among higher organisms, DNA exerts considerable control over death. The common honeybee, for example, can change its age at will. Every beehive needs young workers whose job is to stay indoors to feed and care for newly hatching larvae. After three weeks, these workers grow up and move on to become mature foragers, the bees who fly from the hive to collect pollen from flowers.

At any given period, however, there may be too many young workers or too many old foragers. In the spring so many new larvae may be hatching that the hive lacks mature foragers and needs more very quickly. When that happens, some of the young workers age into foragers in one week instead of the usual three and fly off seeking food. On the other hand, if a swarm of bees splits off to form a new colony, it is likely to be composed mostly of old forager bees. Sensing a shortage of young workers, some of these old foragers will reverse their ages and become young again—they regenerate the hormones of youthful workers and even regrow the withered glands needed to produce food for the hatching larvae.

When bee researchers first discovered this behavior, they were astonished. They realized that aging isn't a one-way process dictated by a fixed timetable for the honeybee, aging is "plastic"—able to go back and forth, slow down or speed up; the real mystery is why this does not hold true for higher life-forms. I would contend that aging is *always* plastic, but that we have cemented it in place through our belief in death, the inevitable end point on the fixed timetable of growing old. "Honeybee colonies are rhythmic entities that must constantly cope with changes in population size and structure, food availability, predators, and weather," wrote bee researcher Gene Robinson. With only slight changes, one could adopt this model for the human body: It is a mammoth hive of 50 trillion cells that grow old or stay young according to what is needed by the whole colony at any given moment.

Floating inside every cell's watery interior is a self-destruct mechanism in the form of sealed packets of corrosive enzymes. These enzymes may or may not be responsible for "normal" aging, but they undoubtedly serve special purposes. After a scavenging white cell, or macrophage, has ingested a large number of bacteria or viruses, for example, it eliminates them by unleashing these digestive enzymes; in the process, the macrophage also dies. This is not a random act of violence but a highly conscious decision. For the overall good of the body, the cell destroys itself.

The same deliberate self-sacrifice takes place millions of times a day in our largest organ, the skin. As a physical object a living skin cell is very frail, far too tender to stand up to the elements. Our outermost layer of skin, the epidermis, is therefore composed entirely of dead cells, which are hard enough to stand up to all the bumping, scraping, jostling, and knocking about that comes our way.

These cells did not perish from exposure to the air. Rather, as a young skin cell is produced in the dermis—the inner lining of the skin—it gets pushed toward the surface by the pressure of newer cells growing from underneath. During this time the cell begins to accumulate a protein inside itself called keratin, the same horny substance as that found in our hair and nails. The keratin replaces the soft part of the cell, making it harder and harder. By the time it actually reaches the air, each skin cell contains enough keratin to protect our bodies against wind, sun, and rain. The cell then fulfills its mission by dying, leaving no trace behind when it gets sloughed off to make way for the next wave of growing cells. By knowing when to die, the skin cell helps to ensure the survival of the whole body.

At the opposite extreme, a cancer cell endangers the whole body by not knowing how to die. A cancer cell is basically a runaway immortalist: It tries to survive on its own terms, disregarding the fate of every other cell. Insane as this behavior seems, it still represents a choice woven into Nature's scheme; every cell's DNA is outfitted with specialized genes, called oncogenes, that apparently switch on before cancer can be triggered. According to another recent hypothesis, there are genes in the first chromosome of human DNA that would allow every cell to divide indefinitely if activated. Scientists have not yet found a reason for cells to pursue their own immortality. Perhaps this switch is a holdover from our ancient evolutionary past. Or is it a latent power we haven't yet learned to tap?

People exert much more choice over their aging and death than we are ready to acknowledge. Although we call ourselves "victims" of old age and death, the stark truth is that for many of us, growing old and dying offer the only escape from an unfulfilling life. Such escapist motives play an important part, I believe, in the phenomenon of early-retirement death, discussed in Part One. Another variation on this theme is "anniversary death," in which someone dies on the same date as a beloved spouse or child passed away. Studies of Chinese and Jewish communities have disclosed that their mortality rate dips dramatically just before important religious holidays, only to rise immediately afterward. People were waiting for one more New Year or Passover before they finally let go. It shouldn't take a study to tell us that people cling to life when something dear is at stake.

The most recent instance I saw of this occurred with an old man, the victim of several severe strokes, and his grandson. The man had finally reached the point of incapacity and was hospitalized with little hope of ever going home again. He drifted along in a weak, semiconscious state; every time he was lucid enough to speak, he pointed to his grandson's picture and mumbled, "Where is he, where is he?"

The dying man's children called the grandson, who rushed to Boston. When he arrived at the hospital, a change came over the old man. He smiled and caressed the young man who meant so much to him. They held hands and chatted quietly, alone together for most of the day. When the grandson left, expecting to return in the morning, everyone told him how much better his grandfather looked. Two hours later the old man died in his sleep. As I think about this incident, I wonder how any researcher could hope to quantify the forces that sustain life as long as there is hope or love to look forward to. From the outside we cannot know with any certainty what a person's body is responding to. The whole affair is much too personal.

When the handbook on suicide, *Final Exit,* became a surprise bestseller several years ago, its primary audience consisted of people afflicted with incurable disease or chronic physical or emotional pain. Nature's form of slow suicide, aging, was not quick enough for them. Appalling as that may sound, a life of pain and sickness would be even more appalling without some release. "If it were not for death," an Indian guru once told his disciples, "we would all be condemned to eternal senility."

Even without senility, life can simply run its course. "I look forward to death," said Redden Couch, a retired farmer from Port Angeles, Washington, "because of all the things I've done that I can't do now. I don't have any fear of death at all. If I were to die right now, it would be just fine. I'm ready anytime." Do these words express resignation, serenity, apathy, courage, defeat? We cannot know. As it happens, Redden Couch made this statement on his 100th birthday and was still alive at 104. Despite his words, his deeper self apparently had more living to do.

All these examples show that death doesn't have just one value, either positive or negative. Dying is a form of change, and as such it has to be seen within the larger framework of non-change. "People have a wrong idea about death," Maharishi once remarked to me. "They see it as an end, but it is really a beginning." You may call that an article of faith, but to me it's a realistic statement of fact. In the flow of life, destruction never has the last word; creation brings a phoenix out of the ashes every time. Every cell knows how to divide to form two cells; every shattered atom can regroup into new atoms; every thought is followed by a new inspiration. How, then, can we learn to live within this continuity that is the wholeness of life? What about a parent's emotional devastation when a child dies, or a wife's when she loses her husband?

These feelings are natural, of course; there is pain at the loss of anyone we love. But the pain does not have to be deep and enduring if you have absorbed the reality of life as an eternal flow in which there is no loss or gain, only transformation. In one of his sonnets Shakespeare wrote, "I weep to have what I fear to lose"—this is the inevitable result of attachment to time-bound awareness. The new paradigm holds that awareness is the source of reality, and two wholly different kinds of reality result from time-bound and timeless awareness.

RESULTS OF TIME-BOUND AWARENESS	RESULTS OF TIMELESS AWARENESS
aging	freedom, autonomy
entropy	youthfulness
confusion	knowledge of reality
fatigue	unbounded energy
repression	liberated emotions
feeling of victimization	expansion beyond body and ego
separation anxiety	peace
conflict	power
grief, sorrow	harmony
imprisonment in ego and body	joy
fear	
death	

All of us experience aspects of both realities, because our awareness is fluid: It can bring us devastating moments of grief and fear and wonderful moments of peace and power. It can choose to identify with the limitations of a physical body and a selfish ego or it can break free into transcendence and expansiveness. This flexibility is the true genius of human awareness, because it leaves all possibilities open. Yet obviously there are great advantages to living permanently in timeless awareness.

India's spiritual masters believe there is a natural tendency for the human spirit to seek unlimited freedom and fulfillment. Like the Gulf Stream invisibly pushing its way through the Atlantic, our human minds contain hidden currents urging our thoughts and emotions toward a higher reality. In India this is called *dharma,* an ancient Sanskrit word that can be translated in various ways. It means law, orderliness, duty, and right behavior. A person's dharma is his work or profession; it is also the duty he owes his family, the higher purpose in his life, and the spiritual ideal to which he is committed.

The root word of "dharma" is a verb that means "to uphold." In the broadest sense, dharma is what upholds the universe; it is the guiding force that makes order out of chaos. Thus, the ultimate way to avoid entropy, aging, and death is to live in dharma. The universe evolves because the stream of dharma guides it; it is the invisible intelligence that weaves the fabric of life. Human awareness is capable of touching dharma directly, of latching onto it and thus guiding its own evolution. This, finally, is what makes us human— that we not only evolve but guide our own evolution. Dharma is not a set of religious teachings but an actual force that can be discovered and used.

In the following In Practice section we will see how this can be accomplished, for with conscious guidance our inner intelligence can create a permanent state of ageless body and timeless mind. All of us experience moments when peace, power, and love arise spontaneously, only to disappear. Far from being random, this drift in and out of Reality reflects the mind's ability to stay on course, for if dharma is followed steadily, there is no end to peace, love, and power. They are the natural results of the most natural kind of awareness—timelessness.

For me the great joy of writing this book was to take a subject fraught with fear—aging—and make it a vehicle for fulfillment. Humans are not trapped in time, squeezed into the volume of a body and the span of a lifetime. We are voyagers on the infinite river of life. This is what Christ meant when he counseled, "Be in the world but not of it." This is what Carlos Castaneda learned from Don Juan when he wrote, "Gone was his feeling of detachment, which was what had given him the power to love. Without that detachment, he had only mundane needs, desperation, and hopelessness: the distinctive features of the world of everyday life."

Although we often identify love with clinging and possessiveness, there is a deep truth here: to lose the power of detachment means losing the ability to love. Detachment is not cold disinterest or lack of feeling. Detachment is a free sense of self unhindered by boundaries. Our voyage does not begin or end in the physical world. Earth is a beautiful green-and-blue jewel hung upon the tapestry of eternity. However long we stay here to drink the pure water and breathe the life-giving air, eternity is more truly our home.

We are of timeless essence. We were born in the bottomless pool that sends up bubbles of time and space. One bubble is a moment, another is a millennium. But the pool itself is pure spirit, and no matter how many stars and galaxies rise from it and burst on the surface like fragile foam, nothing has been taken away or added. Being is deep, clear, permanent, ever the same. It is amazing to think that our everyday existence springs from this infinitely renewable source, but life has no other basis. Unbounded intelligence, freedom, and power are inherent in the unified field that Einstein and the ancient sages shared in their vision. Immortality dawns when you realize that you deserve your place in the eternal flow. Knowing this, you can claim your immortality here and now, in every second, for time is nothing but quantified immortality. Nature waits to lavish this supreme gift upon you. Having nourished us for millions of years, the sea, the air, and the sun are still singing the song we must begin to appreciate once more.

What is Nature saying all around us, in the space between our atoms and pervading every thought? The same breath, the same silent whisper courses through every cell. It is the rhythm of life itself, calling to each of us with gentle insistence. I cherish a verse from the ancient Rig Veda that articulates this eternal song:

> Although my spirit may wander the four cor-
>   ners of the earth,
> Let it come back to me again so that I may live
>   and journey here.
>
> Although my spirit may go far away over the
>   sea,
> Let it come back to me again so that I may live
>   and journey here.
>
> Although my spirit may go far away to the
>   flashing beams of light,

Let it come back to me again so that I may live
and journey here.

Although my spirit may go far away to visit
the sun and the dawn,
Let it come back to me again so that I may live
and journey here.

Although my spirit may wander over the lofty
mountains,
Let it come back to me again so that I may live
and journey here.

Although my spirit may go far away into all
forms that live and move,
Let it come back to me again so that I may live
and journey here.

Although my spirit may go far away to distant
realms,
Let it come back to me again so that I may live
and journey here.

Although my spirit may go far away to all that
is and is to be,
Let it come back to me again so that I may live
and journey here.

Although my spirit may wander in the valley
of death,
Let it come back to me again so that I may live
and journey here.

Read this aloud twice, then be with your body quietly for five
minutes, directing your awareness to every part of your body,
knowing that this awareness is Spirit. Spirit is healing energy, the
flow of life and intelligence in every cell. When we are once more
attuned to the innate joy and delight of our bodies, the signals of
deep wisdom will reappear, creating healing from within. An old
Chinese poem by Chang-Tzu says:

> That which fills the universe
> 　I regard as my body,
> And that which directs the universe,
> 　I see as my own nature.

I hear silent music in these words, reminding me that the cosmic breath is my next breath and the cosmic dance the next beat of my heart.

IN PRACTICE:

The Timeless Way

The deepest reality you are aware of is the one from which you draw your power. For someone who is conscious only of the material world, power is limited to material forces; but at a more profound level there is a creative power shaping mind and body—the power of evolution, or dharma. To get in touch with the core of life, you have to get in touch with the creative power of the universe. That power expresses itself through your personal creativity. When you are in the field of creativity, you lose track of time. Only the flow exists.

There are three forces pervading all life: creation, maintenance, and destruction. All three are present in the life span of cells, stars, trees, planets, and galaxies, since every form must come into being, be maintained, and pass away. Even though each life span unfolds in a sequence over time, the three forces themselves exist simultaneously. The genes of every species include the code for creating new cells, maintaining each cell for a certain time, and destroying it to make way for another generation of tissue. This three-in-one intelligence is what you are trying to affect when you consciously shape your life; it is up to you which aspect—creation, maintenance, or destruction—is most dominant. Because you have the power to shift the balance of forces, you are above and beyond them.

As long as creation dominates your existence, you will keep growing and evolving. Evolution thwarts entropy, decay, and aging. The most creative people in any field intuitively draw on this understanding. They grow with full consciousness that they are the source of their own power, and whatever their field, certain traits are generally shared by them:

1. They are able to contact and enjoy silence.
2. They connect with and enjoy Nature.
3. They trust their feelings.
4. They can remain centered and function amid confusion and chaos.
5. They are childlike—they enjoy fantasy and play.
6. They self-refer: They place the highest trust in their own consciousness.
7. They are not rigidly attached to any point of view: Although passionately committed to their creativity, they remain open to new possibilities.

These seven points give us a practical standard to measure how creatively our lives are proceeding. The following exercise demonstrates how to develop and strengthen these areas.

Exercise 1: Creative Action Plan

Everyone has a set routine that dominates his or her day. Most of us fill our waking hours with the same activities—seeing the same family members and friends, working with the same co-workers, driving the same roads, even thinking the same thoughts (it has been estimated that 90 percent of the thoughts a person has in a day are a literal repeat of his thoughts of the day before). This routine allows little room for genuine creativity unless you choose to make room for it. Yet in quantum terms there is infinite space for creativity, because every second is full of unlimited choice and unseen possibilities. Once you begin to make space for the new and unknown, you open the way for deeper powers to emerge from the gaps of everyday existence. All the most extraordinary historical events took place on ordinary days, and the most extraordinary thoughts arose in minds that were having many ordinary thoughts.

The following exercise gives you a way to open some space for growth in your life, and the more consciously you follow it, the more unlimited the growth will be.

Write out an action plan for the next six months based on the seven qualities of very creative people, listed on p. 319. You don't have to squeeze every point into each day—just make a commitment to allow these aspects of your life to emerge more fully.

1. Experiencing silence

First, block out some time to experience silence. Ideally this would mean a short period of meditation (fifteen to thirty minutes) in the morning before you go to work, then a second period just after you get home in the evening. This is a time simply to be, and yet its very simplicity can make it the most important time of your life. Silence is a precious commodity, particularly in the hustle-and-bustle of modern society. In a world gone more than slightly mad, finding your core of silence is like recapturing the fort of sanity and peace. The mind replenishes itself in silence, the quantum source for all activity. If your life is dominated solely by activity, you are spending more energy than you are gaining; the most basic rhythm of Nature—activity and rest—is being skewed too far in one direction.

Silence is the great teacher, and to learn its lessons you must pay attention to it. There is no substitute for the creative inspiration, knowledge, and stability that come from knowing how to contact your core of inner silence. The great Sufi poet Rumi wrote, "Only let the moving waters calm down, and the sun and moon will be reflected on the surface of your Being."

2. Spending time in Nature

Plan to spend a period of time contacting Nature. There is no healthier way to discharge pent-up energies. The mind-body system throws off its excess energies spontaneously when you remove yourself from the artificial confines of the material world and return to Nature. In city environments it isn't always easy to find a green, open space, an expansive view of sky and clouds, a lungful of pure air. But if you can find a patch of ground to lie down on, shoes off and arms outstretched to the sun, take advantage of it. Short of that, seek out experiences of Nature where you live, getting up early to appreciate the sunrise or stopping for a few moments in the evening to watch the sunset and gaze at the moon and stars.

Your body's cells are exquisitely attuned to the cycles of the moon, sun, and stars. When you drink Nature in through your senses, this invisible connection is strengthened. Even in the heart of congested urban areas, you can tend a windowsill garden so that you can watch a seed grow; walking out onto the roof of your building to absorb the sun also affords some contact with Nature. However you can manage it, capture at least a few moments of freshness and feel the nourishing touch of earth, sun, and sky.

3. Experiencing and trusting emotions

Begin a journal of your feelings. This needn't be a complicated task. Simply make a list of some key emotions and note *one example* of each as it arises in your day. Start with key words for the basic positive emotions, such as:

love	joy
sympathy	acceptance
happiness	friendliness
trust	compassion

Next, make a column for more abstract feelings associated with creativity and personal growth, such as:

insight	intuition
discovery	transcendence
faith	merging
forgiveness	peace
revelation	

Last, note the primary negative emotions, such as:

anger	envy
anxiety	sorrow
guilt	greediness
distrust	selfishness

Look at this sheet of paper in the morning and take it with you to work as a reminder. Although you will get the most benefit by actually writing down your feelings in some detail, making them explicit and reliving how strong each feeling was, what kind of circumstances triggered it, and how much a particular emotion meant to you, you can do very well with a silent journal. That is, glance down the list and simply remember each emotion briefly. Your goals with this journal are as follows:

1. To discover how often you feel things that get over-looked.
2. To permit the spontaneous release of emotions that you would normally repress or try to forget.
3. To truly know your emotions. Many people cannot specifically describe what compassion or insight feels like, for example, but by consciously being on the lookout for an emotion, you will get to know it intimately. This is the first stage of mastering your emotions.
4. To make your emotions enjoyable. The life of feelings is meant to be rich and satisfying, but if your emotions are strangers to you, you cannot enjoy them. Many people have convinced themselves that they have few if any emotions; yet, despite our efforts to repress them, there is a feeling attached to every single thought we have. Bringing all these feelings to light puts you back into the wholeness of the mind-body connection, and wholeness is the most satisfying state in which to live.

In your daily inventory, don't skip over any words on your list and don't dwell on any single category (even if you felt angry several times in one day, think of only one instance, then move on). Also, it's important not to focus too much on negative emotions, which are the easiest for everyone to experience and usually are the most self-serving. I ask you to bring up negative emotions so that you may gain insight into their origin. Being aware of where an emotion comes from permits the dissipation of negative feelings (this is guaranteed to happen, although for stubbornly rooted or repressed negativity, the process will take time). Negative emotions close off and limit the world, while the point of this exercise is to awaken the expansive, creative emotions.

If you take your journal seriously, you will be amazed at how many diverse emotions you have during the day without being conscious of them. Whatever you pay attention to grows, and even though you may feel that words such as *insight* or *revelation* apply to you only rarely, just by looking at your list and focusing on each feeling for a few seconds you will create space for them to grow.

Being genuinely in touch with emotions tends to be tremendously difficult amid work and other activities. Emotions don't follow a routine, and if you have a tendency to be removed from your feelings, the rush of modern life makes it even easier to repress and escape feelings as they arise. Yet nothing is more important than experiencing your feelings. They are the most spontaneous part of your makeup, the most primary expression of your awareness as it relates to the world. You are the totality of all the relationships you have, and the most accurate mirror of them is your emotions.

4. Remaining centered amid chaos

In order to remain centered and calm when everything around you is in confusion, you need to develop skills for finding your center. To do that, isolate two times in your workday when things are most hectic and stressful for you (moments of heaviest workload are an obvious choice, as is the afternoon rush hour going home). Now plan to take five minutes to center yourself just before these two periods, using the following technique:

Find a place where you can be alone, one that is as quiet as possible. Sit comfortably and close your eyes. Pay attention to your breathing, focusing on the passage of air into and out of your nostrils. See the air as faint swirls coming into your nostrils and gently flowing out again. After two minutes, begin to feel your body (i.e., note the sensations inside your body, on your skin, the weight of your limbs, etc.). After a minute, gently bring your attention to the center of your chest and lightly rest it there. Within a few seconds your attention will probably be distracted by a fleeting thought or sensation. Don't resist this, but when you notice what is happening, gently return your focus to your chest. End the exercise by sitting quietly, doing nothing.

Although this is a very simple technique, the discharge of negative energies it produces is often quite dramatic—you can feel a heavy burden lifting off your shoulders and sense a lightness and calm infusing your whole being. Most important, you will begin to experience that being centered is actually the most natural and comfortable way to be in any situation, no matter how hectic. Centering is a way to return to your self and become unmoored from the confusion around you.

5. Being childlike

Write down two or three things you can do tomorrow that are totally childlike. Think of something that evokes childhood for you—eating an ice cream cone, being on the playground, playing games with the shapes of clouds. Begin to incorporate these activities more and more into your present life. Your goal is to find that place inside you where you are still a carefree child. The new paradigm tells us that no event ever disappears; it only recedes out of conscious awareness back into the field. Therefore, your childhood is still there with you, ready to be evoked and integrated into your being.

The activity you choose should be fun but not adult fun; even if you feel you have outgrown hopscotch, jump rope, or toys, find something that irresistibly brings back your happiness as a child (baking a comforting dessert such as apple pie or bread pudding is a good suggestion). When you carry out your childlike activity, *be a child*. Perhaps you will decide to go to a playground to swing or to climb on a jungle gym or just to participate by watching children at play. Put your mind into the innocent, carefree mode that children exhibit. The feeling you are trying to recapture here is not a return to childhood but something much more profound, as stated by the brilliant writer and therapist A. H. Almaas.

"When we look at a child," Almaas writes, "we see that the sense of fullness, of intrinsic aliveness, of joy in being, is not the result of something else. There is value in just being oneself; it is not because of something one does or doesn't do. It is there in the beginning, when we were children, but slowly it gets lost." What usually happens over time is that we lose track of the joy inside us; there may be numerous sources of pleasure and success outside us, but they don't match our feelings, which may remain at very low levels of worthiness and satisfaction.

Ultimately, the desire to be young again is a symbol of the deeper desire to remain new. Babies and young children have no problem with this. By putting yourself back into the most childlike mindset you can imagine, you open the way for learning, as Almaas puts it, that "we are the pleasure, we are the joy, we are the most profound significance and the highest value."

6. Being self-referral

The highest state of consciousness available to us is unity, which erases the distinction between observer and observed. In unity, everything you once thought was "out there" is seen to be part of yourself. What prevents this experience is a false sense of self built from images of past experience. Self-image is necessary to a very limited extent; you have to know your identity and profession and other technical matters. But most people weight their self-image with a multitude of opinions, beliefs, likes and dislikes, and other extraneous baggage. To get rid of this baggage and reexperience yourself as a free, uncluttered person, you have to work at stripping away the crusted varnish of self-image.

Your action plan can take many different directions in accomplishing this goal.

• You can take up a new activity that is totally incongruous with your self-image. Take up aerobic dancing if you are a gray-flanneled business executive, or weight lifting if you're a housewife. Expose yourself to people and situations that challenge you to grow beyond old habits.

• Volunteer to work with the homeless or the disabled. Being confronted with people who are very different from you, learning to overcome your innate fear and resistance to them, and finally seeing yourself in them is a powerful way to find your common humanity.

• Write your autobiography. Putting down every detail of your life as candidly and honestly as possible will help you detach from ingrained attitudes by showing you where they came from. The act of writing also forces you to articulate things you normally take for granted, such as how you feel about your parents and your career. Be as detailed and explicit as possible. Concentrate on how you felt at every period of your life. Don't justify your actions or make yourself out to be better than you are. If you find it difficult to express yourself, try to unlock the flow of words by writing about yourself in the third person: "John was dominated by a father he both loved and feared," rather than, "I was dominated by a father I both loved and feared."

• Resolve to take one step every day to correct some behavior that you know isn't an expression of the real you. For example, you may be an habitual people-pleaser who always says what other people like to hear. The next time you find yourself falling into that trap, say what you really feel. The situation doesn't have to be dramatic or earthshaking. Someone might remark, "The bus is always late, isn't it?" or, "Things are really running down around here." Instead of chiming in to agree with their complaint, state how you actually feel about things. On the other hand, if you are always outspoken and tend to feel that others should listen to you, stop yourself and listen to them for a change. These simple exercises can actually be quite challenging; you need to learn to lower your social facade, and the more you practice, the less critical you will find it is to wear the mask.

• Expand your efforts in meditation, Yoga, creative visualization, or other inner disciplines that take you outside your confined awareness. These practices are useful to everyone, but if you truly dedicate yourself to them, you will walk even faster down the road to discovering the Self.

7. Practicing nonattachment

To be unattached means that you are free from outside influences that overshadow your real self. This lesson isn't one our culture teaches us. Modern people place a high value on being committed, excited, passionate, deeply involved, and so forth, and they fail to realize that these qualities are not the opposite of nonattachment. To be committed to a relationship, for example, ultimately means to have enough love and understanding to let the other person be who he or she wants to be. Being passionate about your work means giving yourself the creative space to approach it from all angles, finding new directions and opportunities. These new opportunities can only come from your inner creative core, which you will not be able to contact if you are immersed in and overwhelmed by the details of your work.

The paradox is that to get the most passion from life, you must be able to stand back and be yourself. Passion and commitment, love and dedication, self-worth and fulfillment—all are born in Being; they are qualities of the essential self that blossom when you are free from narrow attachments. For most of us, the person who loved us most dearly was our mother, but if you reflect on it, this love often implied power and control. As a child you had to do what your mother said or her love might be withdrawn. "I'm your mother, you have to pay attention to me" is the opposite of "I love you, and my greatest happiness is to see you become what you want." The first statement may come from love, but it is not a love that easily permits freedom.

Finding your freedom is necessary, and it involves letting go of expectations, preconceived outcomes, and egotistical points of view. Consider two mothers, each standing in the aisle of a supermarket trying to handle an upset child who is crying loudly and attracting attention. One mother is angry and embarrassed; her primary motive is to stop the child from making a scene, but of course this doesn't work with small children. When they are upset, they are upset. Their feelings are their world, and making a scene in the market doesn't mean anything to them. So when the mother commands, "All right, stop crying. I mean it, stop right now," the child knows that *his* feelings aren't really being heard and therefore he isn't being allowed to really exist. The mother just wants a result; she wants things to turn out a certain way.

The second mother, on the other hand, sees that her child is genuinely upset, and she doesn't care about how she looks to others.

She isn't thinking about the situation as it affects her; instead, she feels for her child and wants him to be happy again. She says things such as, "What's wrong? Did something scare you? It's all right, I'm here." The words she uses are not the critical thing—she might just pick up and caress her child for a moment. The child's quantum mechanical body senses that his feelings have been understood. Therefore, there is no threat, because his mother's intention is to heal, not merely to end a disagreeable situation.

Your quantum mechanical body has all the sensitivity of a child's, and you can use that sensitivity to get back to your true self, which exists above and beyond the troubling circumstances of your life. Again, the matter of self-image is involved. Being oriented to your true self, not to your self-image, is the most basic healing attitude anyone can take. When you are oriented to the self, you use your feelings, your needs, and your values as a jumping-off point for finding that level of your being where feelings, needs, and values are already fulfilled. This self doesn't exist in action, yet paradoxically you can find it through action.

It will appear as a silent witness that stands back from activity simply to observe and appreciate what is going on. Soldiers in battle and daredevil adventurers often feel themselves becoming peaceful, unattached observers completely divorced from the frantic activity around them. Speaking for myself, I've found that moments of nonattachment are characterized by the following:

- I am present with my body.
- My breathing becomes very refined, approaching stillness.
- Mental activity has calmed down.
- I feel no threat; there is a certainty of belonging.
- I perceive my inner world as an open space with no boundaries; awareness extends in all directions rather than being focused on specific thoughts.
- Self-acceptance flows out into the environment. Things "out there" seem intimate to me, an extension of myself.

This experience of unity is also my working definition of love. For most of us love is an emotion that comes and goes; we feel it intensely at times, while at other times we don't feel it at all. But the essence of love isn't a feeling—it is a state of being. Or to be more exact, it is the state in which you are in contact with Being. Someone who is truly experiencing love feels tremendously real and alive, with no desire to do anything except exist within the fulfillment of love. Love's greatest action is simply to be, which is no action. That is why love is a supreme state of nonattachment and yet the most satisfying state.

For your action plan to succeed, you need to find an outlet for your love, a place where you can give it freely. The more openly you experience love, on whatever terms, the closer you will come to finding its essence. Love that doesn't flow is no love at all; it is just yearning and longing. The renowned mythologist Joseph Campbell pointed the way for expressing love when he said, "Follow your bliss." Bliss is the tingling rush of love in action, the flow of Being as it reaches out to meet itself and curl back with delight in contact. Love wants to find itself, and when the circuit is complete, bliss flows. Ask yourself, "Where do I find bliss?" then write down the steps you can take to increase this experience in your life.

Do not confuse pleasure with love. There are many things that give pleasure, such as watching television, with very little love in them. Love certainly brings pleasure but in a more profound way. Carrying a meal to a shut-in is an act of love that is far more pleasurable than watching television, for example, and there is much more to learn from such an action in terms of sharing, compassion, and understanding.

So don't be distracted by superficial pleasures. The deep joy and delight that exist at the core of life must be diligently uncovered. When you make your list, you'll find that many of your most cherished moments of bliss have gone forever. For example, you cannot duplicate the first new feeling of falling in love with the person to whom you are now married. But love has depth after depth. As you make your list, you will remember how you felt the day your children were born, and in that reminder is a clue: Your children can still be a source of bliss, if you resolve to reach deeper into your relationship with them. Nothing is more important than reconnecting with your bliss. Nothing is as rich. Nothing is more real.

Exercise 2: Being Love versus Being in Love

I'd like to explore the state of love further, because it is the surest road back to Being. The ancient sages declared that ultimately everything is made of consciousness, and when we experience consciousness purely, with no extraneous images or assumptions, that is love. The great Bengali poet Rabindranath Tagore declared, "Love is not a mere impulse; it must contain truth, which is law." The merging of love, truth, and reality is the great revelation of unity consciousness, the moment when a person can truthfully say, "I am the All," and, "I am love," in the same breath. Seen from this perspective, love is the feeling-state that is always present when a person is perfectly aligned with dharma, the flow of evolution.

Being *in* love is not the same state as this. When you fall in love, an opening is created for repressed feelings to rush forth and attach themselves to another person. If the love is deep enough, the other person seems ideal and perfect (this has nothing to do with his or her actual state, which could be quite imperfect and even destructive). But the force of love changes reality by changing the perceiver. Why and how does this happen? Physiologists have measured the increase in certain key neurotransmitters such as serotonin in the brains of people who are in love, but chemicals are only crude markers. Clearly, serotonin does not cause people to fall in love; it is only the biochemical basis for the pleasant sensations triggered by being in love.

In a series of revealing experiments, Harvard psychologist David C. McClelland probed the physiology of love. He had a group of subjects view a short film of Mother Teresa in her daily work of caring for sick and abandoned children in Calcutta. The film displayed a profound outpouring of love. As the audience watched the film, McClelland discovered that a marker in their immune systems increased—this was SIgA, or salivary immunoglobulin antigen. High levels of SIgA, as measured in people's saliva, indicates a high immune response; as it happens, an elevated immune response is also characteristic of people who have recently fallen in love. (The popular saying "If you don't want to catch a cold, fall in love" recognizes this connection between emotions and physiology.)

Curiously, when the film was over and the audience was asked their opinion of Mother Teresa, not everyone found her work laudable. Some had objections of one kind or another, centering on differences in religious belief, while others reported feeling disturbed by the sight of children who were starving or suffering from leprosy. Yet all the audience members experienced an increase in SIgA levels; their physical response to love appeared to be more powerful than their rational attitudes. This led McClelland to question one of the most popular definitions of love in modern psychology, which holds that love is a reflexive response that arises when two people meet to fill each other's needs. According to that definition, love would depend on a person's conscious evaluation of the benefits he or she was getting in a relationship. But here were people whose bodies were responding at a much deeper level, deeper even than pleasure.

McClelland also found that the positive effect on the viewers' immune response declined and disappeared an hour or two after they had viewed the film. It remained highest among those subjects who reported a strong sense of being loved in their own lives and having strong ties to family and friends. This implied that some people are already in a state conducive to love. Instead of experiencing it as a passing state, they had incorporated it as a trait. In other words, the statement of the enlightened sage, "I am love," was present in these people, if to a smaller degree.

What is love as a trait rather than as a passing phase? Even the most passionate experience of being in love eventually cools off, leaving people dismayed to find that little real love, in a lasting sense, remains. Pondering this problem, McClelland wondered what had become of the experiences described in the poetry of love. These experiences did not refer to the selfish advantages of being in love but to altruistic, undying devotion. Was Shakespeare simply wrong when he declared, "Love is not love which alters when it alteration finds, or bends with the remover to remove. Oh no! It is an ever-fixed mark that looks on tempest and is never shaken." McClelland also knew of instances cited in the psychological literature where people were in loving relationships that made no sense in terms of gaining any objective benefits. Such people felt deep love and devotion despite the fact that they had no rational reason for feeling that way.

What all this implied to McClelland was that love is a state that transcends reason and whose purpose is simply to allow the experience of a larger shared reality. One critical matter in this regard was a person's reaction to the death of a loved one. If two people were in love just for what they could get, their interdependence would form the basis for loving and being loved. Thus, the death of the loved one would cause great pain as the bond was ripped apart. Certainly this could be observed in real-life relationships, but McClelland felt from personal experience that something very different was possible:

> The death of a loved partner should cause intense suffering and grief, according to this theory. Yet when my wife died of cancer a few years ago, I did not react in this way. We had been very much in love, happily married for 42 years, had raised five children to well-adjusted maturity . . . yet when she died I did not feel the amount of pain that the theory would require that I should feel. . . . What the experience felt like was much closer to the poet's view of love. We had felt that we were part of something that was much bigger than ourselves—which had nurtured and supported us throughout our long life together and which continued to support me after her death.

This describes a step into the realm of timeless love. When two people use their love for each other as a doorway into this realm, the death of the loved one does not close the door or deprive the other of the flow of love. Ultimately, all love comes from within. We are deluding ourselves when we believe that another person is who we love; the other person is a pretext by which we give ourselves permission to feel love. Only you can open and close your heart. The power of love to nurture and sustain us depends on our commitment to it "in here."

It is important to talk about love, to think about it, to seek it out, and to encourage it. To put this in the form of an exercise, make a commitment to yourself to do the following:

1. Think about love. Take time to recall the love you shared with your parents, the times you expressed love to your siblings and friends. Dwell upon what is most lovable about the person who is most loving in your life today. Read deeply the poetry of love, such as is found in Shakespeare's sonnets, and the scriptures of love, such as that contained in the New Testament or in the devotional hymns of the Rig Veda.

2. Talk about love. Express your feelings directly to someone you love. If you cannot do it verbally, write a letter or a poem. You don't have to send it; the exercise is for you, to stimulate the state of love in every cell. But sending it is preferable, for you want to hear expressions of love in return. Don't let your love be something taken for granted. Put a note for your loved one to find in his or her pocket or on the kitchen table.

3. Seek out love. This is possible in many ways. Intimacy in our society is closely identified with sexual encounters, but it is an act of love to give help to the homeless and the sick, to deliver a sincere compliment, or to write a note of thanks and praise. People like to hear that they are loved and appreciated, and if you seek out opportunities to fulfill their needs in this area, their gratitude will be mirrored in your physiology as the bliss of being loved in return.

4. Encourage love. As parents we often teach our children that being openly affectionate and loving is appropriate for babies and toddlers but not for anyone older than that. In teaching manners and respect, we often create a gap that love is too sensitive and shy to cross. We inflict this sense of separation on our children because it was inflicted on us. The story of almost everyone is a story of love waiting to be coaxed out, of affection that has to wait in silence because it is afraid to emerge.

So take it as your duty to give those around you permission to love. Encourage their affection by showing it yourself, without regard for what you may get in return. Real love gains complete satisfaction simply by flowing out to what is loved; if love comes back, that is an added joy, but it isn't required or demanded. Love that has no ulterior motive is rare—all the psychological theories based on selfish love certainly are confirmed by what we observe all around us. But even the most demanding and selfish love is love of a sort. It is a drop taken from the ocean, and if you encourage it, it can swell to become the ocean.

The education of love begins in a moment and ends in eternity. It is sparked by feelings of delight and resolves into the peace that belongs to Being itself. In some haunting lines of poetry Kahlil Gibran expressed this truth:

> Yet the timeless in you is aware of life's time-
> lessness
> and knows that yesterday is but today's mem-
> ory and tomorrow
> is today's dream
> and that which sings and contemplates in you
> is still dwelling
> within the bounds of that moment which scat-
> tered the stars into space.

Use love as your mirror of the timeless; let it nurture your certainty that you are beyond change, beyond the memory of yesterday and the dream of tomorrow. There are infinite ways to discover your true Being, but love holds the brightest torch. If you follow it, you will be guided beyond the limits of age and death. Come out of the circle of time and find yourself in the circle of love.

INDEX

For information on seminars and other programs by Dr. Deepak Chopra, please contact:

Quantum Publications
P.O. Box 598
South Lancaster, MA 01561
800-858-1808